The Bible in the Light of Our Redemption

•

BASIC BIBLE COURSE

By

E.W. KENYON

Edited and Compiled by Ruth Kenyon Housworth

Printed in U.S.A.

Copyright 2011

by

KENYON'S GOSPEL PUBLISHING SOCIETY

ISBN 978-1-57770-016-6
ISBN 1-57770-016-3

E. W. KENYON
Author
(1867-1948)

Twenty-Eighth Printing

Lesson I
THE REASON FOR CREATION

MAN IS confronted with an unexplained creation of which he, himself, is a part. This creation and the iron hand of fixed laws that govern it, reveal to man a Master Designer. By that we mean that the Creator designed Creation that it might fulfill a certain purpose, the reason for its existence.

The purpose in creation seems to be to provide a suitable environment for man. In fact, if we take man out of creation, creation with its resources and its beauty has no reason for existing. If God created the universe as a home for man, He must have had a reason for creating man. Man, in every age of history, has sought in vain for this reason, the reason for his own existence.

Skepticism was born because man was unable to find a reason for creation. The first tendency of science was to become atheistic and materialistic, giving only a mechanical explanation of the universe. However, today, as scientists are delving more fully into the mysteries and wonders of creation, many of them have become God-conscious. They are realizing that behind creation there is an intelligent Creator. However, science has not been able to find Him, or His purpose in creation with just Sense Knowledge . . . knowledge derived from the five senses.

Man's inability to know God is due to the fact that God is a spirit, and that man has no contact with Him. In his own spirit nature, man is alienated from God; and every contact that he has with the universe, or reality, he has through his central nervous system and his five senses. Through these five senses (namely, sight, hearing, touch, taste and smell) man has not been able to contact God. He has learned a great deal about physical nature which is indifferent and many times cruel toward human life, but he has not been able to find God personally, or His reason for creating man.

By this we can see that man in himself cannot find God. God must reveal Himself to man, and God has done this very thing. He has given a revelation of Himself to man. He had to give the revelation upon man's level so that man would be able to contact it. We call this "Revelation Knowledge." It is obtained through our recreated spirits from the Word of God.

The second chapter of I Corinthians, which tells us of this revelation, gives us the following illustration (I Cor. 2:11) : "For who among men knoweth the things of a man save the spirit of a man which is in him? Even so the things of God none knoweth, save the spirit of God." Man, limited to his sense knowledge, is unable to know the inner thoughts of a man. There is a veil of flesh that he cannot penetrate with his sense of sight, hearing or touch. However, a man, by the medium of words, may convey his inner thoughts to another.

So God, in His desire for man to know Him, has formulated His inner thoughts and purposes into words, which man can see with his sense of sight, and hear read or expounded, with his sense of hearing. I Cor. 2:12, 13, "But we receive not the spirit of the world, but the spirit which is from God: that we might know the things that were freely given to us of God. Which things also we speak, not in words which man's wisdom teacheth, but which the spirit teacheth: combining spiritual things with spiritual words."

The Bible is God's revelation to man, and because we have no other channel through which we can know God or contact Him, we turn to that revelation to find out what He has told us of His reason for creating man.

The Earth Is the Reason for the Heavens

Our earth is so small in comparison to the vast number and sizes of the heavenly bodies, that the study of it would be utterly absurd, if it were not for the fact that it is the only planet known to be inhabited by human life.

The first chapter of Genesis reveals that the earth holds a place in the plan and purpose of God that amazes one.

Genesis 1:14-19 declares that the earth is the reason for all the heavenly bodies that swing in their orbits through dark, illimitable space.

Science does not deny the fact that there is not a planet, sun, moon, or star in all this vast universe which does not have its influence upon our earth.

Our sun is approximately ninety-three million miles away, yet it causes climatic conditions of heat, light, rain and winds, which make this planet capable of sustaining human, animal and vegetable life.

"The little earth ball, with its precious freight of human beings, flies softly around the sun amply protected in its transparent case of atmosphere."

To refer once more to the Scripture: "To let them be for signs and for seasons."

We know that the tides of the oceans and seas are influenced by the heavenly bodies. We know that heat and cold, drought and storms, are the direct results of planetary influences. Storms can be predicted for certain localities on this continent by the position and influence of certain planets. We know that frosts and heat waves are predicted months ahead by the sure knowledge of planetary positions.

From these deductions we see clearly that the planets are placed in the heavens to give us seasons, to be signs, and to be continual companions and servants, always ministering to the earth.

The heavens are earth's only perfect timepiece. No watch or clock man has ever made can give us perfect time, but He who knows the path of the stars, knows that every star, sun, or planet will pass a certain given point in the great, unpathed space on schedule time.

The star may not have been seen for thousands of years, but it will appear at the crossroads of the Heavens, not one second ahead, nor one second behind its schedule.

Oh, the wonder of the Architect, the marvel of the Creator, the might of the Sustainer of this great universe. How thrilling it is that this earth of ours, so small that one thousand of them could be lost in the sun, is yet the center and reason for the universe.

The Reason for the Earth Is Man

If the earth is the reason for the stellar heavens, what is the reason for the earth?

Genesis 1 gives the account of Creation. Creation consists of a series of acts by God. These creative acts

11

culminate in the creation of man. When man was created, God's creative activity came to a rest.

Man was the goal of the whole creative movement. Science must here agree with the Biblical account of creation in the placing of man at the summit of creation. He was the last and the highest of God's works.

The earth has no reason for existing outside of man. Unconscious nature cannot enjoy its beauty, contemplate, nor use what it has produced.

Only when God placed upon this earth a man created in His image, was there a reason for the vast universe which had been created. God had endowed this man with the capacities to enjoy the beauty of His workmanship, and to utilize its resources.

Isaiah 45:18, "For thus saith Jehovah that created the heavens, the God that formed the earth and made it, formed it to be inhabited." The Word declares here that God created this earth to be inhabited by man. In His creative acts He met every need that man would have in his life upon earth.

Ages on ages He wrought in storing up treasures of all kinds of wealth for his man. He filled earth's bosom with deposits of iron, copper, silver and gold, and with uncounted varieties of metals, chemicals and forces.

He covered the face of the earth with mountains, valleys, ravines, plateaus and prairies, lovely rivulets, streams and rivers, and with many beautifully colored flowers that thrilled with joy the heart of God's man. Fruits and vegetables supplied food for man. The Great Architect of human need and joy knew man's needs, while yet unborn, and in creation's wondrous plan, these needs were met.

Man is the only creature who can enjoy its beauty or use its resources.

The Reason for Man Is the Father-Heart of God

We have seen that the earth is the reason for the stellar universe, and that man is the reason for the earth. Our problem is not yet solved, however. What is the reason for man? Until we know why God desired to create man, we do not know the reason for creation.

12

Genesis 1:1, "In the beginning God created the heavens and the earth."

The word "God" in the Hebrew is "Elohim." This word is plural, revealing the Trinity at work in creation.

John 1:1-3 and Colossians 1:16 reveal that Christ had a major part in the great acts of creation.

Psalm 104:30 and Genesis 1:2 show the Holy Spirit's work in creation.

The Trinity lies hidden throughout the Old Testament. Many Jews who have accepted Jesus Christ as their Saviour have testified that one of the factors causing them to realize that Jesus was their Messiah, was that they glimpsed, hidden in the Old Covenant, the Trinity.

Israel, however, did not know who composed the Trinity. Not until Jesus Christ, the Living Word, was manifested in flesh, did man know that the Trinity consisted of the Father, Son and Holy Spirit. In His ministry of teaching, Jesus Christ revealed the Father-God.

On several occasions in the life of Jesus Christ, the Trinity is manifested to man's senses. One time is at the baptism of Jesus, recorded in Matthew 3:13-17.

When Jesus was baptized, the Holy Spirit appeared in the form of a dove, descending upon Christ, while the Father spoke in a voice from heaven, "This is my beloved Son in whom I am well pleased."

Matthew 28:19 reveals the Trinity as being the Father, Son, and the Holy Spirit.

From this we can understand that in the beginning the Father, Son, and Holy Spirit created the heavens and the earth.

You see, He was in the beginning a Father-God. In eternity He had a Father-nature. We can understand a father's love and desire for children. Our civilization is built around this fact, for the home is the basic unit of society.

Ephesians 3:14-15 reveals that the human father is just a type of the Father-God. The human father's love exists because in eternity God was essentially a Father-God.

It is natural that the Father-heart of God should long for sons and daughters. This yearning passion took form, and God planned to create a man who would walk with Him as His child.

Ephesians 1:4, 5 (Rotherham), "According as He made choice of us in Him before the founding of the world, that we might be holy and blameless in His presence. In love marking us out beforehand unto Sonship through Jesus Christ for Himself."

Before He created a world, in His dream plan, man was marked out for Sonship. He was to hold the place of a son in the Father-God's love. He was to be the answer to the Father's hunger for children.

Other scriptures that reveal that man was the reason for creation are: Romans 16:25 and I Corinthians 2:7. These scriptures reveal that man was chosen for the place of a son first, then God created this universe to be a home for him.

In our Bible Schools we have listed the attributes of God: His Omnipotence, His Omniscience; but we have overlooked the fact that He is first a Father-God.

The reason for creation is the Father-heart of God.

A few scriptures that reveal the Father's care for His children are: Matthew 7:11; 6:8; 6:25-32; John 16:27; 17:23; I Peter 5:7; Philippians 4:6, 7, 19 and John 14:23.

Satan has been very subtle in blinding our minds to the Father-nature of God. The average Christian has had no real consciousness of God as being his Father. This ignorance has been due to the fact that our minds have not been renewed by the Word of God. Romans 12:1-2 and Ephesians 4:23. Here we see the importance of the study of the Word.

Sense Knowledge has taken the place of the Word of God in our lives. Jesus Christ has been manifested to man's physical senses. I John 1:1, 2, "That which we have handled concerning the Word of Life." Jesus Christ took upon Himself a human body through which He was manifested to man.

Man's mind derives its knowledge through the senses of the physical body. The Father has never been manifested to these senses, as He is a Spirit being; therefore man's mind can form no mental picture of Him.

14

When a man has been born again, past sense knowledge of the life of Jesus Christ has taken the place that the Father should have had in his life. Because man could form a mental picture of Christ, he has developed the habit of praying to Christ, praising and worshipping Him alone. The renewing of the man's mind by the Word of God, brings a consciousness of the Father to him that revolutionizes his life.

The Attributes of God

In this revelation, the Father nature of God has been revealed to us at creation. There are two other laws of His being revealed here: one is that He is a Faith God, and the other, that He is Love. Love caused Him to create a universe, and He created it by Faith. He works by Faith in His Word.

In the first chapter of Genesis there are six creative faith statements. Hebrews 11:3 reveals that God created this universe through faith in His Word. It was through His spoken Word that creation came into being.

QUESTIONS

1. Give and explain the two kinds of knowledge.
2. How has God met man's need of a Revelation?
3. What Scripture reveals that the earth is the reason for the heavenly bodies?
4. Explain as fully as possible why man is the reason for the earth's existence.
5. What is revealed in the word "Elohim"?
6. Give several Scriptures that reveal the Father-nature of God.
7. What is the reason for man? Explain your answer.
8. Why is it that many Christians do not have faith in God and His promises to them as their Heavenly Father?
9. Give two attributes of God's nature that are revealed in creation.

Notes

Lesson 2
THE CREATION OF MAN

WE HAVE seen in our last lesson that man is the reason for creation. In the light of this tremendous fact, we turn to study the man whom God created to meet the cry of His being for fellowship.

Genesis 1 gives the account of the preparation God made for man before He created him.

First, He planned a universe for man, and in the heart of that universe He purposed a home.

When Love laid the foundations of this mighty universe, he planned and purposed it all to be the home for His man.

Genesis 1:25. At the completion, God put His stamp of approval upon it. It will meet man's every need. The home is now ready for man.

Genesis 1:26. God now makes the solemn declaration that He wishes to make man in His own image.

Knowing that fellowship is the reason for man, we can easily understand that man could not meet the reason for his very existence unless he were created in God's image.

In order to partake of God's life, he must be in God's class, in God's realm. He must be made in the image and likeness of his Creator.

He must be created as near like Deity as possible, in order to be God's child and heir.

Man, a Triune Being

Genesis 1:27 records the creation of man in the image of God. Adam was the first man. Genesis 2:7. Through his sin came the fall of man.

Man, after the fall, in his condition of spiritual death, could not know what the image of God was, without a revelation from Him.

John 4:24. Jesus Christ, the Incarnate One, revealed that the Father was a Spirit Being.

I Thessalonians 5:23. Paul in his revelation disclosed the fact that man is a triune being, consisting of a spirit, soul and body.

The spirit is the real man, created in the image of God.

The soul includes the reasoning faculties.

17

The Father-God created man in His own image, a spirit being, with a soul and body.

Man's soul and body fit him for his life upon this material universe which has been created for him.

The real man is spirit. Man was to walk in fellowship with the Father-God in His realm, which is the realm of the spirit.

Your body is not you. Your mind is not you. You have a mind which you use. You possess a body which you use. Your mind and body are merely the instruments of your spirit, the real YOU.

The man who is spiritually dead does not realize the fact that he was created in God's image, to walk with Him.

This is due to the fact that all the natural man is able to know about reality, he gains through the five senses belonging to his physical body.

These physical sense organs of the human body can only receive a stimulus from like substance, matter. Therefore, man's senses can perceive only for him a physical or material realm.

There exists, according to the Scriptures, a spiritual realm as well as a physical.

The Father, the Holy Spirit, the Angels, Satan and Demons, are all Spirit Beings. Our physical senses do not contact this spiritual realm.

Ephesians 6:1-20 reveals the spiritual warfare surrounding us, from which our sense organs receive no stimuli.

We are not aware, through any physical contact, of the presence of the Holy Spirit or Angels.

Read John 16:7-15; Hebrews 1:14; John 14:23; I Corinthians 3:16; I Peter 5:8; Mark 16:17; I John 4:1-6; and James 4:7.

Because the doctor, with the point of his knife, has not been able to locate the spirit of man, the materialists and atheists have said that the body is the whole man.

Romans 1:18-25, 28. Man has refused to have God in his knowledge, because he has not been able to see Him with his physical eye, hear Him with his physical ear, or touch Him.

18

A fish might just as well say there is nothing outside of water, as for a man, limited to Sense Knowledge, to say there exists nothing but matter.

We conclude that man is primarily a spirit being, created to walk with the Father-God on His level. We realize that when He created man, God had no body; yet man's fellowship was perfect and complete with Him.

This reveals that man's body was subordinate to his spirit, and that his spirit was to dominate.

Man's spirit was to rule his mind and his body.

The body exists only for the spirit and soul of a body.

The spirit operates through the soul or intellect, and these in turn operate through the physical body.

At death the man and his soul leave the body. When man has left his body, the body has no reason for existing; therefore, dissolution and disintegration set in at once.

The Will of Man

Another crowning feature which the Father-God gave to His man was man's will. The will has the power of choice, the ability to choose, to determine one's actions.

God assumed a great responsibility in creating a being with a will. Yet, no other type of being could have answered the reason for Creation.

Without this will, God's created one would have been a machine, not a man, a puppet or robot instead of a person.

The desire of the Father is for fellowship. This fellowship must come from man, not as the response to an instinct, but as a result of his deep love, his own choice.

There could be no fellowship with a puppet. Read Luke 9:23.

Obedience to Him is a result of love. John 14:21-24.

The Mind of Man

The Scriptures declare that when man was created, he had a mind, intellectually of such character that he was able to name the entire animal creation.

Genesis 2:19-20, "And out of the ground Jehovah God formed every beast of the field, and every bird of the heavens: and brought them to man to see what he would call them: and whatsoever man called the living creature, that was the name thereof. And the man gave names to all

19

cattle, and to the birds of heaven, and to every beast of the field."

When we realize that there are 500,000 bugs, birds, worms, animals, fish and reptiles that Adam named, we can understand that he possessed intellectual capacities that enabled him to rule creation.

We know that the reason for man's existence is the Father-God's craving for fellowship.

Therefore, man's mental capacities were such that his mind could fellowship the mind of his Creator.

Man's Physical Condition

When man was created, he was planned a perfect human being with an endless human life.

His body was not mortal nor immortal. The word "mortal" means "death-doomed," or "Satan-ruled."

Man was an eternal spirit being in God's class, with an eternal human body.

Adam's body was perfect, and fit to be the temple of God's under-ruler.

Man's Dominion, Authority, and Responsibility

Genesis 1:28. Reading the Scripture through the mind ruled by the senses, we have overlooked the tremendous place man held in the heart of God.

He was the object of the Father-God's love and affection. It was the joy of the Father to give His man dominion over the works He had created. This man had, by creation, the ability to rule the universe.

Psalm 8:3-9 is a revelation of the creation of the first man as the Father-God desired him to be and to live.

Psalm 8:5, "Made him but little lower than God." The King James Version reads "angels," but the correct translation is "God."

The Hebrew word is "Elohim." It is the same word that is used in Genesis 1:1. "In the beginning 'God' (or 'Elohim')."

The thought of the Hebrew is "just a shade lower than God."

Man was created as nearly like the Father-God as was possible.

20

Man was to be God's companion and under-ruler. His dominion reached to the utmost star and planet. His dominion was as far-reaching as Christ's rule shall be when He shall take over the dominion of the universe.

Hebrews 2:5-8 is a revelation of Adam's dominion.

Hebrews 2:8 (last clause) reveals that man no longer holds that dominion (American Standard Version).

Hebrews 2:9 shows that the lost dominion of Adam has been given to Christ, by virtue of His sacrifice on man's behalf.

Hebrews 1:3 gives to us a suggestion as to the way Adam ruled God's creation. Jesus now upholds all things by the Word of His power.

Adam ruled creation by his word. His voice was like the voice of his Creator in its dominion over creation.

Adam possessed such complete authority over creation that he had in his hands the legal right to confer that dominion to another being.

In our next lesson we shall see that he did this very thing.

Man's Responsibility

It is impossible to over-estimate the responsibility of Adam.

He was responsible for the heart-joy of the Father-God, for the human family yet unborn.

God could have spoken the entire human family into existence at once, but He did not choose that way.

Genesis 1:28. He made Adam and Eve fellow-workers with Him in bringing the human family into the world.

God gave to man the ability to reproduce himself or beget children. These children were primarily for the joy and glory of God.

Instead of creating the human race by one single word, the Father-God created one man and woman. He said to them, "I permit you to give birth to My children, to rear, educate, and care for them, teaching them to love Me, and to respond to My yearning."

So man's real business was to give birth to God's children.

This gives a responsibility to man that can only be measured by eternity. Man gives birth to eternal personalities, to children who will live as long as God lives.

Man, then, is the custodian of God's joy.

We have dwelt in detail on the creation of the human race in Adam, for a very definite reason, the renewing of your mind.

Until the time that we were born again, we lived in the realm of spiritual death. We had known of no condition for humanity outside of the bondage of that realm. During that period we all became familiar with the creation of man as given to us in Genesis 1 and 2, but we know it only through the world mind, which is enmity toward God.

In the story of Creation, we did not see that man was the reason for the existence of the universe. To us, man played a minor role. Our spirits, alienated from God, did not grasp the Father-God's longing for children and His joy in creating a man in His own image, with dominion over creation. We saw instead a God for whom we felt no love or nearness, a policeman type of God.

We saw the creation of man as a pitiful failure, the creation of a poor, weak worm of the dust. We saw it as Satan would have us see it.

I Corinthians 15:45-49 (American Standard Version) tells us of two creations: the creation in Adam and the new spiritual creation in Christ. In Adam, we see man marred by the entrance of spiritual death, losing his fellowship with the Father-God and his authority over creation. In Christ, we see spiritual death destroyed and man made a new creature, as free from the dominion of spiritual death as though Adam had never sinned. As you know the place and reason for the first creation, you will know what you mean to the Father-heart of God.

A low conception of the creation in Adam has given to us a low conception of the new creation in Christ.

QUESTIONS

1. Why did the Father-God create man in His own image?
2. (a) What kind of a being is God? Is man?
   (b) Give a scripture for each.

3. Why is it that natural man does not recognize the existence of the spiritual?
4. In what realm was man to live?
5. Why did God give to man a will?
6. What incident reveals the type of mind Adam had?
7. What kind of a body did Adam possess?
8. What scriptures reveal the authority that Adam had before the fall? What authority was his?
9. How near like God had Adam been created?
10. Why is it necessary for us to see the place the first creation held in God's plan?

Notes

Lesson 3
MAN'S TREASON AND RESULTS

THE FIRST division of this course has dealt with the chapters of Genesis which cover the period from the creation of man to the Fall.

To many of us in the past, these chapters have been just a portion of past history, lifeless and uninteresting. We have studied them in a sense of duty to gain essential knowledge.

As we study them now, in the light of our Redemption in Christ, they actually live before us.

In them is portrayed a drama of joy, love, faith, and then unbelief and tragedy, which centers around the Father-God and man.

We see in these chapters, Love's preparation for man, the Father-God's joy in creating man in His own image, and His eagerness to make man His under-ruler, by giving him authority and responsibility.

In this great drama of Creation, the Father-nature and Love of God are clearly revealed.

During the reign of Spiritual Death that followed man's sin, in which Satan ruled in the heart of man, the knowledge of God and His Love became lost.

Not until the coming of Christ was the Father-nature of God again made known to man.

It is a perfect setting for a tragedy.

The Nature of Man's Sin

This is the old problem that has confronted theologians in every generation: What was the nature of man's original sin?

It could not have been broken law, for there had been no law given, as we understand the term, from its connection with the law of Moses.

What kind of a sin was it that impelled the Incarnation and sufferings of Calvary?

Having found that man was invested with such far-reaching authority, that he possessed an intellect of such caliber as to be the companion of Deity, and that he had in his hands the joy or sorrows of God, we can understand now the nature of the sin he committed.

25

High Treason

The sin of Adam was the crime of High Treason.

God had conferred upon him the authority to rule the universe. This Universe-wide dominion was the most sacred heritage God could give to man. Genesis 1:28 and Psalm 8:6.

Adam turned this legal dominion over into the hands of God's enemy, Satan. This sin is unpardonable! High Treason has been so considered in all ages. Adam's transgression was done in the white light of absolute knowledge. He was not deceived by Satan. He understood the steps that led to the crime. His wife, Eve, was deceived, but Adam became the Benedict Arnold of Eternity.

I Timothy 2:13-14. He knew God. He knew Satan. He knew the result of the unthinkable crime he committed.

Genesis 3:1-7. Eve's deception by Satan was due to her unbelief in God's Word. Satan, through the serpent, first questioned the Word God had given to them, and then openly contradicted it. It is thought by some that the serpent originally moved upright like a man, and that it was beautiful to look upon, and perhaps possessed organs of speech. To certain extents naturalists confirm this.

Adam's Treason Recognized by Christ

We have come to one of the most interesting features of the Plan of Redemption. Satan's dominion over Creation.

We have shown how Satan obtained this authority; let us note now some facts in regard to it.

The careful student of the Scriptures will notice the perfect justice of God. He did not take advantage over Satan. Adam had legally conferred to Satan the authority with which God had vested him. Had God not been perfectly just, He would have dispossessed Satan and punished man. Instead of that, His Grace makes provision for humanity's Redemption, showing His love to man, based upon perfect justice.

When Jesus began His ministry, it will be remembered that directly after He was baptized, He was led away by the Spirit into the wilderness to be tempted by the devil.

Luke 4:6-7. During the temptation, the devil led Him up and showed Him all the kingdoms of the inhabited earth in a moment of time. And the devil said to Him, "To thee will I give all this authority, and the glory of them; for it hath been delivered unto me, and to whomsoever I will I give it. If thou therefore wilt worship before me, it shall all be thine."

Now, mark, Satan comes to Jesus and declares to Him that the authority and glory of the inhabited earth has been delivered to him, and that he can give it to whomsoever he wills.

If the devil lied to Jesus and Jesus did not know it, Jesus was not the incarnate Son of God. If the devil lied to Jesus, and Jesus knew that he lied, it was not a genuine temptation.

We believe that the Bible is true, and that this was a genuine temptation. Then Jesus recognized that Satan had authority and dominion over the kingdoms of the human race, which he could transfer at his will to whomsoever he wished.

Satan said, "It hath been delivered unto me." We know that this authority was not given to Satan by God. The Father-God would never confer to His enemy dominion over His creation and man, the object of His love.

Satan tempted man in the garden because of his bitter hatred toward God. Knowing what man meant to the Father-God, it became his object to separate this union and bring humanity under bondage to himself and destruction. He knew this would cause the Father-God the greatest suffering. Yet, Satan, in his malignant character, could not foresee that God would suffer by His own will for this man until He brought him back to Himself.

The sufferings (physical and spiritual) of Calvary reveal the triumph of God by love over His enemy, Satan.

Christ did not yield to this temptation; Love conquered and triumphed over Satan.

The Result of Man's Sin, the Entrance of Death

It was the thwarting of God's plan.

Adam's sin of High Treason brought the entrance of Spiritual Death into the life of humanity.

Romans 5:12 gives to us a picture of Spiritual Death awaiting an entrance into the spirit of man. Man's sin is the door that throws open his spirit to the entrance of this dread nature.

Most of our teaching in regard to the Fall of man has centered in the entrance of Physical Death.

We have seen in our last lesson that the real man is the spirit, and that he was to walk in fellowship with God, a spirit being.

It was into this spirit of man, created in the image of God, that Death entered.

By the term, "Spiritual Death," we do not mean that man ceased to be a spirit being.

Spiritual Death is not a state of non-existence; it is a state of existence in a condition separated and alienated from God, and in union with Satan.

There are three kinds of death that are mentioned in the Scripture: Physical death, Spiritual Death, and the Second Death.

Physical death is a violent and unnatural thing, the separation of man's spirit and soul from his body.

Spiritual Death is more violent and unnatural to humanity. It is the separation of man's spirit from God. (Ephesians 4:18.)

Revelation 20:11-15, the Second Death is an eternal separation of man from God, in a state of existence where the nature of God is no longer, and shall never be, accessible to man.

Spiritual Death Is a Nature

Spiritual death is in reality a Nature. The real powers today are spiritual.

God is a spirit (John 4:24).

Satan is a spirit (Ephesians 6:12).

Man is a spirit (I Thessalonians 5:23).

Man, a creation in the image of God, a higher being, is dependent upon a higher power than he for his spiritual life. He must partake either of God's nature or of Satan's nature.

God is a spirit, and His Nature is Life (John 5:26).

Satan is a spirit also, and his nature is the opposite of God's. It is death.

Ephesians 2:1-5. It was Spiritual Death, this nature of Satan, that laid hold of man's spirit.

There are two words that open the Bible. They are the words, "Life" and "Death."

Without an understanding of those two words, we cannot have a coherent conception of God, and of His Revelation to man, the Bible.

The Primal Death that entered at the Fall was Spiritual Death. Adam had been given his choice.

Genesis 2:9, 16-17. The Tree of Life would have united man with God. The Tree of the Knowledge of Good and Evil united man with Satan.

A Two-Fold Death

When man had been given authority over the Universe, God warned him, telling him that if he disobeyed, he would surely die.

The literal translation of Genesis 2:17 is, "In dying thou shalt die."

This reveals a two-fold death.

The moment Adam committed High Treason, he died spiritually, but he did not die physically for 930 years later.

Spiritual Death came to the earth first. It manifested itself in the physical by destroying it.

Physical death is just a manifestation of its parent, Spiritual Death.

After man had died spiritually, his body became mortal, death-doomed.

Spiritual Death became universal. All humanity was identified with Adam in his Spiritual Death. Adam, the parent of man, the head of God's creation, had died spiritually. He had failed in his responsibility as the custodian of God's joy. Man to whom he will give birth will possess the same nature.

That Spiritual Death becomes the nature of every man born into the world.

Romans 5:12 declares that Death passed upon all mankind.

Romans 5:17-19 says that "through the one man's disobedience, the many were made sinners."

Romans 5:15, "By the trespass of one, the many died." God's dream cannot be realized. Humanity is dead spiritually.

The Nature of Spiritual Death

We have seen that Spiritual Death is as much a substance, a force, a fact, as life.

The difference is that Spiritual Death emanates from the devil, while Life emanates from God.

Satan was originally in Heaven with God, one of those spirits who stood next to the very Throne of God itself, but he turned against God. As he did, his nature changed.

We recognize that in the world there are spiritual forces working that are contrary to each other: Love and Hatred, Joy and Sorrow, Faith and Doubt, Good and Evil, etc. These conflicting forces could not come from the same source. All that is Holy, Good, and Beautiful heads up in Life which emanates from God. All that is evil, bad and corrupt heads up in Spiritual Death which emanates from Satan.

We can understand that out of the Nature of Satan flows hatred, lust, murder, and every unclean and evil force in the world.

There is no understanding in our minds of the condition and problem of humanity without our knowing that Spiritual Death, the nature of Satan, reigns in the spirit of man. It is very clear that when Spiritual Death entered the life of Adam, his spirit underwent a complete change. Man was actually born again when he sinned. He was born of Satan. He became a partaker of satanic nature. He became a child of Satan.

Read I John 3:12, John 5:24, I John 3:14-15, and Ephesians 2:1-5.

Spiritual Death, this hideous monster, seized the sovereignty, the dominion, the lordship over creation.

Romans 5:17, "For if by the trespass of one, death reigned." Death assumed a personality. By the act of Adam's High Treason, death begins to reign. It is in reality the reign of Satan.

Hebrews 2:14 speaks of Satan's holding the authority, the dominion of the realm of Spiritual Death. A literal translation of Romans 5:17 reads, "For if by the trespass of one, death made use of the one to seize the sovereignty."

Romans 5:21 of the same translation reads, "Sin reigned as a king in the realm of death." Here we have the truth stated clearly. Death (the nature of Satan) has seized the sovereignty, and God's creation is under its dominion.

QUESTIONS

1. What was the nature of Adam's sin?
2. Was Adam deceived? Give a scripture.
3. Tell and explain the incident in the New Testament that reveals Satan's authority over creation.
4. Why did Satan desire to bring Spiritual Death into the life of man?
5. Explain Romans 5:12.
6. What is Spiritual Death?
7. What was Adam's "two-fold death"?
8. What are the three main spiritual beings?
9. Give several scriptures that reveal that Spiritual Death passed on all mankind.
10. Give the contrast between the fruits of the Nature of God, and the fruits of the nature of Satan.

Notes

Lesson 4
THE REIGN OF SPIRITUAL DEATH

IN OUR LAST LESSON, we saw the entrance of spiritual death into the life of man.

This explains the dominance and persistence of sin in its kingly sway over humanity.

Man has become a partaker of Satanic Nature, spiritual death. The reign of spiritual death heads up in Satan.

Ephesians 2:1-5 reveals man's condition of spiritual death, a child of wrath, his life ordered by Satan who has become the prince of the powers of the air.

There is no logical reason for man's response to intelligently organized sin, unless man's nature and will are in fellowship with it.

The Father-God had made known His will to man. His will was for man to eat of the Tree of Life, to partake of His Nature.

There are three wills in the world: God's will, Satan's will, and man's will. Just as man is dependent upon God or Satan for his spiritual life, his will must be in harmony with God's will or Satan's.

Matthew 6:24 gives the New Testament explanation. A man cannot serve two masters at once. He will love one or the other. He will serve God or Satan.

Man in the Garden refused God's will. He sought his own will. However, in seeking his will in freedom from God's, that will became in bondage to Satan's will.

We now turn to study the reign of Spiritual Death in the life of man who was created in God's image, and to find the only answer to the spiritually-dead man's need.

The Reign of Spiritual Death Begins

The Dominion of Satan's will over Adam's began the moment Adam obeyed his voice. What a horrible awakening it is to man . . . Satan's nature breathed into his spirit.

Ephesians 2:3. He is now, by nature, a child of wrath.

Genesis 3:8-13. He no longer responds to the call of God. Their fellowship has been broken. Man responds to the call of his new master, Satan.

Genesis 3:22-24. He is an outlaw, an outcast from the garden, with no legal ground of approach to God.

Genesis 3:24, "So He drove out the man, and He placed at the east of the Garden of Eden the cherubim and the flame of a sword which turned every way to keep the way of the Tree of Life." We have not realized the significance of this act on the part of God.

It would have been an unthinkable crime for the Nature of God and the nature of Satan to have been united in one individual, so Adam must not have access now to the Tree of Life. We cannot imagine the kind of being which would have resulted from this union. It is enough to know that it would have made Redemption an impossibility.

Genesis 4:8. Spiritual Death now becomes a hideous reality to Adam. His first son murders his second, lying about it afterwards. The two characteristics of Satan are manifested in the life of man. He is a murderer and a liar.

Adam is made to feel with keenness the effect of his treason. He has not only sinned against God, but also against the human race yet unborn.

Genesis 4:26. A little grandchild is born into the family and Adam names him "Enosh." "Enosh" means mortal, frail, death-doomed, or Satan-ruled. He names the first grandchild in memory's bitter regret of his sin.

Genesis 3:17-19. At the rising of each sun, perfect beauty had gladdened man's eyes; now he lifts them to devastation manifested everywhere. Worms, briars and thorns abound.

The Iron Will of Spiritual Death has breathed hatred into the nature of the animal kingdom. To the ears of Adam come discordant cries of malice and suffering; while before his eyes the carcasses of animals and insects lie rotting in the sun.

Adam himself grovels under the Iron Will of Satan. He finds that his nature is no longer in fellowship with God. He has lost love; his rest, joy and peace are gone.

Spiritual Death and the Birth of Reason

Spiritual Death caused man to cease walking in the realm of his spirit. Hitherto man had walked in the Spirit realm with his Creator. His spirit had dominated and ruled. It had been the Faith Realm, the realm of Omnipotent power where faith spoke words into being and substance.

Romans 4:17. It was the realm of Him who called the things that are not, as though they were.

Adam had walked as the under-ruler of the One who had framed the worlds out of the things which are not, by faith in His Word (Hebrews 11:3).

Now that man's union with God is severed, man's ability is severed from God's ability. Man's word is severed from God's Word.

Man has fallen from the realm of God's ability into the realm of human ability. In this realm he is dependent upon his own resources. The resources of man are limited to his mind and his body. The mind can derive its knowledge only through the senses of man's physical body. The five senses of sight, hearing, touch, taste and smell become the doors and windows of his mind.

Man forms his conception of the world and himself by means of these senses. He orders his life by what he sees, hears, feels, tastes and smells. The senses bring the material to the mind, and reason draws its own conclusions from the material of sensation. Faith has died, the supernatural is lost, and Reason is born.

Romans 8:1-11 gives an exposition of the natural man in his walk and life ordered by the senses of his physical body.

Romans 8:7, "The mind of the flesh is enmity against God." The mind of the flesh is composed of the deductions made from the material of sensation which the mind receives from the physical senses.

In other words, Reason, the product of man's senses, has always been enmity toward the knowledge of God, Faith, or any act that is above the realm of human ability.

Civilization becomes a cultivation of the arts which please the senses. Regardless of how high man's aims may be, he cannot rise above the level of his senses.

The walk in the spirit is lost. The cry of the spirit remains unanswered. At the dawn of human history, reason gains the supremacy.

Spiritual Death and Civilization

The history of the human race has been a revelation of I John 5:19, "The whole world lieth in the embrace of the evil one" (literal translation).

Sin has ruled as a king in the realm of spiritual death, where man lives under the cruel Emperor, Satan.

Every effort of man has failed to eradicate the power of sin. Education has failed. History confesses that every rise in civilization has been accompanied by a decline in morals.

War has dominated in every period of the life of every nation, destroying the youth and strength of humanity. It has brought untold suffering to man. Its cruelty is but a manifestation of Satanic Dominion at work in its destruction of man.

Man has been unable to strike at the root and the cause of sin, sickness and death. The law of disease has fastened itself upon the human body, blighting and scourging humanity. Death is the supreme problem that all men at all periods have faced. It casts its shadow upon every happiness born in the senses of man.

Man, lying in the embrace of Satan, cries in agony against this vain struggle which only ends in a hopeless death and doom. Despite the blighting curse, creation teems with marks of beauty and harmony. The marks and design of an intelligent Creator are yet made manifest. Yet man can see no reason for his short span of life between birth and hopeless death. He is born to die; he brings no joy to himself nor his Creator. His spirit hungers for God, but he cannot find Him.

His reason concludes that his Creator is not a God of Love; therefore, he rejects the revelation of a Father-God.

A scientist, expressing the sentiment of the age, in contemplating on the life of man, said, "The God of the Christians is not a God of Love; the Sisters of Charity are kinder than He."

Man, blinded by his spiritual father, Satan, does not know that at the dawn of human history, Satan, the enemy of God, became the ruler of this world. He does not

36

know that by the trespass of the one, death seized the Sovereignty.

Spiritual Death, the nature of Satan, is the soil out of which has grown sin, sickness, physical death, and every sorrow that has darkened the life of God's man.

Man's Need of Eternal Life

Ephesians 4:17-18 gives a picture of humanity as a result of the entrance of Spiritual Death into the life of Adam. See also Romans 5:12.

Man is alienated from the life of God. He is walking in the Realm of Reason, in the vanity of his mind, and that mind is darkened and blinded by indwelling spiritual death (II Corinthians 4:4).

Man is utterly helpless to redeem himself by his own efforts from his condition. After Adam had obeyed Satan, bringing himself and his authority under Satanic subjection, he had no authority to free himself from that condition. As far as human efforts were concerned, one man had sealed the fate of the human race (I Corinthians 15:22).

No man could ever redeem humanity, for every man would be under Satanic dominion. If man were ever to be Redeemed, someone greater than Satan must undertake on man's behalf. God, Himself, must redeem humanity.

This Redemption demands more than that God merely forgive the sins of man. Although God should forgive the sin of Adam and of all men, man's Redemption would not be touched. The power and authority of sin over the life of man would still remain. It would be necessary for man to be continually granted forgiveness for his sins.

Such was the condition of Israel.

Hebrews 10:11. Every high priest stood daily ministering and offering repeatedly the same sacrifices for the sins of Israel. God's Covenant people were still spiritually dead, and needed continual forgiveness for sins which were the outgrowth of that condition.

Hebrews 10:3. There was continual remembrance in the mind of God of Israel's condition of spiritual death.

Forgiveness of sins alone would not break the relationship that existed between man and his spiritual father, Satan. It would not grant fellowship between God and man, or the Father-God's making His home with man.

Redemption must be more than forgiveness.

Redemption must be the giving of a New Nature, a New Life to man.

Redemption meant a New Creation in the spirit of man. Man's need can only be met by his receiving the Nature of God within his spirit.

First, spiritual death must be absolutely destroyed in the life of man. The nature of Satan must be completely eradicated from man's nature, so that he can stand as free from Satanic authority as though he had never died spiritually.

Romans 6:6. The body of sin, spiritual death, must be done away.

Colossians 1:13. Man must be delivered from the authority of Satan.

Hebrews 2:14. Satan, who reigns in the realm of death, must be dethroned from his position as Lord of man.

Hebrews 2:15. Man must be delivered from even any fear of his old master who had held him in bondage. Then man will be free to receive the Life of God.

Genesis 3:24. We remember that God had driven man from the Garden of Eden, so that man would have no access to the Tree of Life while he was spiritually dead.

Man's need is Life, the Nature of God, but God cannot impart His own Nature to man until He first makes it legally possible for man to be freed from the Nature of Satan.

We see that forgiveness on the part of God, and reformation or education on the part of man, would not strike at the root of sin, spiritual death.

Just as Adam had been born again of Satanic nature when he sinned, man who is by nature a child of wrath, must be born again, born of the life of God (John 3:7).

This will make him a son of God. Read John 1:12 and I John 5:1.

This Life of God within the spirit of man will set him free from the law of sin (Romans 8:2).

I John 2:6. The Nature of God will give to man the ability to walk with the Father as Christ walked with Him.

Jesus Christ, although tempted by Satan, was able to walk absolutely in the Father's will, pleasing Him. See Luke 3:22 and John 5:30.

This was due to the fact that He did not belong to the realm of spiritual death, but possessed the Life of God. Eternal Life within the spirit of man today, makes him an heir of God and a joint-heir with Christ (Romans 8:17). The man who has been born again stands before the Father as Christ stood in His earth-walk, and has the same freedom from Satanic dominion, and ability to please the Father, as Christ had. Read John 17:14-18; John 17:22-23 and I Corinthians 1:30.

Eternal Life will set man free from the law of disease (I Peter 2:24).

Romans 8:11 is not referring to the Resurrection. The word "mortal" means "death-doomed." Therefore, the word "mortal" cannot refer to the condition of our bodies after death, for they are then no longer death-doomed, but destroyed by death, and await immortality at the second coming of Christ. Eternal Life dwelling within these bodies will give Life and healing to them now.

Man's receiving of Eternal Life will make it possible for him to receive the spirit of God and for God to dwell in him. Read II Corinthians 6:16 and Ephesians 3:14-21.

This brings man again into the realm of God's ability, the realm where all things are possible (Matthew 17:20).

Man will be able to walk again in the realm of his spirit —the faith-realm—where he lives by the Word of God (Luke 4:4).

Eternal Life will meet the need of man, and the heart cry of the Father for fellowship; but before Eternal Life can be given to man, he must be declared righteous, and God must have a legal right to take man from the family of Satan into His family.

QUESTIONS

1. Name the three wills that are in the world.
2. Explain Matthew 6:24.

3. Why was man driven from the Garden of Eden after he died spiritually?
4. What incident reveals the working of spiritual death within the sons of Adam?
5. Why did reason gain the supremacy over Faith?
6. How does civilization reveal the fact that spiritual death dwells within the spirit of man?
7. Explain why forgiveness for sins alone will not meet the need of lost man.
8. Why must God undertake for man's Redemption?
9. Why and how will Eternal Life meet man's needs?
10. Explain Romans 8:11.

(Be sure to look up and study carefully all Scripture references.)

Lesson 5

MAN'S NEED OF RIGHTEOUSNESS

MAN HAS ever accused God of injustice in regard to His dealings with the human race. Man declares that He is not a God of Love or Justice, because He created man in the face of the fact that He knew he would fall.

Man questions God's right to send one man to Hell and another to Heaven.

Can God justify Himself in the face of these age-old accusations?

The Father-God had a right to create man just as a good man and a good woman have a right to give life to a child.

Adam was the master of himself. He did not have to yield to Satan unless he chose to do so. He was no "missing link," but he was instead the crown of God's creation, standing in the full light of perfect knowledge.

We have seen that man was created for joy and peace; and that sin, sickness, sorrow or death had no place in God's original plan. These present conditions of society and the world are not normal.

God has vindicated Himself and stands acquitted before the human race because He did not leave man in this condition, but provided a Redemption which man could enjoy through faith in Jesus Christ, that would answer man's every need.

A Three-Fold Problem

Man's need can only be met by his receiving Eternal Life, the Nature of God. God, however, cannot impart to man His very nature and give him the privilege of sonship, until He can do so on legal grounds.

Therefore, as the Father-God undertakes the redemption of man, independent of man's own works, the first problem He faces is man's need of Righteousness.

The Book of Romans, which gives us the legal side of our Redemption in Christ, voices this need in the 26th verse of the third chapter. The footnotes of the American Standard Version read: "That He might be righteous and the righteousness of him that hath faith in Jesus."

41

This was the problem. Man must be given righteousness. God must have a legal right to declare spiritually dead man, a child of Satan, righteous.

Man's need of righteousness involved a threefold problem.

First, God must be righteous in His dealings with man. His transgression must not be overlooked, and the penalty must be paid.

Second, God must act towards Satan on grounds of absolute justice. God must redeem man from his authority on legal grounds.

Third, He must not only be just to man and to Satan, but His actions must also be according to His own righteousness. Righteousness is the very foundation of His throne, and the standard must not be lowered. There must be legal grounds on which God can justly judge the human race and compel them to pay the penalty of sin if they reject His Sin-Substitute.

The Penalty of Man's Sin

When Justice made her demand that man pay the penalty of his crime, man was unable to pay even the interest. There was no mitigation for the crime that man had committed. It was High Treason, an unpardonable sin.

The penalty of man's sin was Hell!

Knowing the nature of man's sin, we can understand the reason for Hell. Man is eternal. Angels are eternal. When men and angels become criminals, they become eternal criminals.

Man is a spirit, and there must be an eternal spirit home for man.

When man became a spirit criminal, it was necessary that after death he be taken to jail, to await the White Throne Judgment. After judgment, at which time he receives his sentence, he must then be committed to the federal prison.

Hell was not prepared for man (Matthew 25:41). Hell was prepared for the devil and his angels.

God intended originally that man should live on the earth eternally. The earth was made for this purpose, and man possessed an eternal human body; but when he sinned and became mortal, it was necessary for Hell to be fitted for his confinement.

Being an eternal criminal, there must be a place of eternal restraint for him. There must be a prison; the criminals must be segregated. If they were permitted to roam indiscriminately through eternity, they would demoralize the new heaven and earth.

We have jails, state prisons, and federal prisons for the criminals who break the laws of man, with life imprisonment for habitual criminals.

Who can raise a protest against God if He has a prison in which are incarcerated the men who violate the laws of Heaven, and who are eternal criminals?

The universal human believes in some kind of Hell or place of confinement for punishment after death, and this testimony is not easily ruled out of court. There is no type of testimony so convincing to a jury and judge as the testimony of universal human consciousness.

God's Justice Toward Satan

God, in restoring righteousness to man, must not take advantage of Satan. Adam's sin of High Treason gave Satan a legal right to rule creation, and made man his legal subject and slave. God, in His omnipotence, is stronger than Satan, but He must strip him of his authority in such a way that he is dealt with justly. The plan that is to be enacted must be upon unquestionably legal grounds.

God's Justice Toward Man

In dealing with man on the grounds of justice, God must recognize the transgression and see that the penalty is paid. Man's redemption must be legitimate, thus allowing the redeemed man to maintain his self-respect, knowing that he was justified on legal grounds.

When man sinned, he became a partaker of Satan's nature; and, as a result of his transgression, he must be incarcerated in Hell. Someone must go there and pay his penalty so that man can be given Eternal Life and a standing before God as though he had never sinned.

This redemption will free man from the penalty of going to Hell. If he refuses it, and persists in his union with Satan, then he must share the fate of such a one.

43

What the Redemption Must Include

The penalty of Adam's transgression must be adequately paid, so that man can be delivered from Satanic dominion. There must also be placed into the hands of man a weapon of defense and offense. Man must be given authority by which he can meet Satan and conquer him in honorable combat.

A resurrection of man's physical body and Immortality must be granted, because man at the beginning had a perfect human body. Man must now be given an immortal body over which death can have no dominion or authority.

Again, there must be a restoration of the earth to the Edenic glory and beauty; it must be on such a basis that there can never again be a recurrence of Satanic dominion.

Man's redemption must include a New Creation, receiving God's Life or Nature, a perfect righteousness, and a perfect reconciliation of fellowship, so that man will feel at home with God once more.

God must be able to give him a son's place in His heart, as well as in Creation, so that righteousness, Sonship privileges, and the fullest fellowship will be man's eternal rights. No redemption that does not give these three great blessings will reach man's needs.

God, Himself, Must Provide a Redeemer

This redemption for man that will restore righteousness to him, must emanate from God. No man himself could meet the demands of Justice on behalf of the human race; for every man born of natural generation is a broken, helpless slave, in the hands of an enemy who rules him, and who has the authority to cast him into Hell. No man can stand before God for himself, for the whole human race is under indictment. Therefore, there is not a man who can represent the human race before God.

The Requirements of the Redeemer

This Redeemer must be a man. This man, however, must not be born of natural generaton. He must be conceived in such a manner that He will not be a subject of Satan. He must not possess within His spirit nature, spiritual death.

44

He must stand before God as the first Adam stood . . . in righteousness, possessing the same dominion and authority.

He must walk on this earth as a man, perfectly pleasing to the Father. He must meet Satan in temptation, as the first man and woman had met him, but He must not yield to Satan's will.

This man must then act as man's substitute. Man's sin, spiritual death itself, must be laid upon this man. Then the judgment of Satan must fall upon Him. He must meet the demands of Justice. In order to do this, He must go to Hell. He must remain there, under judgment, until every legal requirement of Justice has been fully satisfied against the human race. He must stay there and suffer until God can legally acquit every human being who takes Him as Saviour, and every human being who trusted in the Blood Covenant from the beginning.

Not only must this Redeemer be free from Satanic dominion in His earth-walk, but He must be a being greater than Satan . . . One who, after the penalty has been paid, will be able to conquer Satan, taking from him his lordship and legal dominion over man. He must conquer death, bringing life and immortality to the broken, bondaged human.

No angel can act as man's redeemer, for an angel could not meet the demands of justice. No man could fulfill the requirements of Justice for a Redeemer, because of his union with and subjection to Satan.

Only God is greater than Satan; therefore, God and man must be united in one individual. The Incarnation is the only answer to man's need of righteousness. Only the union of God and man will provide a Redeemer Who will walk in righteousness as a man, with the ability to pay man's penalty and conquer Satan.

Deity must suffer for man. God had created a man in the face of the fact that He knew he would fall. The responsibility of such a creation rested on the Father-God. He must provide a Redemption. The only way for humanity to be given Righteousness is the Incarnation of God's own Son.

God's beloved Son must come out of the Father's bosom, lay aside His Glory and Majesty that He had enjoyed with the Father. He must come to earth, taking upon Himself the physical body of a human.

He must walk as a son, pleasing the Father, and conquering Satan in His earth-walk as a man.

Then God must take man's sin-nature, that hideous, monstrous thing, spiritual death, and lay it upon the spirit of His Holy Eternal Son. The Son must go under judgment, and the wrath and indignation of Eternal Justice must be meted out toward Him.

When He has paid the penalty for man, He shall be made righteous, and that righteousness will become man's.

It was through one man that judgment had come; therefore, one man without sin shall be able, on legal grounds, to pay that penalty, so the human race shall be declared free from guilt and unrighteousness if they confess the Lordship of the Incarnate One.

The conclusion of our lesson is this . . . man's need of Eternal Life demands first, righteousness, and man's need of righteousness demands the Incarnation.

A Study in the Scriptures Covered in the Lesson
Scriptures revealing the unrighteousness of man:

Romans 1:18, "The wrath of God revealed against all ungodliness and unrighteousness of man."

Romans 3:9-10, "All under sin: none righteous, no not one."

Romans 5:16-18, "Of one unto condemnation."

Romans 5:19, "The many were made sinners."

Scriptures revealing that judgment rested upon man:

Romans 5:16-18, "Through one trespass the judgment came unto all men."

John 16:8, "Convicted of judgment."

John 16:11, "Of judgment because the prince of this world hath been judged." Satan's judgment became man's.

John 3:36, "The wrath of God abideth on him."

Scriptures showing Hell as the place of confinement:

Psalm 9:17, "The wicked turned unto Sheol."

Revelation 20:13-15, if any was not found written in the Book of Life, he was cast into the Lake of Fire.

II Peter 2:4, "But cast them down to Hell, and committed them to pits of darkness, reserved unto judgment."

Scriptures showing the inability of man to redeem himself:

Ephesians 2:12, "No hope, and without God."

Isaiah 59:15-16, God saw there was no righteousness, no man to act on man's behalf: therefore His own arm brought salvation and righteousness to him.

Romans 3:20, by the works of the law shall no flesh be accounted righteous (footnotes of the American Standard Version).

I John 3:10, "Children of Satan."

John 8:34, he that committeth sin is the bond-servant of sin.

Ephesians 2:2-3, walking according to Satan.

Colossians 1:13, man in the authority of Satan.

Hebrews 2:14-15, Satan holds the dominion of the realm of spiritual death, and man in bondage to him.

Scriptures revealing that Christ, the Incarnate One, did meet the requirements of Justice as man's Redeemer:

In His earth-walk: John 8:29, "For I do always the things that are pleasing to Him."

As man's Sin-Substitute: II Corinthians 5:21; Isaiah 53:4-6; and Romans 4:25.

As the Conqueror of Satan: Colossians 2:15; Hebrews 2:14-15; Philippians 2:9-10; and Revelation 1:18.

QUESTIONS

1. How has God vindicated Himself of the charge of injustice?

2. Why was the penalty of man's transgression Hell?

3. What was involved within the problem of God's justice toward man?

4. What did God's justice toward Satan demand?

5. Why was no man able to redeem humanity?

6. (a) Name the requirements that a Redeemer must meet.
   (b) What is His work on man's behalf to be?

7. What must man's Redemption include?

8. Describe the fellowship between the new man in Christ and God.

9. Give a Scripture showing:
   (a) Man's unrighteousness.
   (b) The judgment that rested on man.
   (c) Man's inability to make himself righteous.
10. Did you study each Scripture?

Lesson 6
MAN'S NEED OF A MEDIATOR

IN OUR LAST TWO lessons we studied the problems that God faced in providing a Redemption for man.

After man had died spiritually, his first need was that of receiving Eternal Life, the nature of God. We saw, however, that God could not impart to man His own nature except on grounds of righteousness, which is the second need of man.

The third need of man was that of a Mediator, some one who could approach God on his behalf.

We remember that after his sin of High Treason, Adam was cast from the presence of God. He had lost his fellowship with the Father-God. Man stood in the unrighteousness of Satan (John 16:11). He had no standing with Deity nor right to approach Him.

The universal man in his condition of Spiritual Death, recognized that he had no standing with his Creator. The temples, altars and priesthoods of all nations eloquently confess man's consciousness of sin, his fear of death and judgment, and his inability to approach Deity in his own righteousness.

India, with its millions of priests struggling in absolute hopelessness, leading their soul-hungry people still deeper into darkness, is an illustration of man's conscious need of a Mediator.

Man's Condition Before God

We have seen in the previous lessons that man's sin united him with Satan.

Man now stands before God, not only as a subject of Satan politically (Colossians 1:13a), but also as one in vital union with him (Ephesians 2:2 and I John 3:10).

This identification of man with Satan caused the judgment and unrighteousness of Satan to become his (John 16:11).

Man became alienated from God (Ephesians 4:18). His mind and understanding became darkened by the god of this world (II Corinthians 4:4).

Romans 3:9-18 gives fourteen charges against the human race in its condition of Spiritual Death.

49

The declaration from the Throne of Deity is that there is none righteous (Romans 3:10), and there is none that understandeth and seeketh after God (Romans 3:11).

Ephesians 2:12 describes the condition of spiritually dead man. He has no covenant claims upon God; he had forfeited every right God had conferred upon him.

In his creation by the hand of God, man had stood in righteousness with legal grounds of approach and communion with Deity. Man forfeited these by his treason, and his condition is described as without hope and without God.

Adam, who had rejoiced in his fellowship with the Father-God, felt immediately after the entrance of Spiritual Death his inability to stand before God. This is shown in Genesis 3:8.

Man then had need of a mediator, one who could stand before God in righteousness and at the same time represent humanity, and approach God on his behalf.

Hopeless, and Godless in a world where Satan holds the authority of death, man's condition is certainly desperate. As far as human efforts are concerned, man's condition is hopeless. He has no grounds for prayer; if God hears his prayer, it is upon grounds of Grace alone.

The Father-God in His love and desire for fellowship with man, immediately made a means of approach unto Himself for man.

To Adam and his children God gave a medium of approach (Genesis 3:21 and 4:4).

Israel's approach to God was through tabernacles, priesthoods and offerings. Outside of God's appointed way, man had, or has today, no approach to the Father-God.

From the time of man's alienation from God at the fall, to the time that Christ sat down at the Father's right hand, no man has had a right to approach God except through a Divinely appointed priesthood, over a bleeding sacrifice, dreams, visions, or angelic visitations.

Man's Inability to Approach God

In the life of Israel we have illustrations of man's attempting to force himself into the presence of God before Eternal Life came through Jesus Christ and justification on the grounds of His Finished Work.

There are many acts of Divine Justice in the Old Testament which are hard to understand except in the light of man's need of a Mediator.

Leviticus 10:1-3 is a recorded incident of one of the lessons that was necessary to cause Israel to know its spiritual condition before Deity.

What a calamitous closing of the dedication of the priesthood. Aaron and his family that morning had been aspiring to the highest point of Divine favor: the tabernacle had been reared; the Shekinah presence had filled it with glory; the majesty of Jehovah was resting upon Israel.

Behind them lay a series of Divine Miracles that had marked them as God's chosen people, and now Aaron's firstborn heir to the priesthood with his brother is suddenly smitten with death before the whole congregation. What had occasioned it?

These two sons, lingering near the tent of meeting at noon, in a spirit of bravado or curiosity, took up censers with live coals, poured incense upon them, and entered the Holy of Holies, contrary to God's appointed way. No one but the High Priest could go there, and he could go only once a year.

Suddenly, the young men stagger, stumble, and fall dead.

As Aaron stands horrified, shocked and stunned in the presence of the dead, Moses cries to him, "Aaron, this is it that Jehovah spake, saying, I shall be sanctified in them that come nigh me, and before all the people I will be glorified." And Aaron held his peace. Israel had learned that man could not approach God uninvited and in his own way.

We have another sample of man's attempt to approach Jehovah unauthorized in Numbers 16. It is the story of Korah and his rebellion.

Korah and a company of the leaders of Israel are jealous of Moses and Aaron, and insist that they have as much right to approach Jehovah as have God's appointed High Priests.

Moses puts the issue to the test in the presence of the whole congregation.

He invited Korah and his followers to appear before Jehovah with their censers, ready for worship.

As soon as they came, Moses warned the people to get up from the tents of these wicked men who dared to approach God uninvited and in their own way.

No sooner had Moses ceased speaking than the earth opened its mouth, and the men with their families dropped down alive into Sheol.

Israel ran away from the scene, frightened, filled with awe and reverence for such a holy God.

Another illustration is given to us in I Samuel 6:19. The Ark of the Covenant had been captured because of Eli's great sin. It had been taken down into Gath by the Philistines; and after a series of judgments that had fallen upon the heathen cities because of their desecration of the Ark, they put it on a cart and sent it back to Beth-shamesh.

The cattle that were drawing the cart turned off the road into the fields. When some of the people laboring in the field saw the Ark, the news spread rapidly over the hillsides until thousands of people gathered from the country round about, reverent and curious.

Then a bolder spirit than the others drew near and threw off the heavy covering from the Ark of the Covenant, and the people for the first time saw that Holy Receptacle of the Ten Commandments.

Suddenly, a plague struck them, and fifty thousand men fell dead upon the ground. Awful fear and consternation fell upon the people; beating their breasts, they turned back to their homes.

It has been shown again that no one can approach God but through a High Priest or over a bleeding sacrifice. Man, because of his Satanic nature, cannot come into God's presence uninvited. He needs a Mediator.

Man's Cry for a Mediator

Job voiced man's cry for a Mediator. The theme of his poetry could be called the question of the ages: "How can man stand right with God?"

The book of Job is the oldest of all the books of the Bible. It was evidently written by Jobab, a cousin of Abraham, about the time that Jacob went to Egypt. Portions of this book show how vital a problem was man's need of a Mediator in Job's day.

Read Job 4:12-17. We have a picture of a man asleep in his tent at night. In a vision he heard a voice saying, "Shall mortal man be just before God? Shall a man be pure before his maker?" (marginal rendering). This is the old and the eternal problem that has confronted the thinking man of all ages. Can mortal man be justified or acquitted before God? Shall fallen man be pure before his Maker? Note the word "mortal." The word "mortal" applies only to the physical body; it means "death-doomed," "frail"; in other words, a subject of the devil.

Man became mortal when he passed under the dominion of the devil. The problem is—shall a mortal man, or a death-doomed, or a Satan-ruled man stand uncondemned in the presence of God? Read Job 9:25-35.

In the ninth chapter Job speaks out the deepest soul agony of universal man. He lies in his tent surrounded by those whom he loves. He opens his heart with perfect freedom, speaking the fear that grips his soul in the death struggle. He gives figures of speech that describe the rapidity with which life passes to the aged.

He continues, "If I say I will forget my calamity, I will put off my sad countenance and be of good cheer, I am afraid of my sorrows. I know that thou wilt not hold me innocent; I shall be condemned."

Every false hope has fled; he is alone with his guilt and despair.

He says, "What is the use in trying to brighten up and put off my sad countenance; I am afraid of my sorrows."

It is the frankness of despair. It is the hopelessness of full-orbed knowledge. "I shall be condemned."

He cries, "Why then do I labor in vain? If I wash myself with snow-water and make my hands never so clean; yet wilt thou plunge me in the ditch, and mine own clothes shall abhor me."

What a picture: "Mine own clothes (or self-righteousness) shall abhor me: for he is not a man, as I am that we should come together in judgment."

Job knows that he cannot face God, for God is not mortal. He is not under the bondage and guilt of sin as is Job. Then Job utters the saddest words that ever fell from the lips of a human being.

"There is no umpire betwixt us, that might lay his hand upon us both."

In other words, there is no Mediator between us who has a legal standing with God, and at the same time can sympathize and understand as well as represent humanity. This is Job's cry for a Mediator; it is not the cry of Job alone, but Job has gathered up the cry of the ages and breathed it forth into one hopeless sob.

How bitterly he says, "Let him take His rod away from me, and let not His terror make me afraid: then I would speak, and not fear Him; for I am not so in myself."

Job 25:4-6, "How then can man be just before God? Or how can he be clean that is born of a woman? Behold, even the moon hath no brightness, and the stars are not pure in his sight. How much less man, that is a worm, and the son of man, that is a worm!"

"How can he be clean that is born of a woman?" The writer here has the fall of man through Eve before his mind.

When he tells us that the stars are not pure in the sight of God, he is referring us to Adam's treason when he turned creation into the hands of the devil. Satan has defiled it so that God cannot look with joy upon it.

In speaking of man as a worm, he shows the depths into which man has fallen. The worm has reference to Satan and the Old Serpent, and man who is termed a worm is spiritually a child of the devil, utterly hopeless and without approach to God.

Job has voiced clearly man's need of a Mediator.

Jeremiah recognized that man had need of a Mediator.

Jeremiah 30:21, "And their Prince shall be of themselves, and their ruler shall proceed from the midst of them; and I will cause him to draw near, and he shall approach unto me: for who is he that hath had boldness to approach unto me? saith Jehovah." The margin reads, "Who hath been surety for his heart that he might approach Me."

Jeremiah realized that no man had a right to stand in God's presence, nor power to do it, and he tells us that there is one being who will be able to draw near, standing uncondemned in God's presence. He foretells of the Mediator whom God will provide for man.

Requirements of a Mediator

We saw that man's need of Eternal Life and righteousness could be met only by the Incarnation of God's Son. Again the Incarnation is the only answer to man's need of a Mediator.

No human being born of natural generation could approach God on man's behalf because of the universality of Spiritual Death.

The requirements of a Mediator for man are the following:

1. He must be a man, for he must represent humanity.
2. He must possess the capacity to understand and to sympathize with the temptations of man.
3. He must also possess a standing of righteousness with Deity.
4. He must not be a subject of Satan; he must be free from all Satanic authority.

These requirements could be met only by the union of God and man in one individual.

QUESTIONS

1. What in human history reveals that universal man recognizes that he has no standing with Deity?
2. Give a description of man's standing before God after his sin. Give Scripture.
3. Why did man need a Mediator?
4. What were the means of approach unto God that were given to Adam and his family?
5. What did the incident in Leviticus 10:1-3 reveal to Israel?
6. Explain the two other incidents in the life of Israel that show man's need of a Mediator?
7. How did Job voice man's need of a Mediator?
8. Explain and give the Scripture in Jeremiah that showed man's need of a Mediator.

9. What were the requirements of a Mediator for man?
10. How could man's need of a Mediator be met?

Lesson 7
THE PROMISED INCARNATION

IN OUR PREVIOUS LESSONS, we saw the entrance of Spiritual Death into the life of man. In studying the problems that the Father-God faced in providing a Redemption from Spiritual Death for man, we saw that man's need of a Redeemer demanded the union of Deity and humanity in one individual. Man's need of Righteousness, Eternal Life, and a Mediator, could only be met by the Incarnation of God's Son.

The Incarnation of Deity with humanity will provide a substitute of Deity and humanity united on such grounds that the Incarnate One can stand as man's mediator. Being equal with God on the one hand, and united with man on the other, He will be able to bring the two together.

Again, being Deity and humanity united, He will be able to assume the obligations of human treason and satisfy the claims of justice, and thereby bridge the chasm between God and man.

God's First Promise of the Incarnation

When man committed the crime of High Treason, he died spiritually. In his existence of spiritual death, his condition is described as "without hope and without God in the world."

Immediately God's love began to work on man's behalf. The Father-God faced man's condition squarely. He knew that man's needs could only be met on legal grounds by the Incarnation of His Son. His love counted no sacrifice too great that would bring man again into His fellowship.

Mercy and truth were met together (Psalm 85:10) and the triumph of love gave to man a promise of a Redeemer.

In His conversation with Satan, God gives to him the first promise of the Incarnation.

Genesis 3:15, "And I will put enmity between thee and the woman, between thy seed and her seed, he shall bruise thy head, and thou shalt bruise his heel."

Let us notice four remarkable statements in this promise:

57

First, "I will put enmity between thee and the woman." That is, there will be enmity between Satan and woman. This is proved by woman's history. She has been bought and sold as common chattel. Only where Christianity has reached the hearts of a country has woman ever received any treatment that would lift her above the brute creation.

In Christian countries she is the heir of our diseases and the victim of the divorce court. Doctors tell us that 95 percent of all the hospital cases are women.

Second, "I will put enmity between thy seed and her seed." Satan's seed is the unregenerate human race, and woman's seed is Christ.

Christ was hunted from His babyhood by Satan's seed, until finally they nailed Him to the cross; and from the Resurrection of Jesus until this day, the church has been the subject of the bitterest persecutions and enmity of the world.

Third, "The seed of the woman." Here is a prophecy that a woman shall give birth to a child independent of natural generation. A child is always called the "seed of man."

Fourth, "And He shall bruise thy head, and thou shalt bruise his heel."

"He shall bruise thy head"—that is, the head of Satan. In all Oriental languages, the term, "bruise the head," means "breaking the lordship of the ruler."

A man has given to Satan his dominion. Satan has just come into the dominion that God had given to man. He is going to exercise that dominion until the Seed of Woman comes. A man is going to break his lordship.

"The heel" is the Church in its earth walk. The long ages of persecution of the Church by the seed of Satan are a matter of history.

This is a remarkable prophecy, and how clearly it has been fulfilled. The Incarnate One has come and brought to nought him that had the authority of death, that is, the devil, and delivered all them who through fear of death were all their lifetime subject to bondage (Hebrews 2:14).

This Scripture has also found its fulfillment in Jesus' bitter persecution, which finds its culmination in His death on the Cross; and then, in the persecution of the Church, which is the Body of Christ, and which carries out His Will upon the earth.

Genesis 3:20, "The man called his wife's name Eve, because she was the mother of all living."

The word "Eve" in Hebrew is "Havvah," which literally means the "living one," or "the life-giver."

Here God tells man that his wife shall be the mother of the "life-giving One," our Christ.

Universal Man's Desire for the Incarnation

The teaching of the Incarnation is not out of harmony with human desire or tradition. It has been believed in by all tribes of people in some form.

Universal man has craved an Incarnation. His spirit hungers for union with Deity, because he was created in God's image with the ability to partake of God's life.

This is proved by man's drinking the blood of human sacrifices, by the naming of his kings after the titles of his deities, and also making his emperor or king an incarnation of Deity.

The gods of the Greeks and Romans were supposed to have been divine and human, showing man's hunger for a union with Deity.

The Incarnation is no more difficult to believe than the creation of the first man. Adam was created by an act of Divine Power: the rest of the human race was generated by natural processes; but this Redeemer, Who is to be born of the woman, is to be formed by a special act of Divine Power. He is God Almighty, and the Incarnation is a possibility with Him.

Satan's Attempts to Thwart God's Plan

We do not know how clearly Satan realized the plan of God for man's Redemption that was given in the promised Redeemer. We know that he did not fully understand it, or he would not have crucified Christ (I Corinthians 2:8).

He thought that crucifixion was the destruction of Christ's life, not knowing that it was the means of man's Redemption.

Nevertheless, Satan must have realized the fact that a Redeemer was coming through humanity who would break his dominion over man.

He, therefore, seeks to destroy the plan of the Father-God.

The working of Satan to thwart the purpose of God follows two lines:

He seeks (1) to destroy the knowledge of God on the earth, and (2) to destroy a Righteous line in humanity.

Through these two he will make it impossible for a Redeemer to ever come through humanity. He desires to separate man from all fellowship with God.

Satan's first attempt to pursue his purpose was in the murder of Abel by Cain (Genesis 4:1-15).

Abel had had witness borne to him that he was righteous by offering a sacrifice in faith according to the revelation that God had given to him.

Genesis 4:4, "And Abel, he also brought of the firstlings of his flock and of the fat thereof, and Jehovah had respect unto his offering."

Hebrews 11:4, "By faith Abel offered unto God a more excellent sacrifice than Cain, through which he had witness borne to him that he was righteous. God bearing witness in respect to his gifts, and through it he being dead still speaketh."

Satan did not know but what Abel would be man's Redeemer, therefore he destroyed his life. In doing this he destroyed the righteous line then existing.

Genesis 4:25, Seth was born to Adam and Eve. Eve seemed to realize that a righteous line had been destroyed and that Seth had been given to fulfill Abel's place. She named him Seth, which means "substitute," and said, "God hath appointed me another seed instead of Abel, for Cain slew him."

The Seed of the Woman

As generations pass, Spiritual Death is at work within the life of man, causing him to walk alienated from God, with his mind blinded (Ephesians 4:17-18).

Satan is attempting to make the seed of the woman so utterly estranged from God that He will never be able to send a Redeemer through humanity.

The only promise so far given in reference to the Incarnation had been very general. Therefore, Satan's bitter war against the seed of the woman is general.

Later on, God makes the promise of the Redeemer more specific and marked; and as we study we shall see a specific working of Satan to the destruction of the righteous line named by God.

Genesis 3:15, the Incarnate One is called the seed of the woman, a general term.

Genesis 12:3, it becomes more marked, and the Incarnate One is specified as being "the seed of Abraham."

Psalm 89:3-4, He is termed the "seed of David." He shall come from the family of David. A family is marked.

And Isaiah 7:14 makes it still more specific when he says, "Behold the Virgin shall conceive and bear a son, and call His Name Immanuel." He says, "the virgin," just as though He had marked her out. An individual is marked.

As we study the history of Israel, we shall see the efforts of Satan directed toward the seed of Abraham, and then the seed of David, and then his bitter hatred and persecution of Jesus Christ, born of the Virgin.

Genesis 5

Genesis 5 gives to us the genealogy of Noah. As Satan works to destroy a righteous line, God is preserving a line through which the Redeemer shall come. He is working toward the Incarnation.

It is well for you to read chapters four and five, that two things may be noticed.

After Cain is brought conspicuously before us by the murder of his brother, his issue is traced for just a little way, and ends in Lamech, also a murderer (Gen. 4:18-23).

The Holy Spirit seeks to interest us in another man altogether, the third son born to Adam and Eve, named "Seth" (Genesis 4:24-26.).

In this line came Noah, Shem, Abraham, Jacob, and then later on, Jesus Himself—the seed of the woman who

61

bruised the serpent's head. In order to fix our attention on Seth, the righteous line, the Divine Author reiterates at the beginning of chapter five the original account of creating man, tracing the history of Adam briefly, and then giving in detail the line of Seth.

This shows us His dealings are now with this line.

Genesis 6

Genesis 6:1-3, "And it came to pass, when men began to multiply on the face of the ground, and daughters were born to them, that the sons of God saw the daughters of men that they were fair; and they took them wives of all they chose."

We notice here the marked distinction between the Cainites and the Sethites, the Righteous line. The Cainites built cities, invented arts and devised amusements to palliate the curse of sin (Genesis 4:21-22).

The Sethites walked with God (Genesis 4:26).

In Genesis 4:25 the word "LORD" in capitals indicates that in the original it is Jehovah, the Covenant name of God. They who believed and had hope in His promise knew and loved that name. It is well to note that the seventh from Adam through the line of Cain, Lamech, was a polygamist, murderer, and worshipper of the god of forces (Genesis 4:16-24); while the seventh in the line of Seth was Enoch, a man who had this testimony, that he pleased God (Hebrews 11:5), and was translated (Genesis 5:21-24).

In the sixth chapter of Genesis we see again the working of Satan to thwart the purpose of God. He causes the intermarriage of the line of Cain with the righteous line. This corrupts the line through which the Redeemer shall come to such an extent that only Noah is left in the worship of the Covenant God.

Genesis 6:5, "And Jehovah saw that the wickedness of man was great in the earth, and that every imagination of the heart was evil continually."

Satan had destroyed the knowledge of God in the heart of man. The thought of every man's heart was evil continually. Only Noah knew and walked with the true God (Genesis 6:8-9).

If humanity were left in that condition, after Noah's death, the knowledge of God would have been completely lost. The Righteous line would have been destroyed, and the Incarnation would have been an impossibility.

Seemingly, Satan had triumphed in his efforts, but God Almighty's purpose was not to be thwarted.

It was a small matter for Him to bring an end to humanity in its corrupt condition (Genesis 6:11-13).

If a righteous line were preserved, and the knowledge of Himself kept upon the earth, God must destroy humanity and continue the line through which the Redeemer would come—through Noah.

In the past, if we have not understood the working of the Father-God toward the Incarnation, perhaps the destruction of humanity by the flood has been hard for us to understand.

Now, in the light of the fact that man's need could only be met by the Incarnation, we can see that the flood was imperative.

QUESTIONS

1. Explain the four statements made in Genesis 3:15.

2. Why does universal man crave union with Deity?

3. How does history reveal the fact that universal man craves an Incarnation?

4. What were the two means Satan used to thwart God's plan of the Incarnation?

5. Give Satan's first attempt to destroy the righteous line.

6. Tell the distinction between the Cainites and the Sethites.

7. Tell what you can of Adam's descendants through Cain.

8. Why is special attention given in Chapter 5 to the line of Seth?

9. What was the purpose in Satan's causing the intermarriage of Cainites and Sethites as recorded in Genesis 6:1-3?

10. Why was the flood necessary?

Notes

Lesson 8

THE ABRAHAMIC COVENANT

IN OUR STUDY of the preceding lessons, we saw that after man died spiritually, his need of a Mediator, Righteousness and Eternal Life, could be met only by the Incarnation of God's Son.

In our last lesson, we traced the working of the Grace of God from the time He gave to man the promise of the Incarnation, to the time of the flood, in His preserving a righteous line through which the Redeemer could come.

We saw that Satan, in his effort to make the Incarnation an impossibility, corrupted humanity to the extent that the flood became imperative.

Noah, who knew God, was spared with his family. He preserved the true faith in Jehovah, and handed it to his sons.

We remember that there were two means Satan used to thwart the purpose of God in the Incarnation. They were: (1) his seeking to destroy the knowledge of God upon the earth, and (2) his seeking to destroy the righteous line.

The Tower of Babel

From the time of the flood until the building of the tower of Babel, there was worship of God. Not that all men accepted it, for many wickedly rebelled against it; but the knowledge and revelation of the true God was too fresh in their minds for them to set up other gods.

We notice that in the ninth chapter of Genesis a command had been given to replenish the earth. In the eleventh chapter of Genesis, we see that the whole earth was of one language and one speech. The unity of the race was untouched. The ark in which Noah and his family were preserved, had rested in Armenia. As men began to multiply, this barren tableland no longer sufficed. Men must either separate and fill the earth as God had told them to do, or a more fertile territory must be found if they are to keep together. The latter course was resolved upon, so they passed down into the rich, fertile lowlands in the plain of Shinar (Genesis 11:2).

They resolved upon a permanent settlement there in order to build a city and tower, that they might not be scattered abroad upon the face of the earth (Genesis 11:4).

Jehovah came down and confounded their language, which caused their being scattered over the earth (Genesis 11:7-9). From there the streams of population poured forth to all parts of the world: northwest to Europe, west to Asia Minor, southwest to Egypt and Africa, south to Arabia, southeast to Persia and India, and east to China. Of course, this was not the work of a day. It took ages and ages for the more distant lands to be settled.

After men had been scattered, the worship and knowledge of Jehovah passed into the worship of the powers of nature and then into idols. Sense knowledge took the place of God's Revelation which had been given to spiritually dead man.

The oldest sacred books and traditions of each nation bear witness to the account in the scripture (Romans 1:18-32), that each nation originally possessed a revelation of God. From these ancient writings and traditions, with the aid of monumental inscriptions, we can get quite a clear picture of the passing from the worship of one God into the worship of many gods and of many idols.

The Call of Abraham

Three hundred and sixty-seven years after the flood, Abraham appears. Noah was alive for fifty years after the birth of Abraham. The world had lapsed into idolatry. Abraham lived among pagans and idolators until he was seventy-five years of age.

He had been born and had lived in Ur of the Chaldees, one of the most splendid ancient cities, until he received his call from God.

We can understand why God revealed Himself to Abraham. The Revelation of God was practically lost. If a righteous line were to be preserved through which God could send His Incarnate Son, He must choose one man who knew Him, and make of him a nation that would preserve the knowledge of Himself upon the earth.

Abraham's countrymen and his father were idolators. If in him a nation was to be founded that would preserve

God's Revelation to man, and a knowledge of man's Redeemer so that He would be recognized when He came, it was necessary for Abraham to be removed from these influences. There are many legends that tell of Abraham's being persecuted for his refusal to worship idols. So, under a call of God, he set out in search of a land where a nation could be founded, free from idolatry (Genesis 12).

Twenty-five years after Abraham had received his call from God, the greatest event in human history until the birth of Christ, took place. It was the Blood Covenant into which Jehovah and Abraham entered.

Before we can understand the significance of this Covenant which God cut with Abraham, we must know the meaning of the Blood Covenant.

The Blood Covenant existed before Abraham. Proofs of the existence of this rite of Blood Covnanting have been found among primitive peoples of every quarter of the globe, and its antiquity is carried back to a date long prior to the days of Abraham.

The Blood Covenant

It is evident that God cut the covenant or entered into a covenant with Adam at the very beginning. A common revelation of the Blood Covenant from God must have been given to primitive man. We saw the scattering of man at the tower of Babel. Noah evidently must have possessed a knowledge of the significance of the Blood Covenant which he handed to his children, so that as the nations were formed, from the dispersion at the tower of Babel, each one possessed a knowledge of the Blood Covenant.

We believe this because of the following facts that are revealed in Dr. Trumbull's book which is entitled, "The Blood Covenant."

"From the very beginning in every nation, Blood . . . seems to have been looked upon as preeminently the representative of Life; as indeed, in a peculiar sense life itself. The transference of blood from one organism to another, has been counted as the transference of life with all that that life includes. The intercommingling of blood has been understood as equivalent to the intercommingling of natures. Two natures, thus intercommingled by the intercommingling of blood, have been considered as forming thenceforth one nature, one life, one soul. The union of natures by the mingling of blood has been deemed possible between man and man, and Deity and man."

A covenant of blood, a covenant made by the intercommingling of blood, has been recognized as the closest, the holiest, and most indissoluble compact conceivable.

There are three reasons for men cutting the Covenant with each other.

If a strong tribe lives by the side of a weaker tribe, and there is danger of the weaker tribe being destroyed, the weaker will seek to cut the covenant with the stronger tribe that they may be preserved.

Or if two business men want to go into business, and one is going to leave the country and travel as a foreign representative, he will cut the covenant with his partner.

Or, if two men love each other as devotedly as David and Jonathan, they will cut the covenant.

The moment the blood covenant is solemnized, every thing that a Blood Covenant man owns is at the disposal of this blood-brother; yet this brother would never ask for anything unless he were absolutely driven by want to do it.

Another feature is that as soon as this covenant is cut, they are called by others "the blood brothers."

That blood covenant goes down through the generations; it is an indissoluble covenant that generations cannot erase. If a man cuts the covenant with his friend, the children of the two families are bound to observe it.

If two men in Africa cut the Covenant—Mr. Stanley tells us and Livingstone bears witness — and one man should break the Covenant, his nearest relatives would seek his death, for no man can live in Africa who breaks the Covenant; he curses the ground.

There is nothing that is absolutely sacred with us, but in Africa, the Covenant is sacred. Mr. Stanley and Dr. Livingstone both testify to the fact that they never knew the covenant to be broken.

The method of cutting the covenant is practically the same the world over. In some places it has degenerated into a very grotesque rite, but it is the same blood covenant. The method which is practiced by the Africans, Arabians, Syrians and Balkans is this:

Two men who wish to cut the covenant come together with friends and a priest. First, they exchange gifts. Then they bring a cup of wine. The priest makes an incision in the arm of each man, allowing the blood to drip into the wine. Then they mingle the wine and drink it. Now they are blood brothers. (Read our book, *The Blood Covenant*.)

The Abrahamic Covenant

The seventeenth chapter of Genesis takes on new meaning for us now. We see that when God appeared to Abraham to make a covenant with him, that Abraham knew what it meant. God was coming into a covenant of strong friendship with him. (The Blood Covenant was called the Covenant of Strong Friendship.) That is why Abraham was called the friend of God (James 2:23; Isaiah 41:8 and II Chronicles 20:7).

Abraham is the only human being who was called the friend of God in the Old Testament.

The Covenant that God cut with Abraham was to bring the Israelitish nation into being as a Covenant people (Genesis 17:7).

Then God gave to Abraham the method of cutting the Covenant (Genesis 17:10-14). The seal of the Covenant was Circumcision. Every male child was circumcised at the age of eight days, and that circumcision was the entrance into the covenant.

Genesis 17:26, in the selfsame day, Abraham was circumcised; and thenceforward he bore in his flesh the evidence that he had entered into the Blood Covenant of friendship with God. To this day, Abraham is designated in the East as the "friend of God."

After the formal covenant of blood had been cut between God and Abraham, there came a testing of Abraham's fidelity to that Covenant. This testing would also give evidence to the future generations of the fact that the cutting of the covenant on the part of Abraham in the rite of Circumcision had not been an empty ceremony, but that in that he had pledged his very life to Jehovah.

Genesis 15:6, "He believed in Jehovah, and He reckoned it to him for righteousness." The Hebrew word, "Heemeem," here translated, "believed in," carries the idea of an unqualified committal of one's self to another. Abraham so trusted Jehovah that he was ready to commit himself to Jehovah as in the rite of the Blood Covenant.

Therefore, God counted Abraham's spirit of loving and longing trust as ready for a blood covenant friendship between them.

Genesis 22:1-19, the testing came when Isaac, a blood covenant child that God had miraculously given to Abraham, was eighteen or twenty years old.

Abraham's Testing

Genesis 22:1, 2, "And it came to pass that God did prove Abraham and said unto him, Abraham; and he said Here am I. And He said, Take now thy son, thy only son whom thou lovest, even Isaac, and get thee into the land of Moriah and offer him there for a burnt offering upon one of the mountains which I tell you of." And Abraham rose instantly to respond to the call of his Divine Friend.

Just here, it is well to recognize the Oriental thought in a transaction like this. An Oriental father prizes an only son more than he prizes his own life. For an Oriental father to die without a son is a terrible thought, but with a son to take his place, he is ready to die.

For Abraham to have surrendered his own toil-worn life, now that a son of promise had been born to him, would have been a minor matter, at the call of God; but for Abraham to surrender that son and to become again a hopeless, childless old man, was a different matter. Only a faith that would neither reason nor question, only a love that would neither fail nor waver, could meet an issue like that. All the world over, men in the covenant of blood-friendship were ready to give that which was dearer than life itself to their Blood-Covenant brothers or their gods. Would Abraham do as much for his Divine Friend as men would do for their human friends? Would Abraham surrender to his God all that the worshippers of other gods were

70

willing to surrender in proof of their devotedness? These were questions to be answered before the world.

Genesis 22:3-10, Abraham showed himself capable of even such friendship as this in his Blood Covenant with Jehovah. And when he had manifested his spirit of devotedness, he was told to stay his hand (Hebrews 11:17-19).

Genesis 22:15-17, then it was that the "angel of Jehovah called unto Abraham a second time out of heaven and said, By myself have I sworn (by my life)."

Here is the foundation of that covenant, Godward. There was nothing that God could swear by except Himself. To the Oriental it meant: "I swear by myself. Now if this fails, I become your slave; you own me. I put myself in bondage to you."

They are bound together; all that God is belongs to Abraham, and all that Abraham is or ever will have belongs to God in this Covenant Relationship.

Now you can understand why so many times He said, "I am Jehovah, who keepeth covenants." He is the Covenant-keeping God.

Back behind Israel was this solemn covenant that God had sealed on His side by putting Himself in utter, absolute bondage to that Covenant.

QUESTIONS

1. Why did God confuse their languages at the building of the Tower of Babel?
2. Why was the call from God (that is recorded in Genesis 12:1-2) given to Abraham?
3. Tell of the significance of the Blood Covenant as it existed among primitive peoples.
4. What were the three reasons for cutting the covenant?
5. Why was Abraham called "the friend of God"?
6. What was the seal of the Abrahamic Covenant?
7. What does the Hebrew word in Genesis 15:6 translated as "believe" really mean?
8. What was the test that was given to prove Abraham's fidelity to the Covenant?
9. What did his obedience to God's command reveal?
10. What did the phrase, "By myself have I sworn," in the promise God gave, mean?

71

Notes

Lesson 9
GOD'S COVENANT PEOPLE

IN OUR LAST LESSON we saw that God entered into Covenant relations with Abraham in order to preserve upon the earth the Revelation of Himself which He had given to man.

Abraham and his descendants were to be God's Covenant people.

Genesis 17:7, "And I will establish My Covenant between Me and thee and thy seed after thee throughout their generations for an everlasting Covenant, to be a God unto thee and thy seed after thee."

Through this Covenant people, God was going to send the Redeemer. Genesis 22:17, 18, "That in blessing I will bless thee, and in multiplying I will multiply thy seed as the stars of the heaven, and as the sand which is upon the sea shore; and thy seed shall possess the gate of his enemies; and in thy seed shall all the nations of the earth be blessed; because thou hast obeyed My voice."

The people who were brought into Covenant relationship with God were also to be His testimony upon the earth.

Palestine was located geographically so that the ancient civilizations had to pass through it in their commercial relations with each other.

God's Covenant people were to be a witness to them of the Revelation of the true and living God.

Isaac, Jacob and Joseph

After giving to us the history of Abraham, the book of Genesis gives to us a brief history of his immediate descendants . . . Isaac, Jacob and Joseph.

All Genesis may be grouped around five names: Adam, Chapters 1-5; Noah, Chapters 6-11; Abraham, Chapters 12-26; Jacob, Chapters 27-37; and Joseph, Chapters 38-45.

We will give just a brief summary of the character of these descendants of Abraham in the Blood Covenant.

Isaac, the most beautiful of the Old Testament characters, a gentle, quiet spirit, has left an impression upon Jewish life that no other of the fathers ever gave. His marriage and love for Rebecca is one of the loveliest of the stories of the founders of that wonderful people.

73

Jacob is another character — crooked, selfish and shrewd. It is doubtful that he ever made anyone happy. He met God at Jabbok and God laid His hand upon him. Jacob is a different man from that day. He had power with God and man. His life proves that God can change the most crooked lives and make them straight.

Joseph is our prince—beautiful. Nowhere in literature is there anything to compare with this young boy, man, statesman, founder and preserver of a nation. The fragrance of this life lingers upon the ages of Israel's history. Many boys have been made good and strong by the influence of his commanding personality.

At the age of seventeen Joseph was sold as a slave into Egypt (Genesis 37:25-28). At thirty years of age he became ruler of Egypt (Genesis 41:37-45). When he was forty years old, Jacob with seventy souls went into Egypt (Genesis 46:1-26).

Reason for Going into Egypt

The Covenant-keeping God remembered His promise to Abraham that He would make of him a great nation.

To save His Covenant people from destruction during the famine that was sweeping the land of Canaan, the Covenant God brought them into Egypt, there to thrive and multiply. Genesis 45:6, 7, "For these two years hath the famine been in the land; and there are yet five years, in which there shall be neither plowing or harvest. And God sent me before you to preserve you a remnant in the earth, and to save you alive by a great deliverance."

God used Joseph to preserve His people. He overruled the work of Satan. He has brought good out of evil throughout the ages.

Genesis 45:8, "So now it was not you that sent me hither but God: and He hath made me a father to Pharaoh, and Lord of all his house, and ruler of the land of Egypt."

What a picture it gives to us of the faithfulness and loving care of the God who said when He entered into the Covenant with Abraham, "By myself have I sworn."

The children of Israel thrived among the ease and abundance and balmy brightness of that land. They were favored settlers. The best of the land had been bestowed upon them. They held honorable and well-paid positions under the Egyptian kings (Genesis 47:1-12, 27).

Above all, the favour of God was upon them. He was keeping His Covenant with Abraham and the word that He spake saying that his seed should be a multitude as the stars of heaven, and as the sand upon the sea shore. Their increase was marvelous. God was making of them a great nation which would be His witness upon the earth.

The Scripture in repeated statements directs our attention to the marvelous growth of God's Covenant people. Exodus 1:7, "And the children of Israel were fruitful, and increased abundantly, and multiplied, and waxed exceedingly mighty; and the land was filled with them."

In the 210 years in which the children of Israel were in Egypt, their number increased from seventy to over three million.

The chronology shows that 210 years were spent in Egypt. This seems on the surface at first to present a difficulty with other passages of Scripture, such as Exodus 12:40, which would seem to give the period of their sojourn in Egypt as 430 years.

However, the Septuagint translation of this reads: "The sojourning of the children and of their fathers which they sojourned in the land of Canaan and in the land of Egypt." Galatians 3:16-17 throws light upon it as showing the period began to be reckoned from the date of the promise to Abraham to the deliverance of the children, which makes precisely 430 years. There passed between the entering of Canaan and the birth of Isaac, twenty-five years.

From the birth of Isaac until the birth of Jacob, there were sixty years. Jacob was 130 years old when he entered Egypt. This whole interval amounts to 220 years, 210 years added to this number makes the 430 years—the 430 years of sojourning from Abraham to the deliverance from Egypt.

The Persecution of God's Covenant People

We saw in the last lesson the working of Satan to destroy "the seed of the woman" through whom the promised Redeemer was to come. Now that the Redeemer has been specified as "the seed of Abraham," Satan seeks to destroy God's Covenant People.

After a period of 100 years in Egypt, during which the Israelites had grown into a mighty people, Satan seeks to destroy them.

Satan put fear into the hearts of the statesmen of Egypt, an ill-grounded fear that the Israelites, who were so mighty in number, would join themselves to the enemies of the Egyptians in time of war (Exodus 1:8-10).

Then followed counsels of systematic oppression and enslavement, determined tyranny and cruelty (Exodus 1:10-14).

The increase, however, of Israel was a part of Divine plan for His Covenant People, and all the world could do nothing to arrest it. The more they afflicted them, the more they multiplied and grew (Exodus 1:15-22).

The treatment that slaves received from the Egyptians was sometimes very horrible. The mutilations and tortures that were inflicted upon the Israelites, with the command that every son be killed or cast into the river, were of Satanic character.

The persecution that Israel receives is so great that they cry to the God of the Covenant for deliverance. He hears their cry and remembers His Covenant with Abraham, Isaac, and Jacob. The Covenant-keeping God comes down to deliver His people from their bondage (Exodus 2:23-25 and Exodus 3:5-8).

"And He said, Draw not nigh hither: put off thy shoes from off thy feet, for the place whereon thou standest is holy ground. Moreover He said, I am the God of Abraham, the God of Isaac, and the God of Jacob."

The second chapter of Exodus gives to us the birth of Moses and his life until the time of his call. We notice two facts here. The hiding of the baby Moses at the river's bank by his mother, and Moses' later renunciation of Egypt, were not rash acts.

Hebrews 11:23-27 shows us that both acts were based upon faith in the Covenant-keeping God.

"By faith, Moses, when he was born, was hid three months by his parents. . . . By faith, Moses, when he was grown up, refused to be called the son of Pharaoh's daughter. . . . By faith he forsook Egypt, not fearing the wrath of the king."

The third and fourth chapters of Exodus give to us the call of Moses, including the story of the burning bush; the revelation of God to him in His plans for delivering the Israelites, Moses' hesitancy to respond, and the permission for Aaron to accompany him. We notice the power given to Moses' rod whereby he might perform miracles. We noticed that God manifested Himself to Moses not only as the Covenant-keeping God, but also as the miracle-working God.

Exodus 4:20-26 reveals the important place that the Blood Covenant held. Moses had neglected the circumcision of his first-born. He had been unfaithful to the Covenant. While on his way from the wilderness of Sinai to Egypt, with a message from God concerning the uncovenanted first-born of the Egyptians, Moses was met by a startling providence and came face to face with death. "The Lord met him and sought to kill him." It seems to have been perceived both by Moses and his wife that they are being cut off from a further share in God's covenant plans for the descendants of Abraham because of their failure to conform to their obligations in the Covenant of Abraham, the circumcision of their son.

In our next lesson, we shall become spectators of the mightiest conflict in history. On one side is arrayed all the power and wealth and splendor of Egypt, its learning, its pride, and its confident dependence upon its gods. On the other hand is a poor, weak, aged, broken and discredited man. He has but one follower, his brother, Aaron. It is no formidable procession which these two make as they pass through the palace gates and ask an audience of the king; and the light-hearted, witty Egyptians must have enjoyed many a jest at their expense. But there was a heart of astonishment behind all the laughter. What generation had ever witnessed such a thing!

Two slaves demanding liberty not for themselves, but for three million people — demanding it again and again after repeated refusal from Pharaoh, the god-king of the mightiest civilization of that day.

We shall see that laughter die down before the persistency of these men, and that astonishment is then changed to fear.

The cheek pales and the heart trembles at the sound of their steps. These two Blood Covenant men hold the fate of Egypt in their hands and leave written upon the land words which lived when its greatness had passed away.

Before we study the exit of the children of Israel out of Egypt, it will help us to note some facts concerning the Egyptian kings.

A prince, in mounting the throne in Egypt, was, so to speak, transfigured in the eyes of his subjects. In the mind of the Egyptians, Pharaoh was equally man and god.

"We may imagine," writes Lenormant, "what prestige such an exaltation in Egypt gave to the sovereign power." The Egyptians, in the eyes of the king, were but trembling slaves compelled from religious motives to execute his orders blindly.

Worship was addressed to him as to Divinity. His ministers and he occupy two different platforms.

He sits apart and alone. When he has spoken, the matter is judged. It is to him alone that God's demand is addressed, and on him the responsibility of refusal and continual injustice is laid.

We now understand why Pharaoh stands forth as the one man in all Egypt with whom the Deliverer of the Israelites has a controversy. Such words as these take on new significance when they are set forth in the light of these facts.

Exodus 8:10, 22, 23, "That thou (Pharaoh) mayest know that there is none like unto Jehovah our God . . . and I will sever in that day the land of Goshen, in which my people dwell, that no swarms of flies shall there be; to the end that thou mayest know that I (emphatic *I* and not thou—I and not thy gods) am Jehovah in the midst of the earth. And I will put a division between My people and thy people."

God and His people are on one side; Pharaoh and his people are on the other side. It is the contest between the true and living God and a pretender.

God has to break the idol to pieces and lay the idol low to deliver His people.

QUESTIONS

1. Explain the place, geographically, that the Israelites held as a witness.
2. Give a brief character sketch of Isaac, Jacob and Joseph.
3. How did God use Joseph to preserve His people?
4. Describe the life of the Israelites in Egypt before their persecution.
5. Who caused the statesmen of Egypt to oppress the children of Israel? Why did he do this?
6. Upon what were based the hiding of Moses by his parents and his later renunciation of Egypt?
7. Why did God come down to deliver the Israelites?
8. Why did God seek to kill Moses?
9. Who were involved in the mighty conflict that took place in the deliverance of Israel from Egypt?
10. Why was it that God had to humble Pharaoh?

Notes

Lesson 10

THE DELIVERANCE FROM EGYPT

A S WE STUDY the great drama of the deliverance of God's Covenant People from Egypt from the story given to us in the Scripture, we notice many facts that show the authenticity of the Scriptural account.

The picture of Egyptian life given to us here depicts a true picture of ancient Egyptian life at that time. The authority that Pharaoh held in his hand over authority that Pharaoh held in this period of history.

The part that is played by the magicians of Egypt in performing miracles is a faithful representation of the power that the ancient priesthood possessed.

The Egyptian priesthood was in reality a corporation endued with magical powers which were exercised on the behalf of the living and the dead.

The Scripture account in every name, incident, and custom portrayed, reveals the very Egypt of this period. The truth and sharpness of the reflection show that it was written by someone who knew the facts. Exodus, giving to us this drama of the miracle-working Covenant God on behalf of His people, was written by someone who knew about the facts. It was not written by a Babylonian Jew about 400 B.C., as some skeptics would claim. It bears the mark of the ancient Egypt which God judged.

Archaeologists have uncovered buildings made of brick in which stubble was used instead of straw as recorded in Exodus 5:12.

The First Miracle

Moses, in obedience to Jehovah, now approaches Pharaoh on behalf of God's Covenant people (Exodus 7:1-7).

Exodus 7:8-13 gives to us Moses' first encounter with Pharaoh and his magicians. The first sign which was given was the casting down of the rod which was instantly changed into a serpent. "Aaron cast down his rod before Pharaoh and before his servants and it became a serpent. Then Pharaoh also called the wise men and the sorcerers; now the magicians of Egypt, they did also in like manner with their enchantments. For they cast down every man his rod and they became serpents, but Aaron's rod swallowed up their rods" (Exodus 7:10-12).

Some may wonder at the power by which the rods of the Egyptian priests turned into snakes also. The spirits which were identified with gods of the Egyptians to whom they made their appeal, did not leave them without an answer. The revival in our day of spiritualism and all the phenomena which cannot be explained away by trickery, shows the working of Satan in miracles when it will bring to him the worship of man.

The conflict between the Maker of Heaven and earth and the gods of Egypt began at the outset. In this light, the miracle in Pharaoh's presence had a startling significance. As the rod of Aaron swallowed up the rods of the magicians, so would the religion which God was about to establish, swallow up the delusive trusts by which the wise men of the world sought a knowledge and a greatness that still left them and their fellows slaves of Satan.

The Plagues

Let us now study the story of the plagues which smote Egypt's strength, and broke its stubborn heart. A sign had been given when the rod had been changed into a serpent. The sign was challenged by the magicians with the result that the power of Jehovah was only more fully manifested. But that was only a sign, and it could be easily forgotten. God must, therefore, have recourse to judgment. The first plague was that by which the waters of Egypt were changed into blood.

The Divine Command came to Moses. "Get thee unto Pharaoh in the morning: lo, he goeth out unto the water; and thou shalt stand by the river's brink to meet him" (Exodus 7:15).

The reader will observe the command to meet Pharaoh at the brink of the river. We at once see a glorious fitness in the time and place that was chosen. The God of the Nile was an impersonation of NU, one of the chief father-gods of Egypt, and an object of profound veneration in this section of Egypt. Over him, therefore, Jehovah, by this plague, asserted His supremacy. It is probable that

Pharaoh went in the morning to offer his devotion to this god.

To the king, then, while standing before the very altar of his god, the message of Jehovah was delivered. It was a startling one. The god and his worshippers were alike to be judged. "And the Lord spake unto Moses: Say unto Aaron, Take thy rod and stretch out thy hand upon the waters of Egypt, upon their streams, upon their rivers, and upon their ponds, and upon all their pools of water that they may become blood, that there may be blood throughout all the land of Egypt, both in vessels of wood, and in vessels of stone" (Exodus 7:19).

The male children of the Israelites had been thrown into the waters, and now God would bring the sin of the Egyptians to their remembrance. The river of blood shall tell the story of their deed to the earth and heaven, and the horror of it shall rise and cling to them.

The second plague was an affliction well-known and dreaded. Its intensity was described in words every one of which must have gone home and filled the breast of every Egyptian who heard the words of God by Aaron with loathing and dread.

"Behold, I will smite all thy borders with frogs, the river shall bring forth frogs abundantly, which shall go up and come into thine house, and into thy bed chamber and upon thy bed, and into the house of thy servants and upon thy people, and into thy ovens, and into thy kneading troughs, and the frogs shall come up both on thee and upon thy people, and upon all thy servants" (Exodus 8:2-4).

Place behind these words the affliction which we know these animals to be in Egypt, and the plague immediately acquires a significance which is terrible. We lose sight of the insignificance of the instrument in the magnitude of the chastisement.

The plague of frogs was not only a terrible chastisement on the people, but also another judgment upon their gods. Frogs were always a great nuisance in Egypt, and from the beginning, the driving of them away was entrusted to a goddess called HEKI. She many times appears with the head of a frog. So important was the office which

83

she was to fulfill that she was supposed to be one of the supreme goddesses in all Egypt. Now the Covenant God of the Israelites, the slaves of the Egyptians, again shows Himself greater than the gods of the mighty Egyptians.

As Pharaoh's heart becomes more hardened, the plagues continue to come upon them. Exodus 8:16-19 and Exodus 8:20-24, give an account of the plagues of lice and then flies.

Another judgment was manifested against the gods of the Egyptians, for the flies also were worshipped in Egypt. First of all, a mere sign had been given when the rod had been changed into a serpent. Then personal discomfort revealed God's power and displeasure. But now, along with the peril brought by the flies, their garments, furniture, and trappings were destroyed: "The land was corrupted by reason of the flies."

In the fifth plague, God still goes further. He lays His hand upon one of their most valued possessions, their cattle.

The matter was not to end when Pharaoh said, "No," to God's demands, or when he promised obedience and then neglected to fulfill his promise.

Again, Moses was sent with the message, "Let my people go that they may serve me"; and Pharaoh is warned, "If thou refuse to let them go and wilt hold them still, behold the hand of the Lord is laid upon thy cattle which is in the field, upon the horses, upon the asses, upon the camel, and upon the sheep: There shall be a grievous murrain."

Exodus 9:1-5. We notice that the separation between the Egyptians and God's Covenant people continues. Nothing was to die of the cattle of the Israelites. Now the possessions of the Egyptians have been touched, the most part of Egypt's wealth. Now in the sixth plague, their bodies are touched. They are smitten with a painful and loathsome disease, which the magicians, their champions in this conflict, confess to be from the hand of God and at once retire from the contest. We notice the mercy of Jehovah in His dealings.

His mercy sent milder chastisements at first to turn them away from disobedience and to save them from the final and awful calamity. When lighter chastisements fail to save, love lets heavier strokes fall, to see whether these may turn the disobedient from his way.

In the seventh plague a distinct advance is made in the severity of the chastisement. There is now to be a loss of life as well as of crops.

Exodus 9:18, "Behold, tomorrow," so ran the Divine Command, "about this time I will cause it to rain a very grievous hail, such as hath not been in Egypt since the foundation thereof until now."

Exodus 10:4-6. As the eighth plague is announced, the word "locusts" had a terrible sound in the ears of the Egyptians.

Exodus 10:7. For the first time we hear a remonstrance in court. The princes and great men who surround the king, and who revere him as a god, are driven to forget the awful distance that stands between them and the throne. They throw aside, in very evident terror, their habitual reverence, and expostulate with the lord of Egypt.

"And Pharaoh's servants said unto him, how long shall this man be a snare unto us? Let the men go that they may serve the Lord, their God; knowest thou not yet that Egypt is destroyed?"

We now come to the ninth plague. This was God's last appeal before the long deferred judgment fell.

Each man was shut in, so to say, with God during those awful three days and nights.

All business was suspended. Everything was laid aside. Each dwelt alone—king, counsellor, noble, priest, merchant, artisan or peasant.

Each was held in God's hand and confronted with the question, spoken in the memory of one plague after another, and reiterated in the consciousness of this: "Canst thou dash thyself against the buckler of the Almighty?" These three days of awe-struck isolation permit us to look into the depths of that infinite compassion which would have saved Egypt from the last stroke which was to break all its stubbornness and pride.

God also showed His supremacy over the sun, which was one of the chief gods of the Egyptians.

The Blood Covenant and Its Tokens in the Passover

There came a time when the Lord would give fresh evidence of His fidelity to His Covenant of blood-friendship with Abraham. Again, a new start was to be made in the history of Redemption. The seed of Abraham was in Egypt, and the Lord would bring thence that seed, for its promised inheritance in Canaan. The Egyptians refused to let Israel go at the call of the Lord.

Now, as we study the last plague which came upon them, we see the significance of the Blood Covenant.

In the original covenant of blood friendship between Abraham and the Lord, it was Abraham who gave of his blood in token of the Covenant.

Up to this time, the Israelites had had to do nothing to avoid the plagues. Now there was to be an act of the shedding of blood, if they were to escape the tenth plague.

The Lord commanded the choice of a lamb, a male without blemish. This lamb was a type of Christ, so it must be perfect.

The blood of the lamb, a type of Christ's blood, was to be put on the two sideposts and on the lintel of every house of a descendant of Abraham.

"And the blood shall be to you for a token upon the houses where ye are," said the Lord to this people; "and when I see the blood (the token of my blood covenant with Abraham) I will pass over you, and the plague shall not be upon you to destroy you, when I smite the land of Egypt" (Exodus 12:7-13). The firstborn was safe when covered by the Blood.

The flesh of the chosen lamb was to be eaten by the Israelites reverently, as the indication of that intercommunion which the blood friendship rite secures, and in accordance with a common custom of the primitive blood-covenant rites everywhere.

The last plague broke the heart of Egypt. Death, terrible everywhere, made an awful pause in the life of this pleasure-loving people. When anyone died in Egypt it especially caused a great mourning.

It may be imagined then, what effect this last affliction had upon the entire people. There was not a house in which there was not one dead. Those who might have mourned with others, had to bow under their own grief. "And Pharaoh rose up in the night, he and all his servants and all the Egyptians; and there was a great cry in Egypt; for there was not a house where there was not one dead" Exodus 12:30).

But, when we have noted the grief of Pharaoh and of all his people because of their dead, we have not summed up all that was accomplished by this judgment. Exodus 12:12 reads, "I will pass through the land of Egypt this night and will smite the firstborn in the land of Egypt, both man and beast, and against all the gods of Egypt I will execute judgment." We notice the phrase, "And against all the gods of Egypt I will execute judgment." Both the words are placed against these: "Both man and beast."

We have seen that animals were worshipped in Egypt and also that the king was esteemed an incarnation, and worshipped as a god. Now Pharaoh, worshipped as divinity, is smitten and chastised in his own land, and in the presence of his people. His heir who had been already hailed with divine honors lay in the stillness of death. It was impossible to doubt that the blow was from the hand of this Covenant people's God.

The firstborn of the Israelites were safe. Not one of the plagues had touched God's Covenant people. A great fear pressed upon Egypt. The hand that had struck might strike again. Freedom was therefore given to the oppressed Israelites. They were thrust out. Pharaoh would not even wait for the day's dawning.

"He called for Moses and Aaron by night, and said, Rise up, and get you forth from among my people, both ye and the children of Israel; and go serve the Lord Jehovah as ye have said, and be gone, and bless me also. And the Egyptians were urgent upon the people that they might send them out of the land in haste; for they said, we will be all dead men" (Exodus 12:31-33).

QUESTIONS

1. Show how Scriptural account gives to us a true picture of ancient Egyptian life.
2. What was the first miracle that was performed in Pharaoh's presence?
3. What spiritual significance may be given to it?
4. In what way did the first plague bring down judgment upon an Egyptian God?
5. What was the second plague and its significance?
6. As Pharaoh refuses, show how the afflictions become greater.
7. How did the ninth plague reveal His mercy before the last plague came?
8. In what way did God give evidence of His fidelity to the Covenant?
9. Describe the effect of the tenth plague.
10. How was it revealed that the plagues were sent by the Covenant God?

Lesson 11
COVENANT PEOPLE IN THE WILDERNESS

WE HOLD uppermost before us this fact that it is the Covenant-keeping God who is delivering His Covenant people. In the Passover, He had reaffirmed His Covenant. As they face the wilderness and its perils, they know that the Covenant-keeping God is with them. Now the institution of this Passover rite of Jehovah's blood-friendship with Israel is to become a permanent ceremonial among them as a memorial of their miraculous deliverance from Egypt as Covenant people (Exodus 12:14-20, 43; 13:16).

Exodus 12:3-8. The Passover Lamb typifies Christ on the Cross. The Lamb must be a male without blemish; he must be taken on the tenth day of the first month (Jewish year) and kept until the fourteenth day when he is slain at even (three o'clock).

Christ was betrayed on the tenth day and was crucified on the fourteenth day, dying at three o'clock. Surely He was the Lamb of God.

The token of this rite is described in the following: "And it shall be a sign for thee upon thy hand and for a memorial between thy eyes that the law of Jehovah may be in thy mouth: for with a strong hand hath Jehovah brought thee out of Egypt" (Exodus 13:16).

In primitive times often when two men cut the covenant, a blood-stained record of the covenant was preserved in a small leather case to be worn upon the arm, or about the neck of him who had won a friend forever in this sacred rite of blood-friendship.

Down through the generations, the Jews have been accustomed to wear upon their foreheads as a crown, and upon their arms as an armlet, a small leather case as a sacred amulet containing a record of the passover covenant between Jehovah and the seed of Abraham, His friend.

Exit with Great Substance

Before the conflict with Pharaoh began, God had said to Moses: "I will give this people favour in the sight of the Egyptians and it shall come to pass that when ye go ye shall not go empty, but every woman shall borrow of her neighbor and of her that sojourneth in her house jewels of silver and jewels of gold and raiment and ye shall put them upon your sons and upon your daughters: and ye shall spoil the Egyptians" (Exodus 3:21-22).

Many have misunderstood this scripture and Exodus 12:35-36, because a mistake was made in the translation. The Hebrew word translated "borrow" means "ask." The word translated "lend" in Exodus 12:35-36 is a form of the same word and means to "let ask," that is, to entertain a request and graciously to give. It was not a case of theft, borrowing with no thought of return. The Israelites asked these things. The question was whether or not the request should be answered or met with angry refusal.

The Covenant God intervened. He gave His people favour in the eyes of the Egyptians. They were looked upon by their enemies in a new light; and the Egyptians gave unto them. These were the spoils of a more glorious victory than any other conquering nation had ever known. In history the conquered have been spoiled, but never willingly. But here, the Egyptians find a joy in giving to those who had mastered them.

The Covenant people who had simply stood and waited for salvation from their God of the Covenant, pass out adorned with the gorgeous raiment and the jewels of those who had so long spoiled them.

More than 200 years before, their Covenant God had predicted this triumph. In Genesis 15:13-14, He had said to Abraham that his seed should be a stranger and afflicted in a land that was not theirs, and that He would judge the nation whom they had served. With it He had given this promise: "Afterward they shall come out with great substance."

Here God had looked forward to the very spoiling of the Egyptians as the end of the sore travail of His people and a compensation for their bondage and slavery.

The Route Changed

On the second day's journey the Israelites followed the usual route to Palestine. This must have led them to the "edge of the wilderness." Across those sands and up along the Mediterranean Coast lay the nearest way to Palestine.

A few marches onward and they would have passed into the territory of the warlike Philistines.

But here the route was suddenly changed. We are told that God led them not through the way of the Philistines, although that was near, for God said lest peradventure the people repent when they see war, and they return to Egypt. But God led the people about, through the way of the wilderness of the Red Sea. Why then, we may ask, were they suffered to make a beginning, which looked as if they were to take the more expeditious road to the land promised to their fathers? Why was the change made in the route so that they had on the third to retrace their steps and march southward on the Egyptian side of the sea?

We may at first be perplexed by the question. It does look as though God's plan had been suddenly altered; but a little reflection will speedily unveil the Divine Wisdom. The whole is explained in those words, "They encamped . . . in the edge of the wilderness" (Exodus 13:20).

God had a twofold purpose. Israel had to bend to the Divine Will. Naturally, they at the outset desired the shortest route. God suffered them to take it and went with them so far—as He often does with us in our wilfulness.

They are brought "to the edge of the wilderness" (Exodus 13:20) ; and then comes reflection. There is nothing inviting in the aspect of that dreary expanse. They begin to think of dreary days of plodding, thirsting, and hunger, through the treeless, waterless, habitationless desert.

Then they think of the embattled wall of fierce, determined foemen through which a way must be forced after the desert has been traversed. There was no murmuring on the morrow when God said: "Speak unto the children of Israel, that they turn" (Exodus 14:2). This brought relief to them.

The Covenant God also had another purpose. The king was carefully watching their movements. God was not going to allow His Covenant people to pass with dishonor from the land of Egypt; they were not going to be allowed to run away. When the Covenant God delivers, it is not through human methods. His deliverance is glorious in its fullness and in its beauty of holiness.

91

Egypt will herself thrust Israel out and compel them to abandon the country, so the route is changed.

Crossing of the Red Sea

The Egyptians are left in their selfish greed and cruelty to misread the change to their own destruction. "For Pharaoh will say of the children of Israel, They are entangled in the land; the wilderness hath shut them in" (Exodus 14:3).

To Egypt this move seemed to be a revelation of unexpected weakness. There was no longer any God among them and Egypt could now enjoy to the full the wild revenge for which it panted.

They said, "I will pursue, I will overtake, I will divide the spoil. My lust shall be satisfied upon them: I will draw my sword; my hand will destroy them" (Exodus 15:9).

The thought which had sprung up in Pharaoh's bosom seems to have flamed up like an answering fire in the bosoms of his people. The heart of Pharaoh and of his servants were turned against the people and they said, "Why have we done this, that we have let Israel go from serving us?"

It seems that all the troops which could be massed together took part in this pursuit (Exodus 14:6-9).

The elaborately disciplined standing army of Egypt was one of the marvels of the ancient world. We can imagine the terror which must have laid hold of the hearts of the Israelites the moment they realized that this fearful engine is directed against them (Exodus 14:10).

It seems that for the moment in mad and hopeless despair, they forget the God of the Covenant. They cry bitterly unto Moses for bringing them into this place of seeming death (Exodus 14:11-12).

Then we hear the words of faith from Moses to fear not, because the Covenant God would work on their behalf that day (Exodus 14:13-16).

Let us note what the miracle-working God performed. His reply to Moses is: "Speak unto the children of Israel that they go forward." Then he, this Covenant man, was bidden to prepare a strange pathway for them.

He was to lift that rod which had hitherto brought judgment upon Egypt; it would command the forces of nature to work salvation for the people of the Covenant.

"And Moses stretched out his hand over the sea; and the Lord caused the sea to go back by a strong east wind all that night, and made the sea dry land, and the waters were divided. And the children of Israel went into the midst of the sea upon dry ground; and the waters were a wall upon their right hand and left" (Exodus 14:21-22).

The forces of nature obeyed His Word. As we stand in the presence of this tremendous miracle, we catch a glimpse into the far past at the time when the first man walked in the realm of God's ability with dominion over the works of His hands. This dominion became lost at the fall. We see glimpses of it now and then under the Old Covenant at such an instance as this, until the time comes when the second Adam walks one with the Father God, with dominion over the forces of nature.

The Pillar of Cloud

We have seen in previous lessons that no man could actually be Born Again of the Spirit of God until the Father-God had a legal right to impart His nature to spiritually dead man. God did not have a legal right to impart His Life to those Covenant people.

We have seen that natural man is limited in his knowledge to that which he gains through the five senses of his physical body. God must manifest Himself to Israel; His presence can be known to them only through their physical senses.

He made His presence known to them by a pillar of cloud which appeared on the second day (Exodus 13:21-22).

They could see the cloud, hear and feel the warmth of this fiery cloud in the night time.

This pillar of cloud was not only a visible manifestation of His presence, but it was also a means of His caring for them.

It became a strange protection from the intense desert heat of the day, and at night it became a mammoth lighting and heating plant. It kept them cool during the day and warm during the cold, bitter night.

When this cloud moved, they knew it was time to break camp and journey on. When it stopped, whether it was day or night, they knew that it was time to make camp and wait His further leading.

This cloud was with them, a protection, a comfort, and a guide during the forty years of wandering in the desert.

At the time that the Egyptians had pursued them, this strange cloud had moved from its position before them and stood behind them. It stood between the camp of the Egyptians and the Israelites. To the Covenant people it was light and warmth; but to the Egyptians, it was thick darkness.

The March through the Desert

Now that eventful period in Israel's history begins, the march through the desert. The peninsula of Sinai is, to this day, a kind of no-man's land. Other regions have been coveted and fought for, but no powers of either ancient or modern times have ever sought for possession of Sinai.

Yet to this isolated, despised district, three million slaves are taken. They have a slave spirit, are untrained and full of criticism and bitterness. In this place the Covenant God is going to reveal Himself and His glory and build from this slave nation a free people with leaders and teachers.

There, separated from idolatry, this nation which is to preserve the Revelation of the true God will learn to walk dependent upon Him.

We now start with Israel on this momentous journey, and as we study it, we find that there are lessons for us to learn.

On the third day of the journey, they arrive at Marah, where the water was bitter. They had been used to drinking the sweet water of the Nile, so famed in the East; and now in childish disappointment, they burst forth in childish, unrestrained complaint against Moses (Exodus 15:22-24).

The Covenant God, ever caring for them, makes the bitter waters sweet.

Then He manifests Himself to them not only as One who shall lead them, care for them and protect them, but as One who will permit none of the diseases of the Egyptians to come upon them. He makes Himself known to them as the God who healeth them (Exodus 15:26-27).

In the blood-covenant rights and privileges, all that He was belonged to Israel. His ability belonged to them. His care, His protection, His healing were theirs.

It is a remarkable fact that during this wilderness period, while they walked in the Covenant, no babies, no children, nor young men and women died. No one died prematurely because of the power of disease. He was the Covenant God that healed them.

NOTE TO STUDENTS

We wish to acknowledge that we are indebted for much of our material in these lessons to Urquhart's New Biblical Guide and Dr. Trumbull's "Blood Covenant."

The reading material covered in this lesson is found in Exodus 12:43 to Exodus 15:27.

QUESTIONS

1. Tell of the Passover rite as it was to exist as a memorial among the Israelites.
2. Explain Exodus 12:35-36.
3. What lost authority of man was manifested at the crossing of the Red Sea?
4. Why did God have to visibly manifest Himself to Israel as in the Pillar of Cloud?
5. What needs did the Pillar of Cloud meet?
6. Describe the land into which God led His Covenant people when they left Egypt.
7. Why were the Covenant people led to this place?
8. Tell of the incident that took place at Marah.
9. Explain Exodus 15:26-27.
10. What has the knowledge of the Blood Covenant meant to you?

Notes

Lesson 12
THE LAW AND THE TABERNACLE
Exodus 15:26 to Exodus 36

JEHOVAH APPEARED many times to Israel in a special manner. Whenever they did wrong, murmured or rebelled, He would manifest Himself to them in the cloud.

It might be signalled to them by plagues or fiery serpents, or it might be a voice that filled them with fear and wonder.

Exodus 15:27. They had camped by twelve springs of Elim, and the hand of God had been upon them. They had murmured at Marah because of the badness of water, but nothing had been said of the lack of bread. They had evidently been bountifully supplied on leaving Egypt. They must have anticipated a wilderness journey. This supply had now come to an end. The discovery of the condition of the three million was soon known. One neighbor going to borrow from another would be met by the assurance that the other was as poor as himself in the matter. In this way the terribleness of their condition would be borne upon them with stupefying effect. Death then seemed inevitable.

The Giving of the Manna

To go forward would make that fate certain. To retreat was equally impossible. They would perish before they could retrace their steps and gain the borders of Egypt.

"And the whole congregation of the children of Israel murmured against Moses and Aaron in the wilderness; and the children of Israel said unto them, Would to God we had died by the hand of the Lord in the land of Egypt, when we sat by the flesh pots, and when we did eat bread to the full; for ye have brought us forth into this wilderness, to kill this whole assembly with hunger" (Exodus 16:2-3).

Now here was a case in which this people could easily have sought help from God. Had He not in every manner proven Himself true to the Covenant? The failure of the bread supply was alarming, but He who had miraculously delivered them from Egypt, led them through the Red Sea, led them by the cloud, and made the bitter waters sweet, could easily provide bread.

What a different story we would have had, and what joy it would have brought to the Covenant God, had they come to Him for this need in assurance that He who had entered a Blood Covenant relationship would meet every need. Instead, they flung away from God. They broke out in rebellious murmuring. They had been shamefully deceived. They had been led away from Egypt, a land of peace and plenty, and they were now entrapped in this terrible wilderness that young and old might die. However, their rebellion could not make Jehovah deny Himself. He heard their murmuring, their unbelief.

Then, He gave to them the promise that He would supply them with bread and meat that they might know that He was their Covenant God (Exodus 16:4-12).

Exodus 16:13-36 gives to us the sending of the bread and meat and the instructions for gathering it.

For forty years, He, their Covenant God, fed them in this miraculous way.

Reason for the Law

As we study the history of Israel, we hold in mind the fact that they are God's Covenant people.

Exodus 19:1-8. In the third month of their journey they came into the wilderness of Sinai. The time has come when the Covenant God is going to give to them the law.

We hold in mind the fact that they have not yet received the life of God. They are still spiritually dead, and a Law must be given to them that will govern every phase of their lives.

Before the Law is given, Moses is called to the Mount. There God reviews to Moses His faithfulness to the Covenant. Now Israel must make known whether or not they will obey Him as their Covenant God.

In these three months they have learned of His faithfulness to His part in the Covenant (Exodus 19:8). Israel promises to obey.

Exodus 19:9-25 gives to us the manifestation of God to His people. We notice that this manifestation of Himself was again on the level of their physical senses. They could see the smoke and fire and hear the voice of the trumpet which waxed loud. They were unable to approach the

Mount because of spiritual death.

The Law that was given is the Law of the Covenant. When the Abrahamic Covenant was fulfilled, it also was fulfilled. There are three divisions that come from this law: The Commandments expressing the Righteous Will of God, Exodus 20:1-27; The Judgments governing the social life of Israel, Exodus 21:1-24; and the ordinances governing the religious life, Exodus 24:12-31.

Three elements formed the Law: the Commandments, the Ordinances, and the Sacrifices. The Commandments were a Ministry of condemnation and of death (II Corinthians 3:7-9). They revealed the spiritual death that reigned in the heart of man.

The Ordinances gave, in the High Priest, a representative of the people with Jehovah.

The Sacrifices gave a covering for the broken law and spiritually-dead Israel.

Giving of the Law

There was a threefold giving of the Law. It was given first orally, recorded in Exodus 20:1-17. This was given with no provision for the Priesthood and sacrifices, and was accompanied by the Judgments (Exodus 21:1-23). Relating to the relations of Hebrew with Hebrew were added directions for keeping three annual feasts (Exodus 23:14-19) and instructions for the conquest of Canaan (24:3-8).

Next, Moses was called up to receive the Tables of Stone (Exodus 24:12-18). Moses on the Mount receives the gracious instructions concerning the Tabernacle, Priesthood and Sacrifices (Exodus 25:31).

Meantime, the people led by Aaron break the first Commandment (Exodus 32). Moses breaks the Tables written with the finger of God (Exodus 31:18; 32:16-19).

Third, the second tables were made by Moses and the Law was again written by the hand of Jehovah (Exodus 34:1, 28, 29).

Scriptures to read: Romans 3:21-27; 6:14-15; Galatians 2:16; 3:10-14, 16-18, 24-26; 4:21-31; and Hebrews 10:11-17.

The Reason for the Tabernacle

Exodus 25:8. God desired to dwell with His Covenant People. He could not dwell in their hearts, because they had not yet received Eternal Life; His Presence must be manifested to their physical senses. Their worship of Him also must be on the same level. There must be a physical dwelling place in which He will dwell, and where they shall meet Him through a physical priesthood.

For the building of the Tabernacle He asked of them free-will offerings (Exodus 25:2). Their hearts must be willing to have His Presence among them (Exodus 25:9).

The Tabernacle was to be made exactly as God revealed it to Moses. From the time that man had died spiritually, God had been working toward his redemption. Now this Tabernacle is to be a type of Christ and the Redemption He wrought for man. Therefore, every detail must be according to His exact pattern.

First, let us notice something that is very suggestive. We saw as we studied creation that God gave the account to us in less than two chapters, and yet the instructions for the making of the Tabernacle take up eleven chapters. We would think that the work of Creation was far more important than the building of the Tabernacle; but, mighty though the work of Creation was, it was simply, as it were, the erection of a stage upon which was to be wrought a far mightier work, the work of our Redemption in Christ.

As in a theater, the actor is more than the stage, so the one who performed that mighty work is infinitely more glorious than the stage on which He performed it.

The Tabernacle, As It Stood among Them

The Tabernacle proper was toward the western end of the court. It was fifty-two feet long, seventeen and one half feet wide, and seventeen and one half feet high.

It was divided into two compartments. The larger of the two was called the Holy Place. The smaller, the Most Holy Place. In the larger, or the Holy Place, there were the Golden Altar, the Golden Lampstand, and the Golden Table; in the smaller, or the Holiest, there were the Ark and the Mercy Seat.

When the Tabernacle had been erected, the only covering visible was the outer covering of badger skins, with a width of the goats' hair curtain above the door. The first set of curtains were fine twined linen; blue, purple, white, and scarlet. Over these were the goat skins, dyed red, and over all was a covering of badger skins.

While the Tabernacle was at rest, the Cloud, the Symbol of the Divine Presence, rested on the rear end of the Tabernacle, and was like a vast umbrella overshadowing the camp.

This cloud was always with them. When they were to journey, it arose from the top of the Tabernacle, going in the direction that God wanted them to travel. When they came to their camping ground, the cloud stopped.

In this way it guided them, showing them the directions, just how far they should go, and when they should encamp.

God had to manifest Himself to their physical senses because they were spiritually dead.

The court was formed of sixty pillars of shittim wood supporting the linen curtain wall. The Tabernacle was a comparatively small building. It was designed to be a place where God could dwell with and meet Israel in the person of their High Priest, so it was not an auditorium as such a place for the assembling of God's people would be today.

The Curtain and Coverings of the Tabernacle

In studying the coverings and curtains we begin on the outside. As we view the Tabernacle from the outside there is nothing interesting in its appearance. It was a long, box-like building, without graceful lines or curves, as if to accentuate its lack of attractiveness.

The unattractive badger skins covered it on the outside; but, if we go inside, what a wonderful change.

On either side the gold-covered boards glint in the light of the seven-branched lampstand. Over our heads is the ceiling formed by the beautiful curtains of fine twined linen with the embroidered cherubims of blue, purple, and scarlet. Before us is the veil; behind us, the door with all the mingled tints of the rainbow. Then there is the gold altar of incense filling the Holy Place with its aroma, and

101

the gold table with twelve loaves of shew bread which also emit a fragrant odor.

In these coverings we see a picture of Christ in His two different aspects. If we look at the outside of the Tabernacle, it has no form nor comeliness—the curtains of badgers' skins covering the beauty of the Tabernacle.

Isaiah 53:2. Christ had no form nor comeliness to the natural man. There was no beauty about Him that man should desire Him. He had nothing in common with man. The badgers' skins are typical of the severity of His separation from man. To the natural eye there was a reserve and severity with Him. It was not within their compass, the compass of men, to understand or enjoy Him. Read John 4:44 and Matthew 16:17.

He was a root out of dry ground. The beauty of Christ was hidden. Only an inner few knew Him; and so the blue, the purple, the scarlet and linen.

Ezekiel 16:10 reads, "I shod thy feet with badger skins." It would suggest separation from evil; sandals protect the feet from the earth, keep them separate from it. Christ took up His place in the Father's will, and all the forces of men and devils in earth and hell could not overcome or hinder His doing the Father's will.

The ram's skin, dyed red, is typical of His mediatorial work, His shed blood.

The inner curtains were in two sets, five in a set. They were held together by fifty taches of gold which fastened into fifty loops of blue, forming, as we read, one Tabernacle. The loops of blue and the fifty taches of gold were typical of His Heavenly Grace and Divine Energy which enabled Christ to perfectly meet the claims of God and man.

These curtains were all of one measure. The blue, ethereal in color, marks the Heavenly character of Christ. Although He was a very man, He was a very God. He walked in the consciousness and dignity of His Divine Mission.

He never once forgot Who He was or where He was going. The purple is typical of His Royalty. He was king of the Jews. He was received into Heaven as a conqueror (Psalm 2 and Philippians 2:9-11).

The scarlet represents His death. A true scarlet color can only be produced by death. His Incarnation, the union of God and man, were not sufficient for our Redemption. He must, on the cross, be made all that man was. By His death, He brought to naught him who had the power of death, and delivered man from his reign (Hebrews 2:14).

The fine twined linen is typical of His spotless purity as a man. There are great depths of spiritual truths in the humanity of Jesus Christ. In order for Him to meet the claims of Justice, and the needs of man, it was necessary that He be absolutely human, and yet at the same time as a man and tempted in every point as we are, and still please the Father as a perfect Son.

It was necessary for Christ to walk as the first Adam should have walked.

(The Study of the Tabernacle will be continued in the next lesson.)

QUESTIONS

1. What should the Israelites have done when they discovered their lack of food?
2. How did the Covenant God meet their need for food?
3. Why was the law given?
4. Why did God manifest Himself to the people through the smoke and fire, and the cloud?
5. What was the purpose of the Tabernacle?
6. How were the materials gathered? Why?
7. Why was it necessary for it to be according to the exact pattern given to Moses?
8. How did the badger skin covering represent Christ?
9. Of what in the Life of Christ were they typical?
10. Show how the inner curtains represent Christ.

Notes

Lesson 13
THE TABERNACLE
(Continued)
The Gate
Read Exodus 27:16-19

IN BEGINNING with the gate we begin where God ended in His instructions which He gave to Moses concerning the building of the Tabernacle.

He begins with the Ark and its Mercy Seat, and works from these out until He comes to the Laver, the Brazen Altar, and then to the gate. We begin, we say, where God left off, and this is very suggestive.

Redemption is complete, and with the completed work, we begin.

As we look at the court wall, the prominent thing is the Door. This gate typifies Christ as the only way to God. Spiritually dead man is on the outside, and Christ came that He might be the divine way of man's coming back to God. "I am the way," Jesus said (John 14:6).

We remember that in the Garden of Eden God drove man from His presence. Now, He provides a way back. There was just one door in the court.

If we were to look at the south side, the north side or the western end, just one long stretch of unbroken white linen would meet our gaze. It was only linen, but to force an entrance would be to rush to certain destruction. The linen stood there marking off the sacred precincts, and whosoever would come to God had to come in the proper way.

As we come to the eastern end and see the door, we see the blue, the purple, the scarlet, and fine twined linen, all typical, as we have seen, of Christ, who is the Door. Read John 14:6 and John 10:7-9.

Any one of the men of Israel could enter by the gate and bring his sacrifice to the altar, but only a priest could go through the door into the Tabernacle.

The Furniture of the Tabernacle

As we have mentioned, in giving the instructions to Moses, God began with the Ark and worked toward the Brazen Altar.

This is typical of the path trod by Christ. Man could not approach God. God must come to man. Christ came from Glory to earth, then to the Cross where He met spiritually dead man, and then back again to the Father. So, from the Ark, which was in the Most Holy Place, to the Brazen Altar that stood near the gate, we see the path which Christ trod from Glory to the cross—where He identified Himself with spiritually dead man and then returned again to the Father. This shows complete Redemption wrought by Christ for man.

The Brazen Altar
Read Exodus 27:1-8

Let us notice the Brazen Altar. Its position was at the gate. It was the place where God met spiritually dead man. Its materials were of brass and acacia wood. It is spoken of as incorruptible wood. It speaks of the Lord Jesus Christ, the One who had no sin. This wood was covered with brass. The candlestick, the Altar of Incense, the Table of Shew Bread, and the Ark were made of gold. but not the Altar.

Brass spoke of sin. It was at the Altar of the Cross that the sin that was man's fell upon Christ. At the Cross, Christ was forsaken of God. The Brazen Altar shows Christ's identification with man on the cross.

God came from the Mercy Seat, which was the throne, to the Altar where He met the guilty Israelite who had, in his obedience to God's command, brought to the Altar a perfect sacrifice.

How very expressive was the act of the one who brought the sacrifice. We read: "He shall lay His hands on the head of the goat" (Leviticus 4:24). That was identifying himself with the sacrifice, confessing that he deserved to die, but that God had provided a substitute. As the fire consumed the sacrifice, there was left no judgment to fall upon the sinner, and the one who had brought the sacrifice could go away from the Altar with the knowledge that his sin was forgiven him.

For Jehovah said, "It shall be forgiven him" (Leviticus 4:26). At the cross we see Jesus Christ taking man's place, identified with all that man was, and God's judgment falling upon Him.

The Brazen Laver
Read Exodus 30:17-21

Beyond the Brazen Altar stood the Brazen Laver.

This Laver also was made of brass, which speaks again of sin.

It was filled with water, with which the Priests washed the dirt of the cursed earth from their hands and feet before they entered the Holy of Holies.

This typifies our daily need of cleansing by the Water of the Word of God.

The Table of Shew Bread
Read Exodus 25:23-30

In the Holy Place was the Table of Shew Bread with the twelve loaves of bread. A loaf is an emblem of the body of our Lord Jesus Christ. I Corinthians 10:17, "For we being many are one bread and one body."

We "are many" just like the wheat in the bread; just as the wheat in the loaf became merged into one loaf through the baking, on the grounds of Christ's identification with us on the cross . . . becoming all that we were, and in burial paying our penalty during those awful three days and nights of separation from God.

In Crucifixion, we see Him as we were.

In Resurrection, we see ourselves as He is.

Romans 6:5-6, "For if we have become united with Him in the likeness of His death, we shall be also in the likeness of His resurrection; knowing this, that our old man was crucified with Him, that the body of sin might be done away, that so we should no longer be in bondage to sin."

He is the Bread of Life. Now we become the carriers of that Life to the world.

The Golden Lampstand
Read Exodus 25:31-40

This Golden Lampstand which was in the Holy Place also speaks forth our identification with Christ in the likeness of His Resurrection.

We see here the union of Christ with His Body. As we read those words, "His Branches," it would seem as though the central shaft were the lampstand and the

107

branches had come out of it, and we are reminded of the words of John 15:5, "I am the Vine, ye are the branches."

Union with Christ was wrought through our identification with His death, burial, and resurrection.

How was this Lampstand made? It would have been comparatively easy to have cast it, but God told Moses definitely how to make it.

It must be hammered out—"One beaten work." As we see the workman bruise the precious metal, our thoughts turn to the scripture in Isaiah 53:5, where we read that Christ was bruised for our iniquities. Only by this bruising could the branches of the lampstand be brought into existence, and only by the identification of God's Son with our Spiritual Death, only by His paying of the penalty that was ours, could we become absolutely one with Him.

It was by His being bruised in our stead, under our judgment, that we are able to take His place as a son of God before the Father.

Resurrection Revealed

Is there anything in this Lampstand that would show definitely that He was portraying our identification with Him in His Resurrection? Yes, we believe there is.

It was to be ornamented with fruit blossoms. Now what fruit shall God select?

He had a wide field from which to choose, and we find that He chose the almond tree. In Numbers 17 we have the act of Aaron's Rod. It, with the other eleven, was laid up before the Lord all night. In the morning it had brought forth buds, bloomed blossoms, and yielded the almonds.

We are branches, bearing fruit because of our union with Him. Like Aaron's Rod, Christ the Living One was cut down in death . . . suffered until our penalty was paid. He has risen to be the first fruits of them that are asleep. When He was made alive, we were made alive with Him.

It must have been a work of considerable difficulty to beat out such a large vessel with its branches so highly ornamented.

Why not make the stand and the branches separately? It would have been so much easier to manipulate them;

those branches could be brazed to the stem, but this would not do. It would not be a true type of the union which existed between Christ and His saints which is vital and not artificial.

So, out of one piece of gold . . . the entire Lampstand is hammered. "One beaten work of pure gold." Gold is a symbol of Deity. We saw that the Altar and Laver were of brass, which spoke of the judgment that rested upon Christ as He acted as our sin substitute; but now in the Resurrection He arises in the fullness of His Divinity, and we are made alive, joint heirs with Him.

The brass shows His being made sin. The gold shows our being made the Righteousness of God in Him.

The Altar of Incense

In the Holy Place before the veil stood the Golden Altar of Incense. The word "Altar" signified place of slaughter, yet no sacrifices are to be offered here.

We saw that the Brazen Altar and the Laver showed forth Christ's identification with our spiritual death, and that the Table of Shew Bread and Golden Lampstand show our identification with Him in Resurrection. Now, this Altar of Incense speaks of His Ascension to the Father. The Altar suggests His blood that had been shed. It was with His own blood that He entered into the Holy of Holies in Heaven, having obtained eternal Redemption for us.

The materials of the Altar reiterate once more the truth about His Person.

The gold proclaims His Deity. The wood shows again His humanity. It brings to us the glorious fact that we have at the right hand of God, a man (I Timothy 2:5).

We are reminded here of the truth that as a man, He is interceding and maintaining our cause in Heaven.

The Ark of the Covenant
Exodus 25:10-22

The Mercy Seat formed the cover of the Ark. At each end was a Cherubim whose outspread wings overshadowed the Mercy Seat.

In Romans 3:24-25, we read, "Christ Jesus; whom God set forth to be a propitiation." The word rendered "propitiation" in the Septuagint is "mercy seat." It would thus read, "Whom God set forth to be a Mercy Seat."

We might ask ourselves, "How could the throne of a Holy, sin-hating God be a Mercy Seat and not a throne of judgment?"

Leviticus 16 gives to us the account of the Day of Atonement. On that day there were two goats brought before the Lord. Lots were then cast upon them. One of these goats was a scape goat; and having had the sins of the congregation confessed over it by Aaron, was sent away into the wilderness to some uninhabited place and let go, never to return.

But it is with the other goat that we have especially to do now. It was spoken of as "for the Lord." While the scape goat spoke of Substitution, this goat spoke of Propitiation. Christ on the Cross of Calvary did a work on the ground of which God can deal with condemned humanity in mercy.

Christ was set forth to be a Mercy Seat where God and spiritually dead man can meet. We shall look at what was done with the goat which was for the Lord, or the one which spoke of Propitiation. It was killed, then some of its blood was carried into the Holiest and sprinkled by the priest on the Mercy Seat seven times. As we see that burning outside the camp, we see in type the Lord Jesus, dying under the judgment of God on our behalf. But as we see Him arise from the dead and pass into the Heavenlies with His own blood, we have what answers to the type of the priest going into the Holiest with the blood of the goat.

There is something very suggestive in the attitude of the cherubim upon the Mercy Seat. The first time we find the cherubim mentioned in the Word of God is in connection with the driving out of the Garden of our first parents. There, the cherubim are seen connected with the flaming sword, but there is no sword in this scene, nothing that would say, "Keep away."

Then we see how their gaze is toward the Mercy Seat, as if they desired to read the meaning of the bloodstains which were put there by the High Priest. Those blood marks tell us how God's throne in Israel became a Mercy Seat, and not a Throne of Judgment. He who sat upon that throne saw in that blood the type of the blood of Him who deemed not His equality with God a thing to be tightly grasped, One whose death would satisfy all the demands of Justice.

Because of that blood He could meet Israel in the person of their High Priest and extend Mercy to them, where they deserved judgment.

It is most instructive to notice where the law was put. "And thou shalt put the Mercy Seat above upon the Ark. And in the Ark shalt thou put the testimony that I shall give thee." Over that law which no spiritually dead man could keep, and which could only condemn, there were the blood stains which reminded God of the Righteous work of His Son.

QUESTIONS

1. How does the gate represent Christ?
2. What great feature of our Redemption in Christ is typified by the general plan of the furniture of the Tabernacle?
3. What do the Brazen Altar and Laver signify?
4. How did the Shew Bread represent the Body of Christ?
5. Show how the Golden Lampstand revealed the sufferings of Christ?
6. How did it show our identification in His Resurrection?
7. What part of the Ark was the Mercy Seat?
8. Why could God's throne in Israel be a Mercy Seat, and not a Judgment Throne?
9. What was suggestive in the attitude of the cherubim?
10. Why was the Law placed in the Ark?

Notes

Lesson 14
THE PRIESTHOOD

THE TABERNACLE and its vessels, and the priesthood and the various ministries connected therewith, formed but one subject, although we divide it, for the sake of contemplating each portion. The Tabernacle would have been useless without its vessels—and the Tabernacle with its vessels would have been of no service but for a living family of priests constantly engaged in various activities within the Holy Place and about the various Holy vessels. They acted as mediators.

Hebrews 8 shows us that the priests who offered gifts, according to the law, serve unto the example and shadow of heavenly things.

Exodus 28:1 gives to us the directions given to Moses concerning the priestly family. Neither Moses nor his sons have any office of priesthood under the Law and that of which Christ is the Head.

(1) The leadership or kingship of Moses, as well as the office of mediator, were in him kept apart from the priesthood, which was confined to Aaron and his sons; and these dignities were thus lodged in different persons; whereas one epistle to the Hebrews is to point out the Lord Jesus in His Resurrection combining in Himself the various offices and dignities of Lord, Mediator, Apostle, Surety, Captain and Shepherd.

(2) The wording of the first verse is remarkable, "Take unto thee Aaron and his sons with him that he may minister." Aaron and his sons formed but one ministry in the priest's office, and Aaron could not exercise his service unless his sons were taken with him. Is there not in this an intimation of the union in priesthood of Christ and His house, and that one great object of His priesthood is that He may minister to God respecting His house (Hebrews 3:1-7)?

(3) The High Priest, under the Law, had compassion upon the ignorant and on them that were out of the way, because he was conscious of infirmities in himself. The very fact of his being himself a sinner was one qualification for that priesthood (Hebrews 5:1-5).

The Lord Jesus, through His human life, was perfected for priesthood. He is able to sympathize because He has been tempted in all points like as we are, yet without sin. He suffered, being tempted, and is therefore able to succor them that are tempted. The dreadful whisperings of the enemy which He was called to endure filled His soul with holy abhorrence and taught Him to feel pity for us who are subject to the assaults of Satan (Hebrews 4:14-16).

(4) The priests of the house of Levi were made without an oath, and in consequence some of them were cut off from the priesthood, as in the case of Nadab and Abihu and Eli's line.

The Lord Jesus was made priest with an oath. "The Lord sware and will not repent." The unchangeableness of God's Word and oath established the Lord Jesus as the Surety of a better covenant (Hebrews 7:20-25).

Hebrews 7:11-17, Aaron was made a priest after the Law of carnal commandment, whereas Christ became High Priest after the power of endless life, the glorious Eternal power of Resurrection. Life received out of death and making manifest His victory over death, constituted Him the great High Priest.

Garments of the High Priest

Let us now proceed with Exodus 28:4, "These are the garments which they shall make; a breastplate, and an ephod, and a robe, and a broidered coat, a mitre, and a girdle." Without these Aaron could not be a High Priest. They typify various powers, responsibilities, and qualities connected with that office.

The priestly garments were considered a part of the work of the Tabernacle.

The robes of the High Priest express the functions and qualities of the High Priest.

The materials are specified, gold and fine twined linen; the others — blue, purple, and scarlet — are colors emblazoned upon the fine twined linen and everywhere interlaced with gold.

The mode in which this is done is described in Exodus 39:3.

114

"And they did beat the gold into thin plates and cut it into wires to work it in the blue, purple, scarlet, and in the fine linen, with cunning work."

The various phases of manhood are typified by the colors. The gold represented His divinity. They were inseparably connected, yet distinct.

Christ's life was a rare and beautiful union of humanity and Divinity. Yet there was a mysterious distinction between His humanity and Deity. With perfect ease He went from the sphere of His human ability to the sphere of His Deity. He was equally at home within one or the other. At the grave of Lazarus, He is seen a very man, a very God.

The ephod, the great priestly robe, was inseparably connected with the shoulder pieces and the breastplate.

The strength of the shoulders and the affections of the heart were devoted to the interests of the people whom He represented. The omnipotent strength and infinite love of Christ, our great High Priest, are ours continually and unquestionably.

The shoulders that sustain the universe uphold the weakest member of His Body. The priesthood was God's provision to bring Israel into His presence and keep them there. It was God's provision for spiritually-dead Israel that they might have an approach to Him.

Exodus 28:15-29 and Exodus 39:8-21 tells of the breastplate with the names of the twelve tribes engraved upon precious stones.

The peculiar excellence of a precious stone is that the more intense the light is, the more brightly it shines.

These were maintained in Divine presence in undiminished lustre and unalterable beauty which belonged to the position in which the Grace of God had set them.

Whatever the failures of Israel might be, their names glittered before Him. Jehovah had set them where no man could pluck them. No one could enter the Holy place to dim their lustre.

Each tribe had its place and its own stone. Each stone had its own peculiar glory and beauty. Each differed from, without rivaling, the other; and each filled its appointed place before God.

God was able to create variety without involving inferiority.

And so it is with the individuals that compose the Body of Christ, and yet Christ is seen in each with a peculiar beauty and glory into which another does not intrude. Each has his place in the Body, a responsibility to magnify Christ, that does not belong to another.

In the view of the Father, the Body shines with the brightness, the Righteousness of Christ. Man cannot see, but God can see us in Christ, in His Righteousness and Beauty.

The Great Shepherd of the sheep will not cease to bear on His shoulders and heart the weakest of the flock until at last He presents him faultless, without blame, before the Father. When the Resurrection morning comes, everyone of the Redeemed will be like Christ, and will be manifested in the same beauty and glory in which he is now representedly upheld on the shoulders of the great High Priest before God.

The Memorial

Exodus 28:12, "And thou shalt put the two stones upon the shoulders of the ephod for stones of memorial unto the children of Israel; and Aaron shall bear their names before the Lord upon his two shoulders for a memorial."

Israel had one feast to which this word "memorial" was peculiarly attached . . . the Feast of the Passover. "This day shall be unto you for a memorial and ye shall keep it a feast to the Lord throughout your generations" (Exodus 12:14 and 13:9).

They had therefore two constant reasons for remembering Jehovah: their deliverance from bondage in Egypt by the blood of the paschal lamb, and their acceptance in the brilliancy and glory of precious stones before the Lord on the shoulders of the High Priest.

There are two memorials to us who are His children: our absolute Redemption from the kingdom of darkness through the blood of the lamb (Colossians 1:13), and our standing before God as His Children, upheld in His presence in all the glory and righteousness (Jude 1:24).

Just as Aaron could not enter the Holy Place without reminding Jehovah of the love and perfection in which Israel stood accepted before Him, we have a constant memorial before Him in our Great High Priest, who brings us before Him. He is our Wisdom, our Righteousness, our Sanctification, and our Redemption.

The Urim and Thummim

Exodus 28:30. The breastplate was made of the same materials as the ephod, and it was doubled or folded to form a bag into which the Urim and Thummim were put. The Urim and Thummim were precious stones bearing significant names which no one has at present ever been able to know.

Urim means "lights" and Thummim means "perfection." These mysterious contents of the breastplate seem to direct our thoughts to the heart of the Lord Jesus as containing all light and perfection, all grace and truth, all mercy and righteousness.

We are told in Ephesians 5:13, "Whatsoever doth make manifest is light." The High Priest with the Urim in his breastplate became the channel by which God made manifest His counsels. The Lord Jesus makes known the counsels and purposes of God. He is light, and in Him is no darkness, and through Him God's will is made known to us.

The Golden Bells and Pomegranates
Exodus 28: 33-35

Around the skirts were placed pomegranates of three colors—blue, purple, and scarlet; and alternated with each pomegranate was a bell of pure gold. The only adornings of this Heavenly Robe were fruits gathered from the earth. The High Priest thus proclaimed on his entrance into the Holiest that he had come from the world, proclaiming his earth walk. Pomegranates are especially mentioned as fruits of the Holy Land.

Between each two pomegranates there was a golden bell. The golden sound was connected with the rich, juicy fruit, and as the High Priest approached the Most Holy Place, his steps sent forth a Heavenly melody, and when he returned again from the immediate presence of the

117

Glory into the camp, his retiring footsteps rang out the unearthly sound. They proclaimed his heavenly walk in the Most Holy Place.

As the High Priest approached Him, God must hear the heavenly sound sent forth by his footsteps, although he came from the midst of a din of worldliness and confusion. His walk, though surrounded by these sins, must be respecting their fruitfulness to God and must not be in regard to earthly ambitions or glory or prosperity. Again, his retiring footsteps from the immediate presence of God were to speak the same truth. He must return into the ordinary occupations of life, still making his footsteps known as from Heaven.

The Mitre

Exodus 29:39 and Exodus 39:28

The word "Mitre" is used for the headdress of the High Priest. It is derived from a verb signifying to "roll" or "wind around," possibly intimating that the High Priest's mitre was wound around his head.

The Mitre covering the head of the High Priest was a type of his being subject to God, and that he was always supposed to be standing in the presence of God.

He was never to lose sight of his glorious calling, but his life was to be spent in the tabernacle, ready to accomplish God's will.

The white, fine linen, of which it was made, is an emblem of that righteousness and purity which must be manifested in one who stands in the presence of God on behalf of others.

The Golden Plate

Exodus 28:36-38 and Exodus 39:30-31

The golden plate is described before the mitre, the object of the mitre being to enable the High Priest to wear this plate of gold before the Lord.

Deeply engraved on this golden plate was the writing:

"HOLINESS TO JEHOVAH"

without which he could not appear in the presence of the Lord in behalf of Israel.

What a volume of truth this little sentence does contain. How expressive of Him who alone has title to bear it . . . the true High Priest.

The forehead is especially that portion of the human countenance on which is depicted the purpose, will and mind. Throughout His earthly ministry, holiness to Jehovah was the ruling purpose of Christ's mind.

Aaron could only present holiness to Jehovah engraved upon the holy crown on his forehead. Christ is holiness to Jehovah. Aaron stood only on behalf of Israel. Christ not only stands on behalf of His people, but they are united to Him in his life.

QUESTIONS

1. Why was the priesthood a necessity?
2. Give at least three contrasts or similarities existing between the High Priest of the Old Covenant and Jesus, our High Priest of the New Covenant.
3. What did the priest's garments typify?
4. Explain Hebrews 7:11-17.
5. (a) Tell of the significance of the breastplate with the names of the precious stones.
   (b) What truth of the Body of Christ is revealed here?
6. What were the two memorials of Israel?
7. What two memorials do we have that correspond to them?
8. Explain the Urim and Thummim.
9. What did the golden bells and pomegranates signify?
10. What does the Mitre signify on the head of the High Priest?

119

Notes

Lesson 15
OFFERING
The Priest's Garments
Exodus 39:27; 28:31-34

THE PORTION of the High Priest's dress called the "Coat" was more properly a tunic. It was derived from the verb meaning "to cover," or "to hide."

The outer garments were distinctly of a representative character; that is, they bore the names of Israel before the Lord.

The Pomegranates around the hem of the robe had relation to that people as bearing fruit to God.

In the under-tunic there was apparently no connection with the people. It was rather a personal clothing of the High Priest. It was an atonement for himself.

The fine white linen coat was typical of that righteousness with which he was covered.

The Girdle
Exodus 28:4; 39:5

The object of the girdle was to strengthen the loins for service. In His earthly ministry, Christ girded Himself with a zeal to do the Father's will that all the forces of men and hell could not shake.

Offerings

There are two distinct types of offerings. One type includes the offering connected with the great Day of Atonement (Leviticus 16).

The other type includes the first three of the five offerings given to us in Leviticus 1 to 4, and the other two for Broken Fellowship (Leviticus 4 to 7). The first three offerings were for Fellowship.

We have seen that the reason for Creation was the heart-cry of the Father-God for fellowship. We saw the entrance of Spiritual Death into the spirit of man which separated him from God. Now we see this desire for fellowship upon the part of the Father-God manifested again as He requests of spiritually-dead Israel to build Him a Tabernacle that He might dwell in their midst. He made provision for their approach to Him through the Aaronic Priesthood and the offerings.

Of the five offerings, the first three were Worship or Fellowship offerings, and the last two were Broken Fellowship offerings. We see that in either case, the object was fellowship. (See Chart.)

Whole Burnt Offering

Read Leviticus 1

Law of Burnt Offering—Leviticus 6:8-13

The Whole Burnt Offering was purely a Fellowship Offering. It was a Love Offering. It was offered by the free will of the individual.

It was to be offered at the door of the tent of meeting. The man laid his hand upon the head of the offering. This identified him with the offering which would make an atonement for him (Leviticus 1:3-4).

The spiritually-dead Israelite could not Fellowship God without first a covering being provided for him.

Leviticus 1:5-9. The man brings his offering and slays it, and cuts it into pieces. The Priests sprinkle the blood around the Brazen Altar. He is able to do this upon the basis of the great Day of Atonement.

The High Priest has no part in this, only the Priests. The innards and feet are washed. The feet have touched the cursed ground, and the innards have been filled with the fruit of the cursed ground.

There was a threefold judgment passed upon the Offering. The man who ordered it examined it to discover whether or not it was without blemish. The priest examined it, and God examined it. It is in this respect a type of Christ.

He was examined by the Law and found faultless. He was examined by the Priesthood that offered Him and found faultless.

They could find no fault in Him.

They had to make false charges.

God found no fault in Him. He cried from Heaven on several occasions, "This is My beloved Son in whom I am well pleased."

Jesus found no fault with Himself. He said, "The Prince of this world cometh and hath no part in me." He also said, "Which of you convicteth me of sin?"

These Scriptures show the sinlessness of Jesus in His own eyes as well as in the eyes of God and the people.

Leviticus 1:9. It was burned upon the Altar for a sweet savour unto Jehovah. It was a sweet savour Fellowship between God and man.

Ephesians 5:2 tells us that the Sacrifice of Christ was an odor of a sweet smell before God. This was because it restored Righteousness to man and brought him back to God. It made possible Fellowship between God and man.

Isaiah 53:10, "Yet it pleased Jehovah to bruise Him." So precious was man in the sight of God that it pleased Him to suffer, and His Son to suffer, that man might be given again the right of Sonship.

The Meal Offering
Leviticus 2

This offering was also a free-will offering — an expression of Love toward the Covenant God. The Worshipper is to bring a basin of fine meal. Everything coarse and unseemly is taken out. The fine flour is a beautiful type of the perfect humanity of Christ, and of His body, the Church.

Oil was poured over it. This is a type of the Holy Spirit's anointing Christ and the Church. It was soaked in oil. He does not give the Spirit by measure.

Frankincense was put upon it. The worshipper then brought the Meal Offering to a Priest. (The High Priest is not seen here.) The Priest took out a handful of the Meal with all the Frankincense and burned it upon the Altar, an offering made by fire, a sweet savour, unto Jehovah. The Frankincense is typical of Worship. Therefore all of it was burned with the portion offered to Jehovah. He received all —the Worship, Love, and Adoration.

The Meal Offering is a type of Christ in the Gospel of Luke. Here we see the beautiful humanity of Jesus. The Incarnation is the fine meal mingled with oil. There was much salt in the life of Christ. This means His wonderful wisdom in all of His conversation. There was no honey, typical of self-indulgence in man. There was no

123

leaven, never a false note. He never accommodated Himself to the ignorance of the people. He is always the true Spokesman from God.

He gave all the Frankincense to the Father. The Father had all the Glory. It took fire to bring out the fragrance of the Frankincense.

It took the Cross to reveal the fragrance and beauty of Jesus.

What was left was to be eaten by the Priest in the Holy Place.

This meal is a type of our feeding upon the Word.

Law of Peace Offering
Leviticus 3; 7:11-36

In the Peace Offering we see the gracious provision that God made for man's fellowship with Him. The Peace Offering is a different type of Fellowship.

In the Meal Offering God had His portion, and the Priest and his family have their portion. In the Peace Offering the Worshipper also has his portion. Jehovah has all the fat of the animal.

The Priest and his family, and the worshipper with his family, both have their share.

We have here a type of Fellowship. Inside the Outer Court sat the Priest and his family and the worshipper and his family, eating, while Jehovah received His share. Eating is a type of the higher order of Fellowship.

One cannot eat and enjoy his food in the presence of enemies.

Revelation 3:20 reads, "Behold, I stand at the door and knock; if any man hear my voice and open the door I will come in and sup with him and he with Me." In this passage, "eating" is used as a type to show forth the Fellowship between the Father and Christ with man as they make their home with him.

The worship of Israel had to be upon the level of the physical senses; their fellowship, also, had to be upon the same level. They could have fellowship only as man desired to express his thanksgiving toward his Covenant God.

Those who were ungrateful probably brought no Freewill offerings.

We see that the Covenant God was not a Despot. Before He had given to Israel the law of the Covenant, He reviews before Moses His faithfulness to the Covenant in delivering them from Egypt and caring for them in their three months' journey. He then gave to them the permission of choosing whether or not they would walk with Him as His Covenant People (Exodus 19:3-9).

Exodus 24:1-8. Before the Law of the Covenant really went into effect, the people first ratified it. God gave the Law orally to Moses, who gave it to the people, who said, "All that the Lord hath spoken will we do and be obedient."

It was so in the building of the Tabernacle. It was to be made of Offerings from willing hearts.

Likewise in the Fellowship Offerings they were to come from those who willed to worship Him.

The Fellowship in the Peace Offering was a threefold Fellowship between God, the Priest, and man. It is a type of our Fellowship today.

We have Fellowship with the Father and His Son, Jesus Christ (I John 1:3).

We also have fellowship one with another.

The Sin Offering and the Trespass Offering

Leviticus 5 and 6

The object of the Sin Offering and the Trespass Offering was to maintain Fellowship.

The Sin Offering was offered when an anointed Priest, Ruler, or anyone of the common people had sinned directly against Jehovah.

Leviticus 6:1-2 is cheating a neighbor over some deposit, or pledge, or theft, or taking advantage of his neighbor in regard to lost property or false oath.

The Trespass Offering was directly against his own neighbor.

As we have mentioned before, it was possible for these five Fellowship Offerings to be accepted because of the foundation that was laid in the Atonement made once a year.

Read the fifth and sixth chapters of Leviticus.

The Sin of Nadab and Abihu
Leviticus 10

The fact that Israel was spiritually dead and needed an Atonement is revealed in Leviticus 10:1.

The Covenant-God desired Fellowship with His people, but because of their condition of Spiritual Death, they could approach Him only through a Divinely Appointed way. Spiritually-dead man needed a Mediator.

The blessing of God had mightily been upon the people. After the dedication of the Priesthood, the Glory of the Lord appeared to the people (Leviticus 8 and 9).

Now a tragedy befalls the family of Aaron. His two sons, who dare to approach Jehovah, uninvited, and in their own way (Leviticus 10:1), are smitten by a fire that devours them (Leviticus 10:2).

Israel learns that they cannot approach God in their own way.

QUESTIONS
1. How did the coat reveal the High Priest's need of an atonement?
2. In what respect was the girdle a type of Christ?
3. What were the two distinct types of offerings?
4. Name the five Fellowship offerings.
5. How was the threefold judgment, that was passed upon the Whole Burnt Offering, a type of Christ?
6. How did the Meal Offering portray Christ?
7. How did the Peace Offering provide a means of fellowship?
8. What was the object of the Sin Offering?
9. What was the object of the Trespass Offering?
10. What was the sin of Nadab and Abihu?

CHART OF THE FIVE GREAT LEVITICAL SACRIFICES

NAME	BURNT	MEAL	PEACE	SIN	TRESPASS
Significance	Highest order of Fellowship	Fellowship between Jehovah and man	Jehovah, Priest and man feasting upon the sacrifice, a type of Christ	To restore broken Fellowship	To restore broken Fellowship
Animal Offered	Bullock, Ram, He-Goat, Turtle-doves, and Young Pigeon	Fine Flour, Oil, Frankincense, Salt, no Leaven	Male or Female of Herd or Flock	Bullock for Priest; He-Goat for Ruler; Kid, Lamb, Birds or Fine Flour for People	Ram without blemish
Where Presented	Door of Tent of Meeting	To Aaron's Sons	Door of Tent of Meeting	Door of Tent of Meeting	Unto Jehovah Unto Priest
By Whom	Anyone	Anyone	Anyone	One who sinned against Jehovah	One who sinned against man
Special Features	A Type of Christ as Son, pleasing Father	A Type of Christ as Pictured in Luke	Type of Believer enjoying Privileges	Type of Jesus, our Advocate	Type of Jesus, our Advocate
Where Offered	Noah — Genesis 8:20	Jacob and Esau — Genesis 32:13	Jacob — Genesis 31:54	Hezekiah — II Chronicles 29:21-24	Philistines — I Samuel 6:4

Notes

Lesson 16
THE GREAT DAY OF ATONEMENT

L EVITICUS, the 16th chapter, gives to us the directions for the Great Day of Atonement.

The Great Day of Atonement is a type of Christ in His Substitutions. Read the 16th chapter of Leviticus through very carefully.

The High Priest's entrance into the Holy of Holies was one of the most significant acts of the Great Day of Atonement.

The bullock is killed for the sin offering. The High Priest takes a basin of blood as far as the laver. There he bathes his body and puts on the white linen garments. Once more he takes the basin and carries it into the Holy Place. There he takes a censer filled with live coals and puts upon it a handful of sweet incense. The smoke from the burning incense fills the Holy Place. He now pushes back the heavy curtain that hides the Holiest of Holies and in a cloud of incense goes in and sprinkles the blood upon the Mercy Seat.

You know the word Atonement means "to cover." He was under a covering of smoke of incense until he could make an atonement with the blood he carried. This sacrifice was made but once a year to cover spiritually-dead Israel.

Leaving the Holy of Holies he goes to the scapegoat that has been held in readiness by a young man, and Aaron lays both of his hands upon the head of the live goat, confessing over him all the iniquities of the children of Israel.

He puts all the sins and transgressions upon the head of the live goat which is to be led into the wilderness to be destroyed by wild beasts. You notice in this that God makes a distinction between what Israel is (that is, Spiritually Dead) and what Israel does (the sins that are a result of spiritual death).

The sins are borne away on the head of the scapegoat. Jesus put away our sin nature and made provision for the remission of our sins when we are born again.

The High Priest going into the Holy Place making the yearly atonement is a figure of Christ's going into the

Heavenly Holy of Holies and making eternal Redemption. Jesus made one sacrifice for sins forever, but the High Priest made an atonement once a year (Hebrews 10:1-21).

NOTE TO THE STUDENTS

In this course we are majoring Redemption. We are studying the Bible in the Light of our Redemption in Christ.

We have seen that Redemption demands the Incarnation. Therefore, God is working toward the time when Redemption shall become a possibility through the Incarnation of His Son. Man had to be redeemed from Satan's bondage in order to become God's child.

The reason for His choosing a covenant people was that through them He might preserve a righteous line through which man's Redeemer would come.

We have studied the cutting of the covenant with Abraham, by which means Abraham's descendants become God's Covenant people. We have seen their deliverance from Egypt by the hand of their Covenant God.

We have learned to appreciate their rights in that Covenant, and what it meant for God to say, "By myself, I have sworn." All of God's resources were theirs if they kept the Covenant.

We have studied the Tabernacle, where God dwelt; the priesthood, who acted as Mediators; and the offerings, a type of Christ and His Redemptive work, God's provision for their fellowship with Him.

Now as we continue to study the further history of this people, we shall touch it only briefly until we come to the Incarnation of Christ.

However, we want no portion of the Word to be neglected, so we are giving in this lesson a chronology in six divisions of the material given to us from Genesis 1 to the birth of Christ. We believe that this chronology which you may use for reference work will be valuable to you.

PERIOD I
FROM THE CREATION TO THE DELUGE
CONTAINING 1,656 YEARS

B.C.

4004 The creation of the world .... Gen. 1:2

4004 Fall of our first parents, Adam and

Eve, from holiness and happiness by disobeying God. Promise of a Saviour Gen. 3

4002 Cain born .... Gen. 4:1
4001 Abel born .... Gen. 4:2
3875 Abel murdered by his brother, Cain ...... Gen. 4:8
3874 Seth born, his father, Adam, being 130 years old .... Gen. 5:3
3382 Enoch born .... Gen. 5:18, 19
3317 Methuselah born .... Gen. 5:21
3074 Adam dies, aged 930 years .... Gen. 5:5
3017 Enoch translated, aged 365 years .... Gen. 5:24
2962 Seth dies, aged 912 years .... Gen. 5:8
2948 Noah born .... Gen. 5:28, 29
2468 The Deluge threatened, and Noah com- Gen. 6:3-22
missioned to preach repentance during II Pet. 2:5
120 years .... I Pet. 3:20
2348 Methuselah dies, aged 969 years .... Gen. 5:27
In the same year Noah enters into the ark, being 600 years old .... Gen. 7:6, 7

PERIOD II
FROM THE DELUGE TO THE CALL OF ABRAHAM
427 YEARS

B.C.

2347 Noah, with his family, leaves the ark after the deluge, and offering sacrifices he receives the covenant of safety, of which the rainbow was the token .... Gen. 9:8-18
2234 Babel built .... Gen. 11
2234 The confusion of languages, and the dispersion of mankind .... Gen. 11
2233 Nimrod lays the first foundation of the Babylonian or Assyrian monarchy .... Gen. 10:8-11
2188 Mizraim lays the foundation of the Egyptian monarchy .... Gen. 10:13
1996 Abram (or Abraham) born .... Gen. 11:26

PERIOD III
FROM THE CALL OF ABRAHAM TO THE EXODUS
OF ISRAEL FROM EGYPT, 430 YEARS

B.C.

1936 Abram called from Chaldean idola- Acts 7:2

131

	try, at 60 years of age	Gen. 11:31
1921	Abram's second call to Canaan	Gen. 12:1-4
1913	Abram's victory over the kings, and rescue of Lot	Gen. 14:1-24
1910	Ishmael born, Abram being 86 years old	Gen. 16
1897	God's covenant with Abram, changing his name to Abraham; circumcision instituted. . . . Lot delivered, Sodom destroyed by fire because of their abominations	Gen. 17-19
1896	Isaac born, Abraham being 100 years old	Gen. 21
1871	Abraham offers Isaac as a burnt sacrifice to God	Gen. 22 Heb. 11:17-19 Jas. 2:21
1859	Sarah, Abraham's wife, dies, aged 127 years	Gen. 23:1
1856	Isaac marries Rebecca	Gen. 24
1836	Jacob and Esau born, Isaac being 60 years old	Gen. 25:26
1821	Abraham dies, aged 175 years	Gen. 25:7, 8
1759	Jacob goes to his uncle Laban in Syria, and marries his daughters, Leah and Rachel	Gen. 28
1746	Joseph born, Jacob being 90 years old	Gen. 30:23, 24
1739	Jacob returns to Canaan	Gen. 31, 32
1729	Joseph sold as a slave by his own brethren	Gen. 37
1716	He explains Pharaoh's dreams, and is made governor of Egypt	Gen. 41
1706	Joseph's brethren settle in Egypt	Gen. 43:44
1689	Jacob foretells the advent of the Messiah, and dies in Egypt, aged 147 years	Gen. 49
1636	Joseph dies, aged 110 years	Gen. 50:26
1574	Aaron born	Ex. 6:20
1571	Moses born	Ex. 2:1-10
1531	Moses flees into Midian	Ex. 2:11-15
1491	Moses commissioned by God to deliver Israel	Ex. 3:2

PERIOD IV
FROM THE EXODUS OF ISRAEL FROM EGYPT
TO THE BUILDING OF SOLOMON'S TEMPLE,
487 YEARS

B.C.

1491 Miraculous passage of the Red Sea by
the Israelites _____ Ex. 14:22

1491 The Law delivered on Sinai _____ Ex. 19-40

1452 Miriam, sister of Moses, dies, aged 130
years _____ Num. 20:1

1452 Aaron dies, aged 123 years _____ Num. 20:28

1451 Moses dies, aged 120 years, Joshua being ordained as his successor _____ Deut. 34

1451 The Israelites pass the river Jordan, the
manna ceases, and Jericho is taken _____ Josh. 1:6

1443 Joshua dies, aged 110 years _____ Josh. 24:29

1155 Samuel born _____ 1 Sam. 1:19

1116 Eli, the high priest, dies, Ark of God
taken by Philistines _____ I Sam. 4

1095 Saul anointed King of Israel _____ I Sam. 10:1

1085 David born _____ I Sam. 16:13

1063 David anointed to be king, and he
slays Goliath _____ I Sam. 17:49

1055 Saul is defeated in battle, and in despair
kills himself. David acknowledged king
by Judah _____ I Sam. 31

1048 Ishbosheth, king of Israel, assassinated
and the whole kingdom is united under
David _____ II Sam. 1

1047 Jerusalem taken from the Jebusites by
David, and made the royal city _____ II Sam. 5

1035 David commits adultery with Bath-
sheba, and contrives the death of her
husband, Uriah _____ II Sam. 11

1034 David brought to repentance for his sin
by Nathan the prophet, sent to him by
the Lord _____ II Sam. 12

1033 Solomon is born _____ II Sam. 12:24

1023 Absalom rebels against his father, and
is slain by Joab _____ II Sam. 16-18

1015	David causes Solomon to be proclaimed king, defeating the rebellion of Adonijah	I Kings 1
1014	David dies, aged 70 years	I Kings 2
1004	Solomon's temple finished, after seven years of building	I Kings 6, 7

PERIOD V

FROM THE BUILDING OF SOLOMON'S TEMPLE TO THE DESTRUCTION OF JERUSALEM AND CAPTIVITY OF THE JEWS IN BABYLON, 412 YEARS

Kings of Judah B.C. Began to Reign	Kings of Israel Began to Reign	Prophets
975 Rehoboam	Jeroboam I	Ahijah, Shemaiah
958 Abijah or Abijam		
955 Asa	Nadad (954)	Azariah
953 "	Baasha	Hanani
930 "	Elah	Jehu
929 "	Zimri	
929 "	Omri	
918 "	Ahab	Elijah, 910-896
914 Jehoshaphat	"	Micaiah
897 "	Ahaziah	Elisha, 896-838
896 "	Jehoram, or Joram	Jahaziel
892 Jehoram	"	
885 Ahaziah	"	
884 Athaliah	Jehu	Jehoiada
878 Joash, or Jehoahaz	"	
857 "	Jehoahaz	Jonah, 856-784
839 Amaziah	Jehoash	
825 "	Jeroboam II	
810 Uzziah or Azariah		Amos, 810-785
784 "	Anarchy (11 yrs)	Hosea, 810-725
773 "	Zechariah	Joel, 810-660
772 "	Shallum, Menahem	
761 "	Pekahiah	Isaiah, 810-698

134

759	"	Pekah	
758	Jotham	"	Michah, 758-699
742	Ahaz	"	Oded
730	"	Hoshea	
726	Hezekiah	(Captivity, 721)	Nahum, 720-698
698	Manasseh	"	
643	Amon	"	Zephaniah, 640-609
641	Josiah	"	Jeremiah, 628-586
610	Jehoahaz, or	"	Habakkuk, 612-598
	Shallum		
610	Jehoiakim	"	Daniel, 606-534
599	Jehoiachin, or	"	
	Ceniah	"	
599	Zedekiah	"	
588	Babylonian		Obadiah, 588-583
	Captivity		

PERIOD VI
FROM THE DESTRUCTION OF JERUSALEM BY NEBUCHADNEZZAR, TO THE BIRTH OF CHRIST, 588 YEARS

B.C.	HISTORICAL EVENTS	PROPHETS
588	Destruction of Jerusalem by the Chaldeans, and captivity of the Jews	
538	Babylon taken by Cyrus	Ezekiel 595-536
536	Proclamation of Cyrus: Zerubbabel, and Joshua	
534	Foundation of the temple	
529	Artaxerxes (Cambyses) forbids the work	
520	Favorable decree of Ahasuerus (Darius Hystaspis)	Haggai 520-518
518	Esther made queen	Zech. 520-518
515	The second temple finished	
510	Haman's plot frustrated	
484	Xerxes, king of Persia	
464	Artaxerxes Longimanus	
457	Ezra sent to govern Jerusalem	
445	Nehemiah sent as governor	
423	Darius Nothus	Malachi 436-420

335 Alexander the Great invades Persia, and establishes the Macedonian or Grecian empire

63 Jerusalem taken by Pompey, and Judea made a Roman province

40 Herod made king

28 Augustus Caesar, emperor of Rome

19 The poet, Virgil, dies

18 Herod begins to rebuild the temple

4 John the Baptist is born

4 Christ born, 4 years before the era known as A.D.

REVIEW QUESTIONS (Each counts 25 points)

1. What was accomplished for Israel on the Great Day of Atonement?

2. During the Old Testament period, toward what event is God working? Why?

3. Tell what you can of the Covenant, the reason for its existence, and its significance.

4. Show how the Tabernacle, Priesthood and Offerings show the hunger of God for fellowship with man.

Lesson 17

SYNOPSIS OF OLD TESTAMENT BOOKS
AND
HIGHLIGHTS OF ISRAEL'S HISTORY

Numbers

THIS BOOK derives its name from the fact that it records the enumeration of Israel. Historically, Numbers takes up the story where Exodus left it, and is the book of the wilderness wanderings of the Covenant people, consequent upon their failure to enter the land at Kadesh-Barnea.

There are some who take the books of the Old Testament typically, such as: Genesis, the book of the creation and the fall; Exodus, of Redemption; Leviticus, of worship and fellowship; and Numbers, of that which should follow — service and walk.

However, we do not give the books in this form of typology. Israel was spiritually-dead, and tested by its wilderness experiences, utterly failed. This cannot be used as a type of the victorious walk and life of the man who has become a New Creation in Christ Jesus, who has passed absolutely from the realm and authority of Satan, into the realm of Life and Christ Jesus.

Numbers is in five chief divisions:

(1) The order of the Host — Chapters 1:1 to 10:10.

(2) From Sinai to Kadesh-Barnea — Chapters 10:11 to 12:16.

(3) Israel at Kadesh-Barnea — Chapters 13:1 to 19:22.

(4) The Wilderness wanderings — Chapters 20:1 to 33:49.

(5) Closing instructions — Chapters 33:50 to 36:13.

The events recorded in Numbers cover a period of thirty-nine years.

Deuteronomy

Deuteronomy is in seven divisions.

(1) Summary of the history of Israel in the wilderness. Chapters 1:1 to 3:29.

(2) A reinstatement of the law with warnings and exhortations. Chapters 4:1 to 11:32.

(3) Instructions, warnings, and predictions. Chapters 12:1 to 27:26.

(4) The great closing prophecies summarizing the history of Israel to the second coming of Christ and a promise of their possession of Palestine. Chapters 28:1 to 30:20.

(5) Last counsels to priests, Levites, and to Joshua. Chapter 31.

(6) The song of Moses and his parting blessing. Chapters 32 and 33.

(7) The death of Moses. Chapter 34. (34:7, Moses was 120 years old when he died. His eye was not dimmed nor his natural force abated. This was because Moses was a Covenant man.)

Joshua

Joshua succeeded Moses as the ruler under God. The government is still Theocratic. The events recorded in Joshua cover a period of twenty-six years. The book falls into four parts.

(1) The conquest. Chapters 1 to 12.

(2) The division of the inheritance. Chapter 13 thru 21.

(3) Incipient discord. Chapter 22.

(4) Joshua's last counsels and death. Chapters 23 and 24.

Judges

This book takes its name from the thirteen men raised up to deliver Israel in the declension and disunion which followed the death of Joshua. Through these men Jehovah continued His personal Government of Israel.

The key verse to the condition of Israel is 17:6, "Every man did that which was right in his own eyes."

There are two prominent facts—the utter failure of the spiritually-dead covenant people, and the grace of the Covenant God.

The book records seven apostasies, seven servitudes to seven heathen nations, and seven deliverances. The events recorded in Judges cover a period of 305 years.

Ruth

This story should be read in connection with the first half of Judges, as it presents a picture of life in Israel at that time. The events recorded in this book cover a period of ten years.

I Samuel

This book gives to us the personal history of Samuel, the last of the judges. It records the moral failure of the priesthood under Eli, and of the judges, in Samuel's attempt to make the office hereditary. In his prophetic office, Samuel was faithful, and in him begins the line of writing prophets. From now on the prophet, not the priest, is conspicuous in Israel.

During this period, Israel repudiated God as a king, and desired a king like the other nations had around them. God gives to them a king, Saul.

This book is in four parts:

(1) The story of Samuel to the death of Eli. Chapters 1:1 to 4:22.

(2) From the taking of the ark, to the demand for a king. Chapters 5:1 to 8:22.

(3) From the reign of Saul, to the call of David. Chapters 9:1 to 15:35.

(4) From the call of David, to the death of Saul. Chapters 16:1 to 31:13.

These events cover a period of 115 years.

II Samuel

This book marks the restoration of order through the enthroning of God's king, David. It also gives to us the establishment of Israel's political center in Jerusalem.

The book is in four parts:

(1) From the death of Saul to the anointing of David over Judah in Hebron. Chapter 1:1-27.

(2) From the anointing in Hebron to the establishment of David over the united Israel. Chapters 2:1 to 5:25.

(3) From the conquest of Jerusalem to the Rebellion of Absalom. Chapters 6:1 to 14:33.

(4) From the Rebellion of Absalom to the purchase of the temple site. Chapters 15:1 to 24:25.

The events in II Samuel cover a period of 38 years.

I Kings

I Kings records the death of David, the reign of Solomon, the building of the temple, the death of Solomon, the division of the kingdom under Rehoboam and Jeroboam, and the history of the two kingdoms to the reign of Jehorab over Judah and Ahaziah over Samaria.

It also includes the mighty ministry of Elijah. Chapter 17 shows the fearless action of this covenant man upon the Word of God.

The events recorded in I Kings cover a period of 118 years.

II Kings

II Kings is in seven parts.

(1) The last ministry and translation of Elijah. Chapters 1:1 to 2:11.

(2) The ministry of Elisha from the translation of Elijah to the anointing of Jehu. Chapters 2:12 to 9:10.

(3) The reign of Jehu over Israel. Chapters 9:11 to 10:36.

(4) The reigns of Athaliah and Jehoash over Judah. Chapters 11:1 to 12:21.

(5) The reigns of Jehoash and Joash over Israel and the last ministry of Elisha. Chapter 13:1-25.

(6) From the death of Elisha to the captivity of Israel. Chapters 14:1 to 17:41. Israel was carried into captivity into Assyria because they had broken the covenant. From this captivity, the ten tribes have never been restored to Palestine.

(7) From the accession of Hezekiah to the captivity of Judah. Chapters 18:1 to 25:30.

The events recorded in II Kings covered a period of 308 years. During this period, Amos and Hosea prophesied in Israel; and Obadiah, Joel, Isaiah, Nahum, Habakkuk, Zephaniah and Jeremiah, in Judah.

I and II Chronicles

The two books of Chronicles together cover the period from the death of Saul to the captivities. They were probably written during the Babylonian captivity, and are distinguished from the two books of Kings in a fuller account of Judah and the omission of many details.

The events in the two books cover a period of 468 years.

Judah was in Babylonia in captivity for a period of 70 years.

Ezra

Ezra records the return to Palestine under Zerubbabel by decree of Cyrus, who laid the temple foundations 536 B.C. Later, 458 B.C., Ezra followed and restored the law and ritual. But the mass of the nation and most of the princes remained by preference in Babylonia and Assyria where they were prospering. The post-captivity Books deal with that remnant which alone remembered the Covenant God. The book is in two parts.

(1) From the decree of Cyrus to the dedication of the restored temple. Chapters 1:1 to 6:22.

(2) The ministry of Ezra. Chapters 7:1 to 10:44.

The events recorded in Ezra cover a period of 80 years.

Nehemiah

Nehemiah, one of the great characters of the Old Testament, has never received the recognition that really belongs to him. He was private secretary to the emperor of the then greatest nation of the world. He was a man of prayer; he was heroic; he was a leader. He was utterly fearless. He left Shushan and came to Jerusalem and by the sheerest bravery and courage rebuilt the wall, restored true worship, gave the law to the common people, and separated Israel from the nations around them.

This book covers a period of about 10 years.

Esther

The book of Esther is one of the most beautiful of Old Testament literature.

Though the name of God does not occur once in it, yet it is a book that shows the hand of God as almost no other book does.

Esther becomes the favorite wife of Ahasuerus. By her absolute obedience to her uncle she becomes the savior of the chosen people. No more beautiful character or heroine can be found in the chronicles of the Old Testament. This book covers a period of about 11 years.

The Poetical Books

We have studied the Historical Books of the Old Testament, and now we take up the study of the Poetical Books. The poetical books are God's song books. Here we find the heart cries of God's people, of their fears and faith and their longings. Job is the first book written. It was written before Genesis. Tradition puts the date about 1700 B.C. Job was a relative of Abraham. He gathers the universal desires of the human race and puts them into this great poem of agony. One of the problems he faces is, "How can man born of woman stand right with God?" He gives to us a suggestion of the fall. Showing the extent of man's treason, he says, "The stars are not clean in God's sight." He recognizes man's need of a mediator, and cries, "Oh, if there were an umpire betwixt us who might lay his hand upon both of us."

He cries for a restoration of righteousness. In these longings of Job we see the longings each race has had and expressed in its human religion. Job stood the tests of Satan. He never lost God's favor. We can see in this book the whole plan of redemption portrayed. He begins in the Garden of Eden and goes through the agonies of the long struggle of suffering man. He gives to us a suggestion of redemption that ends in Eden restored.

The Psalms

The Psalms are Israel's song book. They are the expressions, longings, heartaches, tears and desires of the people of the first Covenant. They represent the daily experiences in some respects; and in others, they are prophecies of something that is utterly beyond them, only found in the New Creation.

The books are generally divided into five sections: 1 to 41; 42 to 72; 73 to 89; 90 to 106; and 107 to 150.

The imprecatory Psalms are the cry for vengeance upon their enemies. These have bothered lots of devout people; but when you realize that Israel was not Christian, that they had never been Born Again, they were just Jews under the blood of bulls and goats, you can understand then how these Psalms could be written. The miracle is that Psalms like the 23rd, 27th, 37th, 91st, could be written by natural men. It proves the inspiration of the Holy Spirit.

The Proverbs

The book of Proverbs is the wisdom of the Old Covenant. It is an interpretation of the law in daily life. It is what the book of James is in the New Covenant.

James is writing for the New Covenant folks and is giving wisdom for their daily walk.

Proverbs should be read with great care. Every boy and girl, every youth in our grammar schools, should read and study the book of Proverbs.

The man who absorbs the wisdom of Proverbs will seldom fall into the snares of modern life.

Ecclesiastes

Ecclesiastes is the most unique book in the Old Testament. It is a picture of the spiritually-dead man trying to find pleasure in the world.

He tries to find it in building, in architectural ambitions. He built great buildings. He tried to find it in horticulture. He had the most beautiful gardens perhaps the world had ever seen up to that time.

He tried it in vast public works. He tried it with wine. He tried it with women and song, and in the conclusion of things he said, "Vanity of vanities, all is vanity."

In the last chapter he sings the song of failure of natural man to achieve the desires of the human spirit.

The Song of Solomon

The Songs of Solomon are the Idylls and Sonnets of Christ and the church. They are filled with beautiful imagery.

It is a love dream put into poetic expressions. It gives pictures of broken fellowship, and of the loneliness of the heart that has lost its love.

It gives the triumphs of fellowship when the heart walks in the fullness of its privileges.

QUESTIONS

1. What portions of Israel's history do Numbers and Deuteronomy cover?
2. What are the two prominent facts revealed in Judges?
3. Who was the last of the Judges? Who was the first king?
4. Read I Kings 17. What was the secret of Elijah's power with God?
5. Why was Israel carried into captivity into Assyria?
6. What was the work of Nehemiah?
7. What problems of the human race are recognized by Job?

143

8. What messages are in the Psalms?
9. What purpose did the book of Proverbs serve?
10. What picture is given to us in Ecclesiastes? In the Song of Solomon?

Lesson 18

THE INCARNATION

WE HAVE now come to the study of the most striking miracle of creation, the Incarnation. We have seen that if man was to be redeemed, the Incarnation was inevitable.

Man's need demanded the Incarnation of God's Son. Man was spiritually dead, a child of Satan, without any approach to God.

The Incarnation of Deity and humanity would provide a substitute of Deity and humanity united in such a manner that the Incarnate One could stand as man's Mediator (I Timothy 2:5).

Being equal with God on one hand and united with man on the other, He could bring the two together, and thereby bridge the chasm between God and man (John 14:6).

Also, being Deity and humanity united, as a man He could assume the obligations of human treason and pay the penalty, satisfying the claims of Justice so that the human race would be freed from the authority of Satan (Hebrews 2:14 and Colossians 1:13-14), and given the right to receive the nature of God (John 1:12).

An Incarnation Fact

The Incarnate One could not be born by natural generation. It was not possible for God to come into a child who had been born of natural generation and make that one an Incarnation.

We have seen that by one man, death (the nature of Satan) entered into the world and passed upon all men; that by the one man, the entire human race died spiritually and was ruled by this Spiritual Death.

Romans 5:12, "Therefore, as through one man sin entered into the world . . . so death passed upon all men." Romans 5:18, "So then as through one trespass the judgment came upon all men to condemnation."

If Jesus had been born of natural generation and God had come into Him, He would have been a child of Satan with God dwelling in Him. That would not have been an

Incarnation. That utterly destroys the thought of a perfect Incarnation of God.

If, on the other hand, God could have eradicated Spiritual Death from the spirit of one man and dwelt in him, making that one an Incarnation, He could have changed the nature of the entire human race in the same way.

To do this would have been an injustice to Satan and an injustice to Himself, for the sin problem had not been settled, the penalty of man's transgression had not been paid.

The Redeemer must be one over whom Satan had no legal claims nor authority. This could only come by a Redeemer being conceived and born as was the Babe of Bethlehem.

Born of a Virgin

God's first promise of the Incarnation is given in His conversation with Satan just after man's sin of High Treason.

Genesis 3:15, "And I will put enmity between thee and the woman, and between thy seed and her seed: he shall bruise thy head, and thou shalt bruise his heel."

The Father-God realizes that man's need can only be met by the Incarnation of His Son. He realizes that the Incarnate One could not be born of natural generation, so He gives a prophecy that a woman shall give birth to a child independent of natural generation, and that it shall be called "the seed of woman."

Isaiah 7:13, "And He said, Hear ye now, O House of David: Is it a small thing for you to weary men, that ye will weary my God also? Therefore the Lord Himself will give you a sign: behold the Virgin shall conceive, and bear a son, and shall call his name Immanuel."

The child is going to be born of the House of David, and the "Lord Himself will give you a sign."

Here He uses the name Adonai; the God of Miracles, Himself, will show you a miracle, a wonder. Something out of the ordinary is going to take place, and we say, "What is it?"

He says, "The virgin" (as though He had marked her out) "shall conceive and bear a son and his name shall be Immanuel."

A virgin is going to give birth to a son in a supernatural way, and she is going to call his name Immanuel, God with us, or Incarnation.

Take in connection with this, Luke 1:31-36, "And behold, thou shalt conceive in thy womb, and bring forth a son, and shalt call his name Jesus. He shall be great, and shall be called the Son of the Most High; and the Lord God shall give unto Him the throne of His Father David; and He shall reign over the House of Jacob forever; and of His kingdom there shall be no end."

"And Mary said unto the angel, How shall this be, seeing I know not a man? And the angel answered and said unto her, the Holy Spirit shall come upon thee, and the power of the Most High shall overshadow thee; wherefore also the holy thing which is begotten shall be called the Son of God." The child, you notice, is conceived of the Holy Spirit. It is a Supernatural birth. She was a cousin of Joseph, who was also of the family of David; so the prophet exclaimed, "Oh, house of David, is it a small thing that ye weary me? I will show you a sign."

He is marking out this daughter of David, who is going to give birth to that wonderful being in a manger cradle in Bethlehem 750 years later.

In Jeremiah 31:22, God declares, "A woman shall encompass a man": more literally, "A woman shall encompass a manchild."

This Incarnate One could not be born of natural generation, because man is a fallen being and his seed is subject to Satan.

This seed must be of one who is not a subject of Satan, and so this wonderful being must be conceived of the Holy Spirit, and the womb of the virgin is to be simply the receptacle of that Holy One until the day He is brought forth.

Isaiah 42:6 says, "I, Jehovah, have called thee in righteousness, and will hold thy hand, and will form thee,

147

and give thee for a Covenant of the people, for a light of the Gentiles."

Adam was created; the rest of the human race were generated by natural processes, but this child that is going to be born, is to be "formed" by a special act of Divine Power.

Paul speaks of His birth in the following words: (Philippians 2:6-8) "Who, existing in the form of God, counted not the being on an equality with God a thing to be grasped, but emptied Himself, taking the form of a servant, being made in the likeness of men; and being found in fashion as a man, He humbled Himself, becoming obedient unto death, Yea, the death of the cross."

Notice those terms: He had existed always in the *form* of God, but now He empties Himself and takes the *form* of a bondservant, being made in the likeness of men and being found in *fashion* as a man.

All these suggest a separate and distinct operation of God, different from natural generation.

Here is a being with whom God performs a Miracle by taking Him out of the Godhead or from the Godhead in Heaven, and placing Him in the womb of a virgin to be united with flesh by a unique conception.

Again Paul says, "Wherefore when He cometh into the world: He saith, Sacrifice and offering thou wouldest not, but a body didst thou prepare for me" (Hebrews 10:5).

God prepared a body, a special body, for this being called the Son of God.

Pre-Existence of Christ

The Incarnation presupposes that this being, who became Incarnate, had a separate existence previous to His coming to the earth.

Seventeen times in the Gospel of John it is declared that Jesus was sent forth from the Father and came to the Earth, and that He again left the earth and went unto the Father.

The entire Gospel of John is based upon the fact that Jesus had a previous existence with the Father, and that while He was walking the earth He remembered His experiences in the other world, and spoke to the Father of these experiences, and also of when He would go back and take up again life with the Father.

John 17:3-5, "And now, Father, glorify thou me with thine own self with the glory which I had with thee before the world was."

Christ, while He is facing crucifixion, remembers the glory He had with the Father before the world was. Read also John 3:16; 8:42; 13:3; and 16:28-30.

Micah 5:2 is a remarkable prophetic utterance of the pre-existence of Christ and His coming to the earth.

"Out of thee shall one come forth unto me that is to be ruler of Israel; whose goings forth are from of old, from everlasting."

Here there is one going to be born of the family of Judah, to be ruler in Israel, and His goings forth have been from of old, from everlasting.

He has traveled up and down through the Eternities and has left His footprints on the Ages.

John 1:1, "In the beginning was the Word, and the Word was with God, and the Word was God."

"In the beginning. . . ." This being existed in the beginning, in Eternity.

"The Word was with God." This Eternal One was with God, with Him in fellowship and purpose . . . working with Him.

Hebrews 1:2, "Through whom also he made the worlds."

John 1:3, "All things were made through him and without him was not anything made that hath been made."

We saw in our first lesson that the word "God" in Genesis 1:1 is "Elohim," a plural word revealing the Trinity at work in creation.

In Genesis 1:26 we hear His words, "Let us make man in our own image."

This Being, who became Incarnate that He might become man's Redeemer, we behold at Creation.

"The Word was God." This Eternal Being, who was in fellowship and companionship with God, was God. He possessed the same nature. He existed in the same form on an equality with God (Philippians 2:6).

149

John 1:14, "And the Word became flesh, and dwelt among us, and we beheld His glory, glory as of the only begotten of the Father."

This Being became flesh. He became man and dwelt among us. He became human, as much man as though He had never been anything else: yet He did not cease to be what He had been. He made His home among us and we beheld the glory of God. He was the Image of the Invisible God (Colossians 1:15).

He was the exact representation of God's being (Hebrews 1:3, Rotherham).

From the time of the entrance of Spiritual Death into the world, until His Birth, God was working toward the Incarnation and repeatedly gave promise of Christ's Coming, Ministry, Death and Resurrection.

His Sufferings: Genesis 3:15; Psalms 22:1-8; 31:13; 89:38-45; Isaiah 53:1-12; Daniel 9:26; Zechariah 13:1; 6:7.

His Death and Burial: Numbers 21:9; Psalms 16:10; 22:16; 31:22; 49:15; Isaiah 53:8, 9, Daniel 9:26.

His Resurrection: Psalms 17:15; 49:15; 73:24; Jonah 2:1-10.

His Ascension: Psalms 8:5, 6; 24:7; 47:5; 68:18; 110:1.

His Future Triumphs: Isaiah 40:10; Daniel 2:44; 7:13, 14, 27; Hosea 3:5; Micah 4:1-7.

The Redeemer: Job 19:25-27; Genesis 48:16; Psalm 19:14; Isaiah 41:14; 43:1; 44:22; 59:20, 21; 62:11; 63:1-9; Jeremiah 50:34; Genesis 22:8; Isaiah 53:7.

Eternally United

We note here that when Christ became man in the Incarnation, He became man for eternity. He did not assume humanity as a garment to be worn for thirty-three years, and then cast off and laid aside, but He became man to be a man forever. Today, at the Father's right hand, there is a man in Heaven, as the result of the Incarnation.

I Timothy 2:5, "Himself man, Christ Jesus."

Man in God's Image

The fact that it was possible for Deity and humanity to become united in one individual for eternity reveals the place the first man held in the plan of the Father-God.

He had created man in His Own Image, just a shade lower than Himself (Genesis 1:26 and Psalm 8:5).

Man had been created so nearly like God that it was possible for God and man to become united eternally in one individual. It was possible that God and man become united.

God can dwell in these human bodies of ours. God can impart His life and nature to our spirits and dwell in our human bodies.

If Jesus was an Incarnation, then immortality is a fact. If we receive Eternal Life for our spirits, we have positive assurance that our bodies will become immortal at the return of the Lord Jesus.

If the Incarnation is a fact, Christianity is supernatural. Every man who has been born again is an Incarnation. The believer is as much an Incarnation as was Jesus of Nazareth. God can now eradicate Spiritual Death from the spirit of man and give man His Life, because the claims of Justice have been met in Christ.

We cannot conceive of anyone's desiring to doubt the Incarnation. It is the only answer to the cry of the human heart for God. It is the only solution to the human problems of sin, suffering, disease and death.

The Incarnation proves the pre-existence of Christ and is the foundation and reason for all subsequent miraculous manifestations of Divine Power. The Incarnation is the basic miracle of Christianity.

QUESTIONS

1. Why could not the Incarnate One be born of natural generation?
2. Explain Isaiah 7:14.
3. What does Philippians 2:6-8 reveal concerning the birth of Christ?
4. Explain John 1:14.
5. Give several Scriptures that show the pre-existence of Christ.
6. In what form did Christ exist before the Incarnation?

7. Give a prophetic Scripture on the following: the birth of Christ, His death, His resurrection, His being man's Redeemer.
8. When Christ became man, did He cease to be what He had been?
9. Give a Scripture that reveals the fact that we have a man at the Father's right hand.
10. What does the fact that it was possible for God to become man reveal concerning the creation of man?

Lesson 19
THE LIFE OF THE INCARNATE ONE
The Fullness of the Time

IN OUR LAST LESSON we studied the need of man for an Incarnation and the promise that the Father-God gave concerning the coming of the Incarnate One. Galatians 4:4. When the fullness of the time had come, God sent forth His Son in the Incarnation. When Christ was born 2,000 years ago, the time was ripe for His coming.

The Civilization of Greece had rendered a great service in preparing the way for Christianity by furnishing it with a worldwide language, the most beautiful, the most flexible, the most expressive the world had ever known.

When Christ appeared, the political power of the world was in Roman hands. Rome had conquered and united under a single government all that part of the world bordering on the Mediterranean. Never had peace so generally prevailed, never had life and property been so safe, never had travel been so easy.

The Romans were great road builders. In their effort to conquer the world and to civilize it they built roads for their armies. Ship lines had been established with the East. These roads and lines became the means of carrying the Gospel to the world.

The Universal Cry for an Incarnation

We see in this that God in His providence had brought about these conditions that the Good News of Redemption might be quickly heralded to the world.

On the other hand, the most deplorable picture of depraved morals in the entire range of history is presented by the Roman world at the time that Christ was born.

In all the world there was nothing to give hope or relief to darkened humanity. In the midst of this condition of despondency and failure, there was a longing for relief.

The hope of a Redeemer lay in the very atmosphere of the age. Jewish prophecy, which had been silent for four centuries, had awakened in the Jew an expectation for the Messiah. Even the pagan mind was yearning for a deliverer.

The wise men from the East who followed the Star represented the universal Eastern longing for a Redeemer. The eyes of the world, in its expectation, were turned toward Palestine. In the fullness of the time, Jesus, the Christ, was born at Bethlehem of Judea . . . the response to the age-long heart cry of universal man, under the bondage of spiritual death.

Only God knew what man's need demanded, and only God could meet that demand. It was the Incarnation.

Man in all ages has hungered instinctively for an Incarnation.

There are three things which natural man has desired. He has desired fellowship with God; he has desired to possess the life of God; and he has desired the strength of God.

Primitive man hungered for an Incarnation. Every ancient human religion has tried to answer that cry.

Dr. Trumbull, in his book, "The Blood Covenant," gives the following, which reveals primitive man's hunger for an Incarnation:

"Beyond the idea of an inspiration through an inter-flow of God-representing blood, there has been in primitive man's mind (however it came there) the thought of a possible inter-communion with God through an inter-communion with God by blood. God is Life. All life is from God and belongs to God. Blood is life. Blood therefore, as life, may be a means of man's inter-union with God.

"As the closest and most sacred of covenants between man and man; as indeed an absolute merging of two human natures into one, is a possibility through an inter-flowing of a common blood so the closest and most sacred of covenants between man and God; so the inter-union of the human nature with the Divine, has been looked upon as a possibility through the proffer and acceptance of a common life as in a common blood-flow.

"Man has counted blood, his own blood in actuality or by substitute, a means of inter-union with God, or with the gods. He has considered that the outflowing of blood toward God is an act of gratitude or of affection, a proof of loving confidence, a means of inter-union with him.

"This seems to have been the universal primitive conception of the race. And an evidence of man's trust in the accomplished fact of his inter-union with God, or with the gods, by blood, has been the also universal practice of man's inter-communion with God, or with the gods, by his sharing in food-partaking of the body of the sacrificial offering, whose blood is the means of the divine-human inter-union."

Every primitive people have drunk the blood of sacrificial victims in seeking oneness with God.

The gods of the Greeks and Romans were Incarnations. Their gods were immortal, superior human beings.

Many times the kings of ancient civilizations were believed to be descendants of the gods, and they were worshipped as Incarnations.

The Present Hunger for an Incarnation

Today, man still hungers for an Incarnation. Education has not eliminated from man's spirit this hunger. Every modern human religion tries to answer this hunger.

Men today, who claim to be Incarnations, receive a large following. It is not only the ignorant who seek an Incarnation, but also the educated.

Certain modern cults that teach that man is Divine and that God by nature dwells in man and is awaiting man's recognition of the fact, receive a great following from the more intellectual and educated classes.

We see that from the time man died spiritually, until the present day, he has hungered for union with Deity, for a God-man.

God Manifest in the Flesh

How desperately man needed an Incarnation. How long and bitter had been the years of separation between man and God. Man, born into a world ruled by Satan, did not by nature know his Creator.

Philosophers have sought in vain to know His Nature. The Incarnation of Jesus Christ has given to the world a true knowledge of the nature of God.

From the time that man had died spiritually, God and man had been separated. Spiritually dead man could

155

not know the nature of his Creator without a Revelation from Him.

Man had rejected Revelation, and in the blindness of his mind how false had been his conceptions of God. A nation's conception of God determines its worship and life.

When we look at the ignorance and untold misery of heathen nations, we realize that it is due to their darkened conception of God.

God had been conceived as the weird, as the cruel, as the grotesque, as the immoral, as the aloof, as impersonal energy, but never had He been conceived as a God of Love, as a Father-God.

Even Israel, which possessed as clear a revelation as God could give of Himself to spiritually-dead man, had no true conception of God when Christ came into the world.

Israel's Need

The product of Israel's conception of God was the Pharisee—proud, bitter, unkind, arrogant and self-seeking. Israel had such a false conception of God that they didn't recognize Him when He stood in their midst.

John 1:14, "And the Word became flesh, and pitched His tent among us. And we gazed upon His glory, a glory as an Only-Begotten from his Father" (Rotherham).

It has been our tendency when thinking of Christ's coming to earth as a man, to dwell upon His self-denial, His sufferings, in coming to earth from Glory. Yet, as we know Him better, we believe that it was a joy to Him who so loved man and so desired man's fellowship, to dwell on earth among men that He might give to alienated man, man who had never known his Creator, a true conception of Him.

How clearly Christ realized and appreciated this phase of His mission. John said of Him, "No man hath seen God at any time; the only begotten Son, who is in the bosom of the Father, He hath declared Him" (John 1:18).

How different was His life from the lives of the greatest philosophers and religious teachers before Him.

They had come as seekers of the truth. He came as the Revelation of the Truth (John 14:6).

He revealed the Creator to be a God of love, a Holy God who could be approached.

John the Baptist, who had been so stern with others, in the presence of this Man, fell back, saying, "I have need to be baptized of thee" (Matthew 3:14).

This man, the best of men, felt his deep need in the presence of this Incarnate One, yet the most sinful of men felt drawn to Him. Publicans and sinners drew near to Him, were pleased to sit and eat with Him (Matthew 9:10. Mark 2:15. Luke 5:30; 15:1). They weren't afraid of His Holiness, they were drawn by His Love.

Children sat upon His knees (Mark 10:13). This Incarnate One showed an interest in children. Christ was the first one who had ever appreciated childhood. There had never been any place for children in any pagan nation. It was only after a child had become a man and of military value to the state, that any value was placed upon his life.

There had never been a strong and pure love for children. Christ alone achieved the elevation of childhood. Our present day appreciation of children is due to the fact that the "Word" became flesh and dwelt among us.

In the same manner, the elevation of woman was achieved. Their privileges, freedom, the blessings they enjoy, are due to His life and teachings.

A God of Love

Here was One who showed by His Life and Words what the heart back of the Universe is like. Creation itself can only bring to us the realization that there is an Omnipotent God. It cannot reveal His Nature to us. We do not ask to know the Omnipotence of our Creator; that would frighten us. We do not desire to know His Omniscience; we could not understand that. We do not ask to understand His Omnipresence; our imaginations could not grasp it.

We want to know the nature of our Creator — His attitude toward us, whether or not He is indifferent toward human beings, or interested in us.

We know now what God is like; we know now His attitude toward us, because He dwelt among us as a man. God is like Christ. The heart of the Creator is like the heart that broke on the Cross.

A certain Yale professor said, "The question to my mind is not the divinity of Jesus, but whether God is like Jesus."

Is it not wonderful that a man lived among us in such a manner that when we think of God we think in terms of this man? We may transfer every moral quality of Jesus to God, and it does not in any measure lower our conception of God. On the contrary, the highest conception that we can have of Him is that He is like Christ. If we try to think of God in any other term than that of Christ, we lower our conception of Him.

The life of Christ has written across this human realm of ours that "God is love," and nothing can erase it. The heart cry of man for an Incarnation has been answered in Jesus. God was manifest in the flesh. God lived as a man among us and we know His nature. We find Him in Christ to be all that we want Him to be.

Christ not only revealed Him to us as a God of Love, but also as a Father. No other religion had ever had a Father-God.

What excitement was caused among the Jews when Christ called Him "Father."

John 5:18. They sought to kill Him because He called God His Father.

From the following scriptures—John 14:20; 6:46; 7:29; 8:18 and 10:15—we know that the revealing of the Father-God to man was the center around which Christ moved.

Let us look at the life of this Incarnate One. He had become man in the fullest sense of the word, yet wherein did He differ from other men?

The difference between His life and the lives of those around Him did not lie in the fact that He was any less human than they. It lay in the fact that He did not belong to the realm of spiritual death.

John 5:26. For as the Father hath life in Himself, so has He given the Son to have life in Himself. Christ was the first man from the time of man's treason that had been able to make a statement like that. He stated that He possessed the Life of God.

Satan had no dominion over Christ, because Christ was not spiritually dead. He walked in oneness with the Father-God. He lived in the realm of His omnipotence.

Disease had no dominion over the body of Christ, because disease was a child of spiritual death.

For the same reason, the body of Christ was not mortal. The word "mortal" means "death-doomed." Man's body became death-doomed when he had died spiritually. Spiritual death had never entered the spirit of Christ. Therefore as He walked this earth His body was not subjected to death. The Body of this Incarnate One was neither mortal nor immortal. He possessed a perfect eternal human body, the kind of a body that Adam had had before he died spiritually. It was impossible for man to have taken the life of Christ before His time had come.

On the cross Christ died physically, because He had first died spiritually.

When He was made to be sin (II Corinthians 5:21) for us, His spirit underwent a change. Spiritual death was laid upon it, and His body became mortal as did Adam's when he died spiritually.

The Hebrew word for death in Isaiah 53:9 is a plural word, showing that Christ's death on the cross was a two-fold death — first a spiritual, and then a physical, as man's substitute.

In the life of this man we see the life that the Father-God had planned for man. How utterly free and rich and full was the life of this Incarnate One. As a man, He walked this earth free from Satan's dominion.

Because He was an Incarnation, He possessed ability to live with men, and as a man reveal to them their Creator, and also free them from the bondage of Satan.

Questions

1. Explain Galatians 4:4.
2. How does history reveal that ancient man hungered for an Incarnation?
3. Does man today still seek an Incarnation?
4. Why had man no true conception of God?
5. Explain John 1:18.

6. What effect did the life of Christ have upon the childhood and womanhood of the world?
7. How do we know that God is love?
8. How did Christ reveal God as a Father-God?
9. Why did disease and death have no power over the body of Jesus?
10. Why was Christ as a man independent of Satan?

Lesson 20
REDEMPTION

The Object of the Incarnation

THE OBJECT of the Incarnation was that man might be given the right to become a child of God (John 1:12). Man could only become a child of God by receiving the nature of God. Therefore Christ came that man might receive Eternal Life (John 10:10).

Man could receive Eternal Life only after he had been legally redeemed from Satan's authority (Col. 1:13-14).

Therefore the step in our study after the Incarnation is Redemption, which was really the object of the Incarnation. We have seen that the qualifications of man's Redeemer demanded an Incarnate One. Now we shall study how the Incarnate One legally redeemed man from the authority of Satan, and made it possible for him to receive the nature of God.

Man's Redemption is legal. It swings around the law of Identification. Identification is twofold. It includes man's Identification with Adam and his Identification with Christ.

The entire plan of Redemption revolves around this twofold identification of man with Adam and with Christ.

Paul's Revelation

God gave to Paul the revelation of the finished work of Redemption and the present ministry of Christ. Paul speaks of the fact that this revelation was given to him, in the following scriptures:

Romans 16:25-26. He calls it "my gospel." It is a revelation of Jesus Christ, not from man but from God. Galatians 1:6-17. This tells where Paul received his revelation. It is a revelation that had been kept silent but now has been made known.

Ephesians 3:1-12. He reveals that his understanding in the mystery of Christ that had not been known to other generations was due to the fact that he received it by revelation.

Within this revelation which Paul received, as the basic foundation was the revelation of man's identification with Adam and with Christ. When a child of God grasps clearly this two-fold identification, the foundation has been laid for the renewing of his mind.

Before we study this revelation of identification we shall study why it was necessary for a revelation of Redemption to have been given after Christ had arisen, and ascended to the Father.

Necessity of Paul's Revelation

We saw in the first lesson of this course that there exist two kinds of knowledge. One kind of knowledge is the knowledge of natural man. It is derived by means of the five senses of the physical body. The other kind of knowledge is that which is given to man by the Holy Spirit. It is called Revelation knowledge. The Word of God is this Revelation.

In the Incarnation the Revelation of Christ that was given to man was given to him on the level of the senses of his physical body.

John said in I John 1:1-2, "That which we have heard, that which we have seen with our eyes, that which we beheld, and our hands handled, concerning the Word of Life."

Man saw with his physical eyes Christ and His deeds.

The life of the Son of God, man saw lived before him. He heard with his ears the words that He spoke, and he could touch Him with his hands. The knowledge that man possessed of Christ during His life on earth was gained purely by his physical senses. This physical revelation of Christ was not alone sufficient for man's faith in Christ as the Son of God or his understanding of Redemption in Him.

Matthew 16:15-17. Peter made his declaration that Christ was the Son of God. Then Christ made a strange statement. He said: "Flesh and blood has not revealed it unto thee, but my Father who is in heaven." That which Peter had seen, that which he had heard, and that which he had handled concerning the life of Christ, by means of the five senses of his nervous system (which lay embedded within his flesh) had not given this knowledge.

It had come as a special revelation from the Father. However, it was only a temporary Revelation, for when Peter saw with his sense of sight the death of Christ and perhaps handled His lifeless body, all hope fled from his heart.

162

The Death and Resurrection of Christ
as the Disciples Saw It

The disciples knew the meaning of the Crucifixion of Christ, His Burial, and His Resurrection, only through their physical senses.

They saw the beating of Christ; they saw the nails driven into His hands and feet. They heard His words, "My God, my God, why hast thou forsaken me." They saw and handled His body in the process of embalming it, as it was laid away for burial.

They saw the stone rolled away from the tomb and the empty grave clothes. They saw and heard and handled the resurrected body of Christ. They saw Him ascend into Heaven.

This physical knowledge, however, gave to them no insight into the meaning of the spiritual significance of Christ's death, burial, and Resurrection. In the crucifixion of Christ, they saw only His physical suffering. They knew nothing of the spiritual suffering of Christ as His spirit was made sin. They knew not where Christ's spirit was or what He was doing during the time His physical body lay in the tomb. They knew nothing of the conquering of Satan by Christ in His Resurrection. They knew nothing of the Ascension of Christ with His own blood into the Holy of Holies. They knew nothing of the ministry of Christ at the Father's right hand after He had left them.

A Revelation Needed

It was necessary that the Holy Spirit reveal the complete Redemption that was wrought in the Spirit of Christ in His Death, Burial and Resurrection.

I Corinthians 2:6-16 speaks of this Revelation—this wisdom, as it is called. Verses 9-10, "Things which eye saw not, and ear heard not . . . unto us God revealed them through the Spirit."

This Revelation that was needed could not be given until after Pentecost, when the Holy Spirit came to guide them into all truth.

Now that we have seen the necessity of a Revelation of Redemption, we shall study Identification, the heart of the Revelation of Redemption.

Identification with Adam

Romans 5 : 12 - 21 gives to us a clear picture of Identification.

Genesis 3 gives to us Adam's sin of High Treason, but for 4,000 years revelation had been silent upon this subject. Now, Paul reveals that the human race was identified with Adam in his transgression.

Romans 5:12, "Therefore, as through one man sin entered into the world, and death through sin; and so death passed unto all men." The death that entered Adam passed unto all men.

We notice here that it is not only physical death, but spiritual death, the nature of Satan.

Romans 5:14-19. This death ever reigned over those who had not committed high treason, for by the one, or through identification with him, the many had died.

Romans 5:18. Through identification with Adam the judgment came upon all men.

Adam's judgment became the judgment of every man. Romans 5:19. Through Adam, or because of Identification with him, all men were made sinners.

So Paul reveals that down through the ages and to the present day, sin has reigned in the realm of death where Satan is Lord, because of the fact that the human race was identified with the first man, Adam.

There are two sides to Redemption, the legal and the vital. The legal is what God did for us in Christ; the vital is what God does in us in Christ. So also there is a legal side and a vital side to the fall of man. The legal is what Satan did to us in Adam and the vital is what Satan does in us when by nature we are children of wrath.

Vitally, we were not in the garden with Adam; but legally, his death, his bondage, his judment and all that spiritual death made him, became ours.

Now God has redeemed man completely from every result of Adam's treason through the identification of the human race with His Son. This is the message that this revelation is bringing to us in Romans 5:12-21.

If the Lordship of Satan over the human was due to the identification of humanity with Adam in his crime of high treason, it is legally possible for the works of Satan to be destroyed by the identification of the human race with the Son of God, the second Adam.

Christ's Identification with Man's Humanity

We shall now study the steps whereby the Son of God and humanity became identified in the legal side of man's redemption.

The first step was Christ's identification with our humanity. This took place in His Incarnation—John 1:14 and Hebrews 2:14, "Since then the children are sharers in flesh and blood, He also Himself in like manner partook of the same."

As we saw in our last lesson, He walked as the first man should have walked, doing the will of the Father-God.

This, however, was not a complete identification with man. He had not identified Himself with the nature of man. If Christ had partaken of the nature that reigned in the spirit of man at His Incarnation, He would have been spiritually dead during His earthly ministry. He could not have revealed Him to man. Therefore, His identification with the spirit nature was during His Crucifixion, when the time had come for Him to fulfill the purpose for which He had come into the world.

Isaiah 53:4-6. The direct translation from the Hebrew into the English reads as follows: "Surely our diseases he did bear and our pains he carried;

"Whereas we did esteem him stricken, smitten of God, and afflicted. But he was wounded for our transgressions; he was crushed because of our iniquities. The chastisement of our welfare was upon him and with his stripes we were healed. All we like sheep have gone astray and the Lord hath laid on him the iniquity of us all."

This translation is taken from the Jewish translation of the Old Testament.

Christ's Identification with Man's Sin Nature

The Revelation that Paul received in II Corinthians 5:21 is that God actually made Him to become sin for us.

He not only bore our sins, but the sin-nature itself was laid upon Him, until He became all that spiritual death had made man.

165

In the mind of God, it is not Christ who hung on the Cross, but it is the human race. So each one of us may say with Paul, "I was crucified with Christ" (Galatians 2:20).

In the garden we were not with Adam vitally, but we were legally. In the same manner we were not on the Cross vitally with Christ, but we were there legally. The identification of the human race with Christ was just as complete as was its identification with Adam.

Now that the Identification of Christ with humanity was complete, the steps in Redemption began.

The first step was to pay man's penalty. The judgment that was man's fell upon Him and He was forsaken of God.

Isaiah 53:8, "By oppression and judgment He was taken away: And as for His generation, who did reason? For He was cut off out of the land of the living. For the transgression of my people to whom the stroke was due."

The judgment, the stroke, was due man; but it fell upon Him, because they had become one.

He died under our judgment and we died with Him. And as He paid our penalty in Hell we were identified with Him. Psalm 88 gives to us the picture of a righteous man in Hell upon whom all the wrath of God lay hard. The wrath of God lay hard upon Him, because He was one with us in identification.

Acts 2:24-28 shows to us the suffering of Christ in Hell. It tells us that His soul was not left in Hell (verse 27) but that God raised Him up, having loosed the pangs of death. The Greek word "pangs" means "intense suffering," showing that when Christ was raised His spirit was loosed from the intense suffering that He bore as our sin-substitute.

Christ suffered until God could justify the human race.

I Timothy 3:16 reveals that Christ was justified in Spirit. He, in identification, had become so utterly one with us that He Himself needed justification when man's penalty was paid. (Rotherham says that Christ was declared righteous in spirit.)

The next step in Redemption was that He who had been made sin be begotten of God.

Hebrews 1:5, in speaking of the resurrection of Christ, says that the Father-God said to Him, "Thou art my Son, this day have I begotten thee."

Acts 13:33, "That God hath fulfilled the same unto our children, in that He raised up Jesus; as also it is written in the second Psalm, Thou art my Son, this day have I begotten thee."

Jesus Christ, when man's penalty had been paid, had to be born of God and pass from death into life just as man, because He had become identified with our Spiritual Death. After Christ had been justified in spirit and born of God, He conquered Satan as a man. It is evident that Satan tried to hold Christ within his authority. Satan did hold Christ until God could declare man righteous.

Romans 6:9 (Rotherham), "Who was delivered up for our offenses and raised on account of the declaring us righteous." When we were declared righteous, I Timothy 3:16 reveals, He was made righteous. Then He was begotten of God, and in the power of His Deity, He met Satan and triumphed over him as a man.

Colossians 2:15, "Having put off himself the principalities and the powers, He made a show of them openly triumphing over them in it." He displayed them as His conquests. Christ was the first man to free Himself from Satan's grasp and triumph over him. When He arose as a man, Satan's forces were put under His feet. (Ephesians 1:20-23).

QUESTIONS

1. What was the object of the Incarnation?
2. Give three Scriptures telling of Paul's Revelation.
3. Why was it necessary for a Revelation to be given?
4. What place does identification hold in Redemption?
5. What became man's by his identification with Adam?
6. Give five Scriptures showing man's identification with Adam.
7. Why did Christ identify Himself only with man's humanity in the Incarnation?
8. When was Christ identified with our spirit nature?

167

9. Why was it necessary for Christ to be made alive in the spirit?
10. When did Christ conquer Satan as a man?

Lesson 21
OUR IDENTIFICATION WITH CHRIST

IN OUR LAST LESSON we studied the steps whereby our Redemption was wrought for us in Christ from the time of His Crucifixion to His Resurrection.

When Christ ascended into Heaven, with His own blood He had obtained eternal redemption for us upon the basis of His substitutionary death and resurrection on our behalf.

Hebrews 9:12, "But with His own blood entered in once for all into the holy place having obtained eternal redemption for us."

Hebrews 10:12-14, "But He when He had offered one sacrifice for sins forever sat down on the right hand of God; henceforth expecting till His enemies be made the footstool of His feet. For by one offering He had perfected forever them that are sanctified."

When Christ sat down at the Father's right hand, man had been perfectly redeemed because he had been legally identified with Christ in His Redemptive work.

We saw in our last lesson that man's spiritual death was due to the fact that he had been legally identified with Adam in the fall.

Now we shall study the steps in man's identification with Christ, whereby he became legally redeemed from spiritual death.

There are six steps.
I WAS CRUCIFIED WITH CHRIST
Galatians 2:20, "I have been crucified with Christ." The King James Version erroneously translated this verse as, "I am crucified."

Romans 6:6, "Knowing this that our old man was crucified with him that the body of sin might be destroyed, that so we should no longer be in bondage to sin."

Romans 4:25 gives this to us, "Who was delivered up for our trespasses and raised for our justification." He was delivered up on the account of our trespasses. On the cross, God made Him to become sin for us. It was our spiritual death and our trespasses that He bore. He became Identified with us on the cross. He was our Substitute.

169

I DIED WITH CHRIST

Romans 6:5, "For if we have become united with Him in the likeness of His death"; and Romans 6:8, "But if we died with Christ." As He died we died with Him. Christ would not have died physically if He had not first had our spiritual death laid upon His Spirit.

So there followed as a result of our identification with Him in crucifixion, the death of His body which had then become mortal, "subject to death," as had Adam's when he died spiritually. We died with Him. As His spirit left His physical body and went into Hell we were identified with Him.

There may arise in the minds of some a question concerning the meaning of the words of Christ spoken to the thief while He was upon the Cross.

Some may ask, "What did the Master mean when He said to the thief on the cross, 'Verily I say unto thee, Today shalt thou be with me in Paradise'?" A better translation punctuates it as follows: "I say unto thee today, thou shalt be with me in Paradise."

He did not say, "I will be with you in Paradise today," but, "I am telling you today, I will meet you in Paradise." Jesus could not go to Paradise until He had paid the penalty of the Old Covenant transgressions that were blood-covered.

I WAS BURIED WITH CHRIST

Romans 6:4, "We were buried therefore with Him through Baptism into death"; and Colossians 2:12, "Having been buried with him in baptism."

Baptism is a type of our burial with Christ; His body lay in the tomb, but His spirit suffered in Hell as He paid the penalty that was due man. He could adequately pay man's penalty and meet the demands of Justice because He had been identified with man. The penalty He paid was not His, but man's with whom He had been made one. In the mind of God, it was you and I there in that place of torment, bearing the judgment that was due us. On the basis of this identification the man who receives the Redemptive work of Christ need not go to Hell but goes free, while the man who refuses Christ's redemption on his behalf must go there.

When the penalty of man's high treason was paid, man was freed from his bondage to Satan.

In Romans 6:1-11, in which we have given to us our identification with Christ in crucifixion, death and burial, we have the following facts revealed:

The body of sin, or the body of spiritual death, was destroyed (Romans 6:6).

Man was released from spiritual death (Romans 6:7 Revised Version footnotes) because he died in Christ and adequately paid his penalty.

When the penalty had been paid, man stood before God justified or declared righteous. We are glad that we know the meaning of the word "righteousness."

Socrates, called the father of philosophy, taught that one, before he could speak intelligently on any subject, must be able to define the terms he used. The word, "Righteousness" means "the ability of man to stand in the presence of God as free from sin and condemnation as though there had never been any spiritual death within his spirit."

When God could declare man righteous and legally freed from spiritual death, He had the right to impart life, His own nature, to the spirit of man.

So, after Christ had been declared righteous in *His* spirit, because *our* penalty was paid, He was made alive. The identification of man and Christ that had been complete upon the cross, continues and the next step is:

I WAS MADE ALIVE WITH CHRIST

Colossians 2:13, "And you being dead through your trespasses and the uncircumcision of your flesh, you did He make alive together with Him"; and Ephesians 2:5, "Even when we were dead through our trespasses made us alive together with Christ."

When God raised Christ from the dead, He said, "Thou art my son; this day have I begotten thee" (Hebrews 1:5 and Acts 13:33).

He was the firstborn from the dead. He was the first man to be born out of spiritual death into Eternal Life.

171

He was the first man over whom the dominion of death was broken.

Romans 6:9-10, "Death no more hath dominion over Him, for the death that He died, He died unto sin once." When He was identified with us on the Cross, Death had dominion over Him, but when He paid our penalty, the dominion was broken. He was released.

He died unto sin and He was begotten of God in the realm of life.

Romans 8:29, "For whom He foreknew He also fore-ordained to be conformed to the image of His Son that He might be the firstborn of many brethren."

The "many brethren" were legally identified with Him in His Birth out of death into Life, but He was the first one to vitally experience it, the first-born. In legally being made alive with Christ, we were conformed to His Image.

The word "conform" means to make exactly like. It means to be made according to a certain pattern.

In His being made sin in Crucifixion, He had been conformed to our image of spiritual death. When He was made alive, we were made alive with Him. With Him we are conformed to the Image of this first-born. All that He is we become. That is why we are joint-heirs with Him. We were legally born out of death into Life with Him.

In Romans 6:11, He tells us that we are to reckon ourselves dead unto sin and alive unto God in as much reality as Christ is dead unto sin and alive unto God. The reason for it lies in the fact we were together born again, made alive legally.

A man, vitally receiving this Life of God, is actually born out of death into life when he personally accepts Jesus Christ as his Saviour.

Our identification with Christ in His death and resurrection in reality means this. It is as though Adam had gone to Hell, suffered the judgment that was due him and had been released, freed from the bondage of spiritual death, legally acquitted from his crime of high treason, and given the right to receive Eternal Life and walk in fellowship with God.

If Adam could have done this, the human race that had been identified with him in his spiritual death would never have been under the dominion of death, but Adam could not do this. God in His great love wherewith He loved us, sent His Son to do it.

In Adam, all humanity died spiritually, and as a basis of identification with Christ in His death, burial and resurrection, all humanity legally has been made alive.

I Corinthians 15:22, "For as in Adam all die; so also in Christ shall all be made alive."

The man or woman who has accepted Christ as Saviour and Lord may walk in fellowship with the Father and as free from Satan's dominion as though Adam had never sinned or been spiritually dead.

At the New Birth a man passes from the authority of Satan into the Lordship of Christ. Colossians 1:13, "Who delivered us out of the authority of darkness and translated us into the kingdom of the Son of His Love."

This is because when Christ was released from death into Life, man was really released with Him. All that Christ did was not for Himself, but for man.

After Christ had been released from Satan's authority, the next step was to put off from Himself the forces of Satan.

The Word tells us, in Ephesians 1:20-23, that when God raised Christ from the dead that He raised Him far above "all other government, and authority, and power, and dominion and every title of sovereignty used either in this Age or the Age to come."

I WAS RAISED WITH CHRIST

Ephesians 2:6, "And raised us up with Him."

Our battle in this world is with the principalities and powers and world rulers of this darkness, with the spiritual hosts of wickedness in the high places.

Ephesians 6:12, "For ours is not a conflict with mere flesh and blood, but with the despotisms, the empires, the forces that control and govern this dark world, and the spiritual hosts of evil arrayed against us in the heavenly warfare" (Weymouth).

173

These are the rulers that Christ disarmed and displayed as His conquests in the very throne room of Satan.

Colossians 2:15, "And the hostile princes and rulers He shook off from Himself and boldly displayed as His conquests when He triumphed over them" (Weymouth).

Hebrews 2:14, "That through death He might bring to nought Him that had the authority of death, that is, the devil."

Another version of the Greek reads, "He rendered powerless him that held the dominion of death, that is, the devil."

We were identified with Christ in this victory over Satan. It is only because of our identification with Him that He was thus triumphing over Satan. He always was greater than Satan.

It was because of His Identification with us that as a man He must meet Satan in his own dominion and conquer him. He went there as our Substitute representative. His victory was our victory. When He stripped Satan of his authority, it was as though we had done it.

After Jesus' Justification, Satan no longer had dominion over Him.

Our identification with Christ makes us as free as Jesus is.

I WAS SEATED WITH CHRIST

After Christ's spirit had been freed from Hell, He entered His body, raising it to immortality.

Acts 2:31, "He foreseeing this spake of the resurrection of the Christ, that neither was He left in Hell nor did His flesh see corruption." Before His Ascension to sit down at the Father's right hand, He appeared to His disciples, telling them that all authority in Heaven and earth had been given unto Him. Matthew 28:18, "All authority hath been given unto me in heaven and on earth."

As a man, He possessed authority over the world rulers of this spiritual darkness. With that authority, He sat down at the Father's right hand. It was for us.

Acts 2:34-35, "For David ascended not into the heavens; but he saith himself: The Lord said unto my Lord,

Sit thou on my right hand till I make thine enemies the footstool of thy feet." In Hebrews 1:13, we have a song of praise, addressed to the Son, in which the Father said: "Sit thou on my right hand till I make thine enemies the footstool of thy feet."

Hebrews 10:13 tells us that He is waiting for His enemies to be made the footstool of His feet. Let us study this in connection with Ephesians 1:20-23: "Which he wrought in Christ when He raised Him from the dead, and made Him to sit at His right hand in the heavenly places far above all rule and authority, and power, and dominion and every name that is named, not only in this world but also in that which is to come; and He put all things under His feet, and gave Him to be head over all things to the church, which is His body, the fullness of Him, that filleth all in all."

He legally put all things under His feet (that is, under His body, the Church) in His Resurrection, and He is waiting today for those enemies of His (man's enemies, Satan, sin, sickness) to be vitally put under His feet.

We are seated with Him. (Ephesians 2:6, "And made us to sit with Him in the Heavenly places.") He is waiting for us in His Name to vitally take what legally is ours and in His Name put every enemy of ours under our feet that we might reign as kings with Him.

Read and study very carefully Romans 5:17.

The identification of man and Christ has destroyed the work of Satan in humanity through man's identification with Adam.

IDENTIFIED

In crucifixion on the Cross
With Jesus Christ identified,
In death for man's eternal loss
With Jesus Christ identified.

In burial 'neath the cursed ground
With Jesus Christ identified,
In hell's deep dungeons where He's found
With Jesus Christ identified.

175

In resurrection might and power
With Jesus Christ identified,
At God's right hand this very hour
With Jesus Christ identified.

—E. W. Kenyon

QUESTIONS (Answer fully)

1. Give and discuss fully the six steps in our identification with Christ, giving scripture for each.

Lesson 22

GOD'S TWO CREATIONS

IN OUR LAST LESSON, which was on Identification with Christ, we studied the steps whereby God brought forth a New Creation in Christ.

After Christ was made alive out of spiritual death, He arose, the firstborn of many brethren.

Romans 8:29, "For whom He foreknew He also fore-ordained to be conformed to the image of His Son that He might be the firstborn of many brethren." He was the firstborn of many Sons of God.

He was the Firstborn from the dead.

Hebrews 1:5-6, "For unto which of the angels said He at any time, Thou art my son, this day have I begotten thee and again, I will be to Him a Father and He shall be to me a Son and again when He bringeth the firstborn into the world let all the angels of God worship Him." He was the first man in all the ages of human history to be born out of spiritual death into the realm of life.

Colossians 1:18, "And He is the head of the body, the Church who is the firstborn from the dead that in all things He might have the preeminence." He is the head of a New Creation. He is the head of a New Species, a new type of men.

He is the head of a creation of men who are free from the dominion of Satan.

Whenever a man accepts this Son of God as Saviour and Lord, he passes out of death into life (John 5:24).

II Corinthians 5:17, "Wherefore if any man is in Christ he is a New Creature: the old things are passed away; behold all things are become new."

This New Creation in Christ, a Spiritual Creation, is just as much of a reality as the Creation in Adam. In this study we are going to compare the two.

Creation in Adam

The Creation of the universe and the creation of man, the crown of creation, points us to an intelligent, omnipotent Creator. Only a man whose mind is blinded by a determination not to believe God will believe otherwise.

We will give just a brief summary showing what a man must believe if he refuses belief in an intelligent Creator.

The first fact that man faces is this: he exists. Here at least his knowledge is certain. He is, but how did he come to be? He lives in a world that teems with life, but how did life begin? To say that man is descended through numbered or innumerable generations merely puts the difficulty back.

From whence did the first man come? How did life begin? To the present day science has been able to offer no answer—not even a guess. The only answer which science can make is that life sprang out of death, out of nothing. The scientist who rejects God must accept as a very foundation of his belief a theory which is not only void of proof, but a contradiction to all our present-day knowledge upon the subject. Every scientific experiment has proven that life cannot be generated independent of antecedent life, that inanimate matter cannot become living except under the influence of matter already living, and that Life is produced only by Life.

The man who rejects a Creator answers that although we cannot prove that spontaneous generation has ever taken place, it may have taken place billions of years ago. He also says that only one germ of living matter would have been necessary. This primeval life germ he must take for granted. But he must believe that it had inherent within it all the possibilities for the development of life in every realm.

Which is easier to believe? Can an honest man believe that there happened to be a living germ of matter which possessed the capacities for the development of the universe with its highly complicated and intelligently organized forms of life, more readily than he can believe in an intelligent Creator? Can he believe that an intelligent, conscious being like man, who thrills with a desire for immortality, could have been developed from unintelligent, unconscious matter?

No! The creation of man points to an intelligent creator. The creator of man in Adam points to an intelligent creator of the most tender love and care for man.

As we study creation — either through the most powerful telescopes, which reveal that the planets, the stars and the comets all perform according to a schedule of order and law; or through the most powerful microscopes, which reveal that the same law and order prevail in the most infinitesimal forms of life — we find that the utmost painstaking care and thought have been lavished upon all forms of life.

The same Creator, who has with marvelous skill painted a sunset and a rainbow, has touched with the most brilliant colors each feather in the wing of a fly. Because the Creator knew that man would become curious and study life under the most powerful artificial lenses in care and thoughtfulness, He delicately and beautifully made every minute form of life. Some forms of life are so small that twenty of them can be found in one single drop of moisture; yet, every one is exquisitely and beautifully designed.

The Place Man Held

We ask to what purpose this care and thoughtfulness we see manifested in all creation? The answer is Man.

Every step in creation points to man as the goal. The earth with its fields, fruits, vegetables, its forests, its cattle, its beauty is for man. We find that in preparing this home for man, the Creator gave His personal attention to every particle of dust as well as to every star.

What care, what thoughtfulness, what love is manifested in His provision for the man He created in His own image to rule creation with Him.

The creation of man in Adam, the first creation, reveals the infinite love of the Creator for man and the place man holds in His plans. But now let us turn to this New Creation in Christ to see what it reveals to our hearts of the Creator.

Creation Blighted

We have seen in our past study that a catastrophe has blighted this creation and the life of the one created in God's Image.

Spiritual Death, the nature of Satan, entered the spirit of man, alienating him from God (Genesis 3).

In their condition of spiritual death, men have looked upon this Satan-cursed creation and thought that God, if there be a God, has been inactive, just a spectator upon the world's affairs. The forces of nature that are so benevolent toward man are at the same time so destructive, so indifferent toward human life. It seems that in every element there is a blessing and a cursing. The sun, the winds, the water, the fires, bring ofttimes suffering and death.

But during this reign of spiritual death the Creator has been far from inactive. He has been no more inactive and thoughtless toward man than He was in His preparation for man's advent into this world.

Down through the ages of human history, every step, every dealing of God with man, has been toward one goal—a New Creation, a spiritual creation of man that would free man completely from spiritual death and satanic dominion.

No less thought, no less care, no less love has been lavished upon the preparation for the New Creation than was poured out upon the Old Creation of man.

If the first creation reveals the love of the Creator for man, how much more does the New Creation!

If the first creation gives to us a glimpse of the place man held in God's plan for man, how much more does the New Creation.

No creative power alone could bring forth this New Creation. It could not be created in paradise.

The New Creation in Christ

We, in our last lesson, studied the steps whereby the New Creation was brought forth. Only the Son of God, by taking our place in spiritual death, by taking our penalty and paying it, could make the New Creation a possibility. Has the God of Creation been inactive during the ages of human woe and misery? No, He, the Creator, has assumed the liabilities of man's sin. The Son of God, the One who existed on an equality with God, has not only been touched with his suffering of spiritual death but has assumed it, borne its penalty, and suffered in humanity's stead that man need not suffer.

The first creation was brought forth in a paradise, fresh from the hands of the Creator. The New Creation in Christ was brought forth in Hell. Hell had been prepared for Satan and his hosts, and in this dread place the Son of God suffered until the claims of justice had been paid. Then He was made alive out of death and we were legally made alive with Him.

Ephesians 2:5, "Even when we were dead through our trespasses made us alive together with Christ."

This was the place where the New Creation was legally brought forth. It was here that spiritually-dead man, when he had been justified, was legally conformed to the image of God's Son.

Romans 8:29, "For whom He fore-knew He fore-ordained to be conformed to the image of His Son that He might be the firstborn among many brethren."

And Christ arose the firstborn of many brethren because we had been declared righteous.

Romans 4:25, "Who was delivered up for our trespasses and raised on account of our being declared righteous."

His soul was not left in Hell.

Acts 2:27, "Because thou wilt not leave my soul in Hell."

Acts 2:21, "He foreseeing this spake of the resurrection of the Christ that neither was His soul left in Hell nor did His flesh see corruption."

Acts 2:24, "Who God raised up having loosed the pangs of death." When God made Christ alive He was loosed from the intense agonies He had suffered in His condition of spiritual death.

This was the birth of the New Creation in Him.

The first creation had been created in the image of God as the crown and climax of all creation.

The New Creation was brought forth in Hell, conformed to the image of God's Son, a joint-heir with Him.

This is the price the Father-God paid for the New Creation. Words cannot give an estimation of what the New Creation means to Him.

We have been dealing here with the legal side, that which God did for man in Christ. A man enters into it vitally and actually by receiving Christ personally as Saviour and Lord (Romans 10:9-10).

II Corinthians 5:17. He is then made a New Creation in Him.

Let us now study the Father's attitude toward the New Creation today.

Is this Creator today indifferent toward the New Creation in Christ? His inheritance is the New Creation. Every dream, every plan for man only finds its fulfillment in the New Creation.

Let us now study what God has said about the New Creation. He declares that the New Creation has been made righteous.

Romans 5:1, "Being therefore declared righteous by faith" (a literal translation from the Greek).

He also states that Jesus, His own Son, is the righteousness of the man who has become a New Creation in Him.

I Corinthians 1:30, "But of Him are ye in Christ (this is a description of the New Creation begotten of God in Christ) who was made unto us wisdom from God and righteousness, and sanctification and redemption."

However, these statements cannot describe the righteousness of this new man He has brought forth. He can say nothing more when He says that the New Creation has become the very righteousness of God in Him.

II Corinthians 5:21, "Him who knew no sin He made to become sin on our behalf that we might become the righteousness of God in Him."

The New Creation is as free from Satan's dominion as is Christ. The new man has been delivered absolutely out of the authority of Satan.

Colossians 1:13, "Who delivered us out of the authority-of darkness and translated us into the kingdom of the Son of His Love."

As far as the New Creation is concerned, Satan has no existence.

Hebrews 2:14, "That through death He might bring to nought him that had the authority of death, that is the devil."

Satan is the father and lord of natural man and ruler of the dominion of death, but to the New Creation he legally is as nought.

Romans 6:1-13 shows that the New Creation is as free as Christ is from the dominion of spiritual death.

The first man was God's under-ruler, but the new man is a joint-heir with Jesus Christ.

Romans 8:14-16, "The Spirit Himself beareth witness with our spirit that we are children of God, and if children then heirs; heirs of God and joint-heirs with Christ."

The Father-God looks upon the New Creation as He looks upon Christ. The new man does not belong to the world and has no more part in his relation to Satan than Christ had.

John 17:16, "They are not of the world even as I am not of the world."

The Father-God loves the new man even as He loves Christ.

John 17:23, "That the world may know that Thou didst send me and lovest them even as Thou lovest me."

The Father hears the requests of the New Creation even as He heard Christ because that one prays in the Name of Jesus. This new man can bring the Omnipotent Creator to action on his behalf by using the authority of the Name of Jesus.

John 16:23-24, "Verily, verily I say unto you, if ye shall ask anything of the Father, he will give it you in My Name." How limitless in power and authority is the life of the one who has been made a New Creation in Him!

QUESTIONS

1. Explain the following phrase of Romans 8:29, "That He might be the firstborn of many brethren."
2. What must a man who rejects God accept concerning the creation of man?
3. Show why the Creation of man points to an intelligent Creator.
4. How does creation reveal the care of God for man?
5. Show how creation was blighted at the fall.
6. What price did God pay for the New Creation?
7. Why was it necessary for a New Creation to be brought forth?

8. Tell how limitless in power and authority is the life of the one who has been made a New Creation in Him.
9. How righteous is this New Man in Christ?
10. What is the Father's attitude toward him?

Lesson 23
THE NAME OF JESUS

WE STUDIED in our last lesson that God has brought forth in Christ a New Creation. We have seen that upon the grounds of this Redemption in Christ, that a man by receiving Christ into his life is made a New Creature, a new person.

We have seen that an actual New Creation takes place within his spirit when he receives Jesus Christ as Saviour and Lord. Spiritual death is eradicated from his spirit, and he is taken completely out of Satan's dominion of death.

Colossians 1:13, "Who delivered us out of the authority of darkness and translated us into the kingdom of the Son of His love."

Then Eternal Life, the nature of God, is imparted to his spirit. This is the New Creation that takes place. His spirit is begotten of God.

I John 5:1, "Whosoever believeth that Jesus is the Christ is begotten of God."

I John 5:12, "He that hath the Son hath life; he that hath not the Son of God hath not life."

This one who has become a New Creature in Him (II Corinthians 5:17) has become a child of God and joint-heir with Christ.

Romans 8:16, 17, "The Spirit himself beareth witness with our spirit, that we are children of God: and if children, then heirs; heirs of God, and joint-heirs with Christ."

II Corinthians 5:17, "Wherefore if any man is in Christ, he is a New Creature: the old things are passed away; behold, they are become new."

Need of the Name

Although the one who has been made a New Creation in Christ is transferred out of Satan's authority, he is still in a world ruled by Satan.

In II Corinthians 4:4, Satan is called the god of this world: "Whom the god of this world hath blinded."

In Ephesians 2:2 he is called the prince of the powers of the air. "Wherein ye once walked according to the prince of the powers of the air, of the spirit that now worketh in the sons of disobedience."

Christ called him the prince of this world.

Satan and his forces still have an opportunity to attack the child of God through temptations and trials. The very air about us is filled with hostile forces which are attempting to destroy our fellowship with the Father and deprive us of our usefulness in the Master's service.

Our Father in His provision has given to us a weapon to use in this combat with Satan, not only for ourselves but also for Satan-ruled men around us.

That weapon is the Name of Jesus.

Before we study the authority invested in that Name, we shall study how Jesus obtained it.

The Threefold Greatness of the Name

There is authority within the very Name of Jesus because He inherited His name, because He achieved the authority of His name by conquests, and because His name was conferred upon Him.

We cannot measure the vastness of the power of the Name of Jesus when we realize that He inherited His name from God, the Creator.

Hebrews 1:2-4, "Hath at the end of these days spoken to us in His Son whom He appointed Heir of all things, through whom also He made the world, who being the effulgence of His glory, the very image of His substance . . . He hath inherited a more excellent name than they."

As the One who is the very image of the Father's substance, His very outshining, and the heir of all things, He has inherited His name, the Greatness of His Name, from His Father. The power of His Name then can only be measured by the power of God.

Secondly, He achieved the authority of His Name by conquests.

Colossians 2:15, "Having despoiled the principalities and powers, He made a show of them openly triumphing over them in it." The picture given to us here is of Christ in awful combat with the hosts of darkness. It gives to us a glimpse of the tremendous victory He won before He arose from the dead. The margin reads, "Having put off from Himself the principalities and the powers."

It is evident that the whole demon host, when they saw Jesus within their power, simply intended to swamp Him, overwhelm Him, and they held Him in fearful bondage until the cry came forth from the throne of God that Jesus had met the demands of justice, that the sin problem was settled, and man's redemption was a fact.

When this cry reached the dark regions, Jesus arose and hurled back the hosts of demons, and met Satan in awful combat, as is described in Hebrews 2:14:

"In order that through death He might paralyze him that held the dominion of death, that is the devil" (Rotherham).

In other words, after Jesus had put off from Himself the demon forces and the awful burden of guilt, sin, and sickness, that He carried with Him down there, He grappled with Satan, conquered him, and left him paralyzed, whipped and defeated.

The words that Jesus used in Luke 11:21-22 are fulfilled: "When a strong man fully armed guardeth his own court, his goods are in peace, but when a stronger man than he shall come upon him and overcome him, he taketh from him his whole armor and divideth his spoils."

So, when Christ arose from the dead, He not only had the keys of death and of hell, but He had the very armor in which Satan trusted. He had defeated the devil; He had defeated all Hell, and He stood before the three worlds, Heaven, earth and Hell, as the undisputed victor over man's ancient destroyer.

He conquered Satan before his own cohorts, his own servants in the dark regions of the damned, and there He stood, absolute Victor and Master.

Is it any wonder that fresh from such victories He should say to the disciples, "All authority has been given unto me in Heaven and earth" (Matthew 28:18)? He stands as the Master and the ruler of the Universe.

All this authority over Satan's dominion is invested in that Name. The deliverance of man from sin, sickness, or any other Satanic influence or power is invested in that Name.

Thirdly, the greatness of His Name was conferred upon Him.

In Philippians 2:9, 10, we find: "Wherefore also God highly exalted Him and gave unto Him a Name that is above every other name, that at the Name of Jesus every knee should bow, of the beings in Heaven, and the beings upon earth and the beings under the earth, and that every tongue should confess that Jesus Christ is Lord to the glory of God the Father."

The inference is that there was a Name known in Heaven, unknown elsewhere, and that this Name was kept to be conferred upon someone who should merit it, and Jesus as we know Him, the Eternal Son as He is known in the bosom of the Father, was given this Name, and at this Name every knee shall bow in the three worlds— Heaven, Earth and Hell — and every tongue shall confess that He is the Lord of the three worlds to the glory of God the Father.

Why Was It Given?

We now ask, why was this name given?

We notice this tremendous fact, every mention of the Name that He inherited, achieved, or had conferred upon Him, shows that He received the greatness of His Name after His resurrection from the dead.

Hebrews 1:3-7 shows to us that He inherited His Name when He was made alive out of spiritual death (verse 5). It was when He said to Him, "Thou art My Son, this day have I begotten thee."

Acts 13:33 reveals that this took place at His Resurrection. "That God hath fulfilled the same in that He raised up Jesus even as it is written in the second psalm, Thou art my Son, this day have I begotten Thee."

It was after His resurrection that He revealed that all authority in heaven and earth had been given to Him.

Ephesians 1:19-23. He was raised above every power and dominion.

Philippians 2:8-10 reveals that it was after His resurrection that the Name above every other name was conferred upon Him, when the Father-God highly exalted Him.

We ask, why was this Name conferred upon Him — why was it invested with such vast authority and dominion? Was it for Himself?

During the period of almost two thousand years that He has been at the Father's right hand, has He used it or had need of it? The Scriptures give to us no inkling of the fact the Jesus Himself has used His Name or has needed it. He rules creation with His Word. He exists on an equality with God.

Every mention in the Scripture of the use of the Name of Jesus has reference to His Body. The Name was given to Him that the Church might use it. The ones who have need of the use of His Name are those who have become joint-heirs with Him and are here in contact with men and women who need deliverance from Satan.

All that He is by inheritance is in that Name, and all that He has done is in that Name, and that Name is for man.

God has made this investment for the church. He has made this deposit on which the church has a right to draw for her every need. The Name that has within it the fullness of the Godhead, the wealth of the Eternities, and authority over every other power or authority known in Heaven, earth and Hell, has been given to us.

If we could search Heaven, with all of its power and omnipotence, if we could search the dark regions of Hell's domain, with its dominion over mankind, and if we could search the whole world through, we could not find a dominion, an authority, or any power greater than the Name of Jesus.

We have the right to use that Name against our enemies.

We have the right to use it in our petitions. We have the right to use it in our praises and worship.

That Name was given to Him for us, and is ours today. It has lost none of its power.

The Use of the Name

Let us now study what this Name means to us.

We shall first look at the prayer promises Jesus made in regard to His Name.

189

We have the charter promise given to us in:

John 16:24. Jesus says, "Hitherto ye have asked nothing in my name. Ask and ye shall receive that your joy may be made full."

Jesus says, "Hitherto (or up to this time) you have never prayed in my Name, but now whatsoever ye shall ask the Father in my Name, He will give it you."

This promise is the most staggering statement, perhaps, that ever fell from the lips of the Man of Galilee; that we are to have the use of His Name, that Name of Omnipotence.

He does not say, "If ye believe, or if ye have faith."

He has given to us His Name. It is ours, and what is ours we do not have to have faith to use.

When we were born into the Family of God, the right and privilege to use the Name of Jesus became ours.

The Name of Jesus takes the place of Jesus in performing miracles, delivering from Satan's authority, and brings God upon the scene.

The disciples, while Christ was with them, had no need of the Name of Jesus. He met every need. But now that the time has come for Him to leave them, He said to them that whatsoever they would ask of the Father in His Name, the Father would give to them.

Jesus gave another tremendous promise concerning His Name in John 14:12-14.

He had spoken to the disciples of His departure from this world. Their hearts had been saddened and troubled at the thought that Jesus should leave them.

To them, it meant that everything would cease. His ministry on earth would come to an end, and all of His marvelous works that had brought healing and deliverance to multitudes would cease.

Now Christ says this to them: "Verily, verily, I say unto you, He that believeth on me, the works that I do shall he do also, because I go unto the Father, and whatsoever ye ask of the Father in My Name that will I do that the Father may be glorified in the Son."

His works, He tells them, are not to cease. On the other hand, they are to be multiplied.

While Christ was here in the flesh, He was limited by His human body, He could only be in one place at a time. But now when Redemption shall have been completed so that man may become a child of God, each child of God will be able to do locally what Jesus could do locally.

The reason for this is the authority of the Name. Jesus said, "You will do greater works than I do because I go to my Father, and whatsoever ye shall ask of the Father in my name I will do." He is really saying this: "You will take my place down here on earth. I will be your representative in Heaven, and whatsoever you ask in my name I will make good. It will be as though I were on earth asking of the Father."

He realized that the heart of our conflict would be with Satanic forces, so He said, in Mark 16:17, "In my name ye shall cast out demons." He has fully equipped us for our place as His representatives by giving us authority over every Satanic force and influence. In Mark 16:18, He tells us that in His Name we shall lay hands on the sick and they shall recover. Demons and disease must obey the Name of Jesus as they obeyed His words.

Oh, that our eyes were opened, that our souls would dare to rise into the realm of Omnipotence where the Name would mean to us all that the Father invested in it.

This is practically an unexplored tableland in Christian experience.

Here and there some of us have experienced the authority vested in the Name of Jesus, but none of us have ever been able to abide where we might enjoy the fullness of this mighty power.

QUESTIONS

1. Why does the New Creation need a weapon to use against the forces of Satan?
2. What is the threefold greatness of His Name?
3. What authority is vested in the Name of Jesus as a result of His conquests?
4. Show how Christ's words in Luke 11:21-22 show a picture of Christ.

5. When was the greatness of the Name of Jesus conferred upon Him?
6. Does Jesus Himself need the use of His Name?
7. For whom was the Name given? Why?
8. What is deposited in that Name?
9. How may we use the Name of Jesus?
10. What possibilities for your own growth do you see in this lesson?

Lesson 24
THE WORD, GOD'S REVELATION TO MAN

WE HAVE recently been taking up several phases of our Redemption in Christ. We are now going to study the means whereby God has made known to us our Redemption, the means whereby man becomes a New Creature in Christ. Our Father has given to us a Revelation of Himself. In this Revelation He has given to us a Revelation of our Redemption in Christ. He has also given a Revelation of the New Creation in Christ. This Revelation is not only a witness of Himself, but also a witness of the New Creation, his privileges, authority, and responsibility.

That Revelation is His Word, the Bible. Words can give no adequate estimation of the place the Word of God holds in Redemption and the life of God's child. It is our aim in these lessons to show forth the utter sacredness of the Word to the Father, and the vital place it holds in the life of every Christian . . . as fulfilled today. His people are destroyed, their lives are powerless for the lack of the knowledge of His Word.

God Works Through the Word

Satan has always bitterly and subtly fought God's Word, because God works through His Word. When God desired to create a universe, He brought it into being by the power of His spoken Word.

Hebrews 11:3. The worlds were created by the Word of God.

Every child of God was begotten, born of the Word. James 1:18, "Of His own will He brought us forth by the word of truth."

I Peter 1:23, "Having been begotten again not of corruptible seed, but of incorruptible, through the Word of God which liveth and abideth forever."

Then, after man has become God's child, the food, the sustenance, and the maintenance of his spiritual life is the Word of God.

Matthew 4:4, "Man shall not live by bread alone, but by every word that proceedeth from the mouth of God." It is the Word which builds us up.

193

Philippians 2:13, "For it is God who worketh in you both to will and to work for His good pleasure." He is working in us through His Word.

Colossians 1:5-6, "Whereof ye heard before in the Word of truth of the gospel which is come unto you even as it is also in all the world bearing fruit and increasing as it doth in you since the day ye heard it."

Satan's Battle Against the Word

Every period of spiritual declension has been marked by a low conception of God's Word. When Satan found that the torturing and martyrdom of the Christians, and the destruction or burning of Bibles would not stop the church from growth, he employed a more successful method. That method has been subtly attacking the Word so that it is made powerless and ineffectual in the life of man.

For a period of one thousand years before the Reformation, the Word was not given its place in Christian circles. James Lord, in his writing, "Beacon Lights of History," shows that it was Oriental philosophy that for a period of one thousand years usurped the authority of the Word, and ruled and controlled the Christian world.

When the Word lost its place, Redemption lost its place, and faith became unknown. For a thousand years the Bible was locked up in monasteries, locked in a language that the common people could not understand. It was written in Latin only, and just the clergy had access to it. This is the reason for the spiritual darkness of the Middle Ages. This is why God seemed inactive during that dark period. When His Word lost its place, He lost His place in the lives of men. It was out of Oriental philosophy that penance, purgatory, monasteries, and the Crusades grew.

The Place of the Word in the Reformation

When the Reformation came, it came when the Word began to work in the lives of a few men. Those men caught a glimpse of its place and gave it to the common people. It was the working of God's Word in the lives of men that brought Light and Life to humanity. The spread of Bibles into the homes of the common people cannot be separated from the Reformation.

Yet Satan has not ceased to try to make the Word inactive. When he could no longer lock it up within monasteries and a language the people could not understand, he locked it up within creeds and doctrines.

The Reformation and the cheaper means of printing made it possible for every home to possess the Bible.

Satan's Battle Against the Word

Then Satan caused men to build creeds and doctrines about the lives and teachings of the leading men of the Reformation, thus hindering themselves from growth and development.

No single leader of the Reformation possessed all the light. God raised up these men and gave to each a portion of light. Yet these men themselves were largely the product of the Middle Ages. Whenever a man locks himself up within a set of creeds, he shuts out further light on the Word, and hinders his growth. This has caused the divisions within the church and made her a reproach to the world.

This has hindered a true presentation of Christianity to the world so that Redemption has never had a fair chance to work in the lives of men.

This has caused a furious battle to be waged over the Deity of Christ and the authority of the Scriptures that has resulted in the present-day condition.

Many churches are preaching, in the place of the Word, other themes which they consider more practical and in harmony with modern civilization.

While on the other hand, those who today are preaching the truth, and are considered the most spiritual, have no true conception of the sacredness of the Word of God, and the place it should hold in their lives.

Mental Assent, and Its Origin

The utter commonness of the Word, which should have been our deliverance from ignorance and bondage, Satan has used to hinder the working of the Word in our midst.

The greatest weapon that Satan is using today to make the Word ineffectual, is the weapon of Mental Assent. This weapon is utterly dangerous because it is so subtle. Mental Assent is hard to recognize, because it comes clothed in the term "Faith."

195

Before we can understand the difference between Mental Assent and Faith, we must understand the meaning of each.

Mental Assent . . . versus Faith

Faith is action upon the Word. Believing is fearlessly acting upon the Word. Mental Assent is agreement to the fact that the Bible is true, but it is void of action.

Perhaps a few illustrations will make it clearer.

A man seeking to become a Christian, who really believes, says the following: "I believe that Christ was raised from the dead. I take Him as my Saviour and confess Him as my Lord. Therefore, I am saved, because His Word in Romans 10:9-10 declares so." He confesses that he is saved before he receives the witness within himself. He believes the Word to be God's. Therefore, he acts fearlessly upon it, regardless of his feelings, because he knows it cannot be broken. He boldly makes the Word his confession. There is no believing that does not result in confession.

A Mental Assenter, who is seeking to become a Christian, will speak similarly the following: "I believe the Bible is God's Word. I believe Jesus Christ is the Son of God. I have been trying to be saved for a long time. I've asked Him in, but I am not saved." This one would be insulted if he were told that he did not believe, yet his attitude is one of Mental Assent.

He professes to believe, yet he has no conception of acting upon God's Word. If he had believed, he would have said, "God's Word is true. I believe, therefore I have Eternal Life." (John 5:24)

Mental Assent produces no action; it has no confession. Mental Assent has robbed many of receiving healing.

A believer says this, "By His stripes I am healed." The disease may be manifest in his body, yet he is acting upon the Word which declares that by His stripes he is healed. It may be that after he has been prayed for, he has witnessed no healing; yet he says, "I am healed, because the Word declares that in Christ's Name they shall lay hands on the sick and they shall recover."

A Christian who is a mental assenter has the following attitude: "I believe the Bible is true. I have believed these

Scriptures all my life. I have had so many pray for me, I can't understand why I am not healed." How many of God's children have suffered years with a disease, not realizing their difficulty, thinking that their Mental Assent was Faith.

Many Christians who are living in the realm of Mental Assent today are living barren and fruitless spiritual lives. They, all their lives, have been seeking power with God in their lives and prayer. They have never learned to live by the Word. They live in weakness and failure and want, because they have no conception of the real meaning of believing God's Word, of really acting upon the Word. The Word declares that they have been made New Creations in Christ (II Corinthians 5:17) ; that they have been made the very righteousness of God (II Corinthians 5:21); that they are joint-heirs with Christ (Romans 8:17); that the authority of His Name is theirs in prayer (John 16:23-24) ; and that God shall supply every need of theirs (Phil. 4:19).

Yet they have no consciousness of righteousness, authority in the Name of Jesus, or strength. This is due to the fact that their attitude has been one of Mental Assent, and Satan has robbed them of their Inheritance in Christ.

Cause of Mental Assent

The cause of Mental Assent has been our utter familiarity with the Word. Perhaps all of us have had a Bible in the home from childhood. We have always been familiar with its teachings.

Many of us, long before we accepted Christ as Saviour and Lord, personally believed the Bible to be true. However, our attitude all these years toward it was Mental Assent. We professed to believe it was God's Word, long before we acted upon it.

After we were Born Again, this same Mental Assent followed us through life. We will explain this more completely.

As a child, our attitude toward it was Mental Assent. Through life this attitude of Mental Assent followed us. Perhaps for years the Bible lay on the bookshelf, on the study table; yet we never studied it, as we were so occupied with other things.

However, if anyone had refuted the fact that it was God's Word, we would have earnestly taken our stand for it. Perhaps many times we professed our faith that it was God's Word. Yet, if this attitude had been more than Mental Assent, we would have zealously studied it, continually seeking to discover what God really had for us in His Own Word or Message to us.

We said we believed it, but our actions were contrary. We didn't study it, we didn't speak of it often.

Later, the time came when we actually were Born Again. The Bible became a New Book to us. We were able to understand it. We found it to be our help, our food. Yet how much of our attitude toward it was still Mental Assent. How little we really dared to act upon it.

We lived in weakness. We felt that our prayer life was powerless. We didn't possess the ability to testify and pray for the sick. We felt our need was a deeper experience that would fill our lives with power. We sought experiences, we received blessings many times, yet we realized that the life of victory was still in the future. We didn't realize that the heart of our difficulty was the fact that in our Mental Assent we were not acting upon the Word. We didn't realize that God had already made us what we were trying to be. We didn't realize that the authority which we sought was already ours.

We memorized Scriptures and quoted them often without ever really acting upon them. In the presence of His Word which declared that God had made Christ our Righteousness (I Corinthians 1:30), and that we had actually become the Righteousness of God (II Corinthians 5:21), we spoke of our sinful and weak state. We considered it a form of humility to approach God as unworthy worms of the dust, confessing and repenting continually of our sinful nature. We made more of sin and its power than of Redemption which had made us absolutely Righteous. Righteousness is the ability to stand in the presence of God as free from sin or condemnation as if sin had never entered the world.

Prayer was a weeping and crying for God to hear us and answer us.

We didn't realize that our place as joint-heirs with Christ, and the authority of the Name of Jesus, gave to us legal rights in prayer. However, we knew all the prayer promises.

One translation of James 1:26 is the following: "Faith without corresponding actions is dead." This is a definition of Mental Assent. Faith, without corresponding actions, is Mental Assent. It means nothing to the Father. It robs us of our Inheritance in Christ. If I profess to believe the Word, and yet I do not act upon it, my actions do not correspond.

The secret of a life of victory in Christ which everyone may possess is found in Revelation 12:11.

He declares that we overcome by the blood of the Lamb, which signifies the completeness of our Redemption in Christ, and the Word of our testimony, which means acting fearlessly on the Word. We make God's Word our confession in the midst of every circumstance.

We say, "I am the righteousness of God, because His Word declares it. Sin shall not have dominion over me. I have authority over Satan. I am healed by the Stripes of Christ. In all things I am more than a conqueror. My God shall supply every need; I will not be anxious."

In the face of every contradictory circumstance we hold this confession. We make His Word our word. What He declares we fearlessly declare, because we are freed from Mental Assent and have learned to act on His Word.

In our next lesson we will see what will bring us to a place of action upon the Word.

QUESTIONS

1. What has God made known to us in this Revelation which He has given?
2. What place does the Word hold in the New Birth and life of God's child?
3. When Satan found that the martyrdom of Christians would not keep the church from growth, what other means did he employ?
4. Why was God seemingly inactive during the Middle Ages?
5. What brought the Reformation?

6. Why was the church hindered in growth after the Reformation?
7. What method is Satan using today to keep the Word from prevailing in our lives?
8. What is the origin of Mental Assent?
9. Show the difference between Mental Assent and Faith.
10. Show how Mental Assent robs us of our inheritance.

Lesson 25

THE PRESENT MINISTRY OF CHRIST

WE HAVE STUDIED in our course the working of God for a period of four thousand years in the preparation for Christ's coming (Galatians 4:4). We have studied the earthly life of our Lord Jesus Christ and His death and Resurrection for us through which He redeemed us from Satan's authority (Hebrews 2:14).

Now we are going to study the present ministry of Christ, what He is doing now for us, and what He has been doing for almost a period of two thousand years. This present ministry of Christ has been neglected by most Christians. So many, when they think of His giving His life for us think only of His death and Resurrection. They do not know that when He sat down on the Father's right hand, that He began to live for us in as much reality as He had died for us. How few Christians have a clear conception of the present ministry of Christ.

There are three views of Jesus' ministry for us: Jesus beyond the cross as the lowly "Man of Sorrows"; Jesus on the cross as the "Son made Sin" (II Corinthians 5:21); Jesus seated at the right hand of the Majesty on high, the "Exalted One, with a name above every other name" (Philippians 2:9-10).

As we study our hymns, we realize how few teachers and song writers have understood this present ministry of Christ. Many see Jesus beyond the cross, the lowly Jesus. Another group see Him only on the cross. A very small number have looked beyond the cross and the tomb to the Christ seated at God's right hand.

He is no longer the meek and lowly man of Galilee. He is no longer the Son made Sin, forsaken of God. He is the Lord of all who conquered Satan, sin, disease and death.

He is the One who possesses all authority in Heaven and in earth (Matthew 28:18).

We can today act fearlessly upon His Word, because He is the surety of it. He is the surety of this New Covenant.

Hebrews 7:22, "By so much also has Jesus become the surety of a better covenant."

The surety of the covenant is the Word.

Hebrews 8:6, "But now hath he obtained a ministry the more excellent by so much as He is also the mediator of a better covenant which hath been enacted upon better promises." The New Covenant has been enacted, is based upon the Word, and He is the Surety. This man today at the Father's right hand, is the Surety of this Word.

He who possesses all authority in Heaven and earth makes good every word in these promises. Let us now study what He is today to us in this New Covenant.

In the revelation which Paul received, God has drawn aside the veil and given to us the present ministry of Christ. He sat down as our "High Priest," our "Mediator," our "Intercessor," our "Advocate," our "Surety" of the New Covenant.

Jesus, Our High Priest

We have studied the High Priesthood of the Old Covenant. The High Priest of the Old Covenant was a type of Jesus, the High Priest of the New Covenant.

Once every year the High Priest under the Old Covenant had entered into the tabernacle on earth with the blood of bulls and goats to make a yearly atonement for the sins of Israel. Read Hebrews 9:25; 10:1-4.

The priests stood daily ministering and offering the same sacrifices for the sins of Israel (Hebrews 10:11).

Christ entered into Heaven itself with His own blood, having obtained eternal redemption for us. (Hebrews 9:12, 23-27).

When God accepted the blood of Jesus Christ, He signified that the claims of Justice had been met and that man could be legally taken from Satan's authority and restored to fellowship with Himself.

By the sacrifice of Himself, Christ had put sin away (Hebrews 9:26).

The crime of High Treason of Adam had been met and settled by His one sacrifice for sin (Hebrews 10:12).

By the sacrifice of Himself He had sanctified man (Hebrews 9:10-14).

"To sanctify" means to "set apart," "to separate." He had separated man from Satan's kingdom and family. We had become as separated from Satan's dominion as He was (John 17:14).

When Christ met Mary after His Resurrection (John 20:17), He said to her, "Touch me not, for I am not yet ascended unto the Father." He was then on His way to the Father with His own blood, the token of the penalty He had paid, and He could not be touched by man.

Jesus' ministry as High Priest did not end with His carrying His blood into the Holy Place, but He is still the minister of the Sanctuary (Hebrews 8:2).

The word, "sanctuary," in Hebrews 8:2, in the Greek means "Holy things." He is ministering in the "Holy things." These "Holy things" are our prayers and worship. We do not know how to worship Him as we ought, but He takes our ofttimes crude petitions and worship and makes them beautiful to the Father. These "Holy things" are our "Spiritual Sacrifices" which He makes acceptable to the Father. Every prayer, every worship is accepted by the Father when it is presented in the name of Jesus.

I Peter 2:5, "Ye also as living stones are built up a spiritual house to be a holy priesthood, to offer up spiritual sacrifices acceptable to God, through Jesus Christ."

Study the High Priestly ministry of Christ as it is given to us in the book of Hebrews. He is a merciful and faithful high priest (Hebrews 2:17-18). He is a High Priest who can be touched with the feelings of our infirmities (Hebrews 4:14-16).

He is High Priest forever (Hebrews 6:19).

Jesus, the Mediator

When Christ sat down at the Father's right hand, He had satisfied the claims of Justice and He became the Mediator between God and man.

I Timothy 2:5, "For there is one God, one mediator also between God and man, himself man, Christ Jesus."

Jesus is man's mediator for two reasons. He is man's mediator because of what He is, and He is man's mediator because of what He has done.

First: Jesus is man's mediator by virtue of what He is. He is the union of God and man.

203

John 1:14. He is the Word "Who was with God and was God . . . the Word made flesh" (John 1:1).

He is the One who existed on an equality with God, made in the likeness of men (Philippians 2:8-9).

He has bridged the gulf between God and man. He is equal with God and He is equal with man. He can represent humanity before God.

This, however, was not a sufficient ground for a mediation between God and man. Man was an eternal criminal before God. Man was alienated from God (Ephesians 2:12) and under the judgment of Satan (John 16:11).

This brings us to our second fact. Jesus is man's mediator because of what He has done.

Colossians 1:22, "Yet now hath He reconciled in the body of His flesh, through death, to present you Holy, and without blemish and unreprovable through Him."

II Corinthians 5:18, "Who reconciled us unto Himself through Christ." There could have been no mediator between God and man if there had not been first a Reconciliation made between God and man. Man was unrighteous in his condition of spiritual death. While he was in that condition of spiritual death, He could not approach God. Neither could any Mediator have approached God for him.

Christ has reconciled us unto God through His death on the cross, so that He now presents man holy and without blemish before God. Therefore, man has a right to approach God through Christ, his Mediator.

From the fall of man until Jesus sat down at God's right hand, no man had ever approached God except over a bleeding sacrifice, through a Divinely-appointed Priesthood, or by an angelic visitation or dreams.

On the ground of His High Priestly offering of His own blood, He perfected our Redemption, satisfied the claims of justice, and made it possible for God to legally give man Eternal Life, making him righteous, and giving him a standing as a son.

Every unsaved man now has a legal right to approach God.

Jesus, the Intercessor

Jesus, as High Priest, carried His blood into the Holy of Holies, satisfying the claims of Justice that were against natural man. As Mediator, He introduces the unsaved man to God.

John 14:6, Jesus is the way to God, and no one can approach God except through Him. As soon as a man accepts the reconciliation work of Christ, he becomes a child of God. Then Christ begins His intercessory work for him.

Jesus is Mediator for the sinner, but He is intercessor for the Christian.

The first question that comes to us is: "Why does the child of God need someone to intercede for him?"

We can find the answer to that in Romans 12:2.

At the New Birth, our spirits receive the life of God. The next need is that our minds be renewed. For the number of years that existed before we were born again, we walked according to Satan (Ephesians 2:1-3). He ruled our minds.

Now that our spirits have received the Life of God, our minds must be renewed so that we will know our privileges and responsibilities as children of God. Ephesians 4:22-24 shows us the need of a renewed mind. The New Birth is instantaneous, but the renewing of our minds is a gradual process. Its growth is determined by our study and meditation of the Word.

During this period we need the intercession of Christ. Many times we strain our fellowship with the Father, as in our ignorance of His will we many times say and do things that are not pleasing to Him.

Then again, we need His intercession because of demoniacal persecution against us.

Matthew 5:10, "Blessed are they who are persecuted for righteousness' sake." This isn't the persecution of men but the persecution of demons.

Matthew 5:11-12 refers to the persecution we receive from men.

Demons persecute us for righteousness' sake. They hate and fear us because God has declared us righteous.

Because we have not fully learned of our authority they cause us to stumble many times.

Regardless of this, He is able to save us to the utter-most because He ever lives to pray for us (Hebrews 7:25).

No one can lay anything to the charge of God's child. God has declared him righteous. There is no one to condemn him. Jesus is living to make intercession for him (Romans 8:33-34).

Jesus, the Advocate

We came to the Father through Christ, our Mediator. We have felt the sweet influences of His Intercession on our behalf. Now we want to know Him as our Advocate before the Father.

How many Christians today who are living in broken fellowship would be living victorious lives in Christ if they had known or knew that Jesus was their Advocate?

Because of our unrenewed minds and Satanic per-secution, we sometimes sin and cause our fellowship to be broken.

Every child of God who breaks fellowship with the Father goes under condemnation. If he had no advocate he would be in a sad position.

The Word shows us that if we do sin we have an advocate with the Father.

I John 2:1, "My little children, these things I write unto you that ye may not sin, and if any man sins we have an advocate with the Father, Jesus Christ, the Righteous."

I John 1:3-9 is God's method for maintaining our fellowship with Him. If we sin so that our fellowship is broken, we may renew that fellowship by confessing our sin.

Jesus' ministry as an advocate is a work of Jesus on the part of God. However, He is unable to act as our advocate unless we confess our sins. The moment we confess them, He takes up our case before the Father.

The Word declares that when we confess our sins, He is righteous and faithful to forgive us our sins and to cleanse us from all unrighteousness. God can forgive our sins and be perfectly righteous in doing it, because Christ bore them (Isaiah 53:6).

He is also faithful and ready at the moment we confess to wipe them out as though they had never been.

It is absolutely essential that Christians know Jesus as their advocate. Many who are out of fellowship have confessed their sins many times without receiving a sense of restoration, because they did not know Jesus was their Advocate. They did not take forgiveness when they confessed their sins. They do not act upon the Word which declares that the Father forgives the moment they confess.

No Christian should ever remain in broken fellowship any longer than it takes to ask forgiveness. What the Father forgives He forgets. A child of His should never dishonor Him by ever thinking of his sins again.

Jesus, the Surety

Jesus is our personal surety. This is the most vital of all the ministries of Jesus at the Father's right hand.

Under the law the High Priest was the surety of the Old Covenant. If the High Priest failed, it interrupted the relationship between God and Israel. The blood of the atonement lost its efficacy.

Under the New Covenant, Jesus is the High Priest and the Surety of the New Covenant.

Hebrews 7:22, "By so much also hath Jesus become the surety of a better covenant."

Our position before the Father is absolutely secure. We know that throughout our lifetime, we have, at the right hand of God, a Man who is there for us.

He is representing us before the Father. He always has a standing; we have One representing us before the Father. Our position is secure.

QUESTIONS

1. What are three views of Jesus' ministry?
2. Show how the High Priest of the Old Covenant was a type of Jesus, the High Priest of the New Covenant.
3. What did the acceptance of Christ's blood by the Father signify?
4. Give two reasons for Christ's being man's mediator.
5. Why does the child of God need an intercessor?
6. What are the two kinds of persecution mentioned in Matthew 5:10-12?
7. When does Christ act as our advocate?

8. Why is it essential for every Christian to know Jesus as his Advocate?
9. What does Jesus as the Surety of the New Covenant mean to you?
10. Name five phases of Christ's present ministry, and give a scripture for each.

Lesson 26
HEALING

THE SUBJECT OF HEALING is one over which there has been much controversy. Today there exist at least three different attitudes toward healing among the Christians.

One group teaches that healing is not for us today. They base this upon the theory that healing is a miracle and that miracles do not belong to the present day; that they belonged only to the Apostolic Age.

Another group teaches that God heals today in answer to special prayer or a special act of faith, and that according to His own will in the matter.

The third group teaches that healing for the body is the legal right of every child of God, and that he receives healing for his physical body upon the same grounds that he receives remission of sin for his spirit.

Let us now examine these three teachings in the light of the Word.

The first attitude can be easily shown to be erroneous by a definition of a miracle. A miracle, according to Webster, is an act or happening in the material or physical sphere that apparently departs from the laws of nature or goes beyond what is known concerning these laws. It is really an intervention of God into the realm of natural laws, or the realm of human activity. It is God coming upon the scene.

Whenever God comes into immediate contact with men a miracle is performed. Every answer to prayer, regardless of its smallness, and every New Birth is a miracle.

An act of healing whereby God comes into immediate contact with man's physical body is no more a miracle than the New Birth, in which God comes into immediate contact with the spirit of man, imparting to it His own nature.

Man asks God to perform a greater miracle than healing when he asks Him to save his soul, and as great a miracle as healing when he asks Him to answer a request, regardless of how slight it might be.

To say that miracles belonged only to the Apostolic Age would be to say that God must take the place of a mere spectator or cipher in the world He had created, from the Apostolic Age to this.

We can easily see the utter fallacy of this teaching. Let us now seek to find what God's Word declares about the issue of the other two beliefs. If the second attitude is the correct teaching, the third is not.

If God heals only in answer to a special act of faith, and that only when He wills to, healing does not legally belong to the child of God and was not included in Redemption.

If, on the other hand, healing was a part of man's Redemption in Christ, healing belongs to every child of God, and no special act of faith is required to obtain it. There need be no questioning as to whether it is God's will to heal; if it is in the Redemption, it is His Will. We will now consider what God's Word says about this.

Origin of Sickness and Disease

Before we are able to understand healing we must understand the origin of disease, sickness and death. We have seen that as a result of Adam's crime of High Treason, Spiritual Death gained an entrance into the spirit of man. This Spiritual Death, which has reigned in the human race, has been the soil out of which has grown the reign of sin, disease and death over man. Sickness, disease and death in man's physical body are but the manifestation of Spiritual Death within the spirit. If man had never died spiritually, disease and death would never have had a part in man's physical body. When Satan became the god of this world, one of the results of his reign was the peopling of the air with disease germs so that from then to the present time, disease microbes too small to be seen with the naked eye have been one of the greatest enemies of man.

The fact cannot be denied that in this world there exists evil. The existence of evil has caused many earnest people to reject belief in a God of love; they have not understood that evil was the result of Satan's reign over humanity as the prince and god of this world.

There are philosophers who have been so impressed by the reign of evil that they have arrived at the conclusion that the central principle of the universe is evil. They are wrong. It is not the Creator, but the Usurper, Satan, who is the source of evil.

The two divisions of evil are pain and sin. Pain may have several sub-divisions, but the major body of pain known and experienced by humanity is the pain caused by disease.

In conclusion, sin and disease are twins, born of Spiritual Death. They are both the work of Satan. Sin is a disease of the spirit; sickness, as we see it, is a disease of the physical body.

God's Attitude Toward Disease

God looks upon disease as He looks upon sin, the work of Satan in the life of His Creation, man.

Christ came to reveal the Father-God, to make known His attitude toward man. By carefully following the life of Christ we may learn the attitude of God toward sickness.

Christ Was the Will of the Father

Christ's ministry from the beginning to the close was a twofold ministry. He brought peace to the souls of men and healing to their bodies. Healing had a major place in the ministry of Christ. Throughout His ministry He delivered all those who were oppressed of Satan. This deliverance included healing for physical bodies. If disease did not come from Satan, it must have had a place in God's original plan for man.

Read Matthew 8:16-17 and Mark 1:32-34.

If this were the case, then Jesus' ministry would have been contrary to the Father's will. He was the Father's will revealed to man and He revealed that it was the Father's will to break the power of disease over man's body and set him free from pain and suffering. Christ's ministry proclaimed healing and blessing to the physical part of man's nature, as well as to the spiritual side.

There are several instances where the attitude of Christ toward disease is clearly shown. One is in Luke 13:10-17. After loosing a woman on the Sabbath from an infirmity which she had had for eighteen years, Christ was criticized by the rulers of the synagogue.

His answer was, "Ought not this woman, whom Satan hath bound, lo, these eighteen years, to have been loosed from this bond on the day of the Sabbath?"

He clearly stated that Satan was the cause of the infirmity which had bound her physical body.

Another incident is found in Mark 2:1-21. A man with palsy is brought to Christ to whom Christ said, "Son, thy sins are forgiven."

When the scribes questioned the statement Christ had made, He answered them with this, "Which is easier, to say to the sick of the palsy, Thy sins are forgiven; or to say, Arise, and take up thy bed, and walk?"

In reality Christ is saying this, "Which is easier? Wherein is the difference—to forgive sins which are the results of Spiritual Death in man's spirit, or to heal the disease of his physical body, which is the result also of the same Spiritual Death." In either case Christ was dealing with the bondage of man to Satan. To see more fully the attitude of Christ toward disease and the place healing played in His ministry, read the following:

Healing in Redemption

I John 3:8 tells us that Christ was manifested to destroy the works of the devil. He came to destroy what Satan had wrought in humanity when he became the spiritual father of man as a result of Adam's crime of High Treason. He came to bring Satan to nought in his relationship and power over man.

Hebrews 2:14. He came to completely redeem man from the effects of Adam's sin by identifying Himself with humanity. Study carefully Romans 5:12-21.

If man's redemption from Spiritual Death is to be a complete redemption it must be a redemption from disease as well as sin. God realized this, and He has clearly shown us in His Word that He has made provision for the healing of man's body.

Isaiah 53:4-6. God lifts the curtain through the prophets and lets us see Him dealing with sin and sickness.

Literally it reads, "He was despised, and rejected of men; a man of pains, and acquainted with sickness."

Fourth verse, "Surely He hath borne our sicknesses, and carried our diseases; yet we did esteem him stricken, smitten of God and afflicted."

He was stricken of God with our diseases. He was afflicted with our pains.

"He was wounded for our transgressions, He was bruised for our iniquities; the chastisement of our peace was upon Him; and with His stripes we are healed."

Tenth verse, "Yet it pleased Jehovah to bruise Him, He hath made Him sick; when thou shalt make His soul an offering for sin."

The old version which reads "griefs and sorrows" is not correct.

Every literal translation gives "disease and sickness."

God not only laid upon Jesus our iniquities, but our diseases.

He was made sick with our diseases. He was made sin with our sins. In the Father's mind, and in the mind of Jesus, and according to the Word, our diseases and sins were borne by the Master.

If they were borne by Him, then it is wrong for us to bear them.

Sense Knowledge has attempted to repudiate this, but the truth remains that God laid our diseases and our sins on Jesus.

He could not be raised until man was declared righteous (Romans 4:25).

When He arose from the dead, the body of sin, of Spiritual Death, had been destroyed (Romans 6:6). Sin had lost its power and so had disease.

Isaiah 53:10 reads as follows in the Hebrew: "Yet Jehovah hath delighted to bruise Him; He hath made Him sick." God made Jesus sin with our sins, and He made Him sick with our sicknesses: He delighted to do it because of one reason . . . it meant healing for man.

Christ bore our sins and the penalty that we might be free from sin, its power, and its judgment.

Upon the same grounds He bore our disease and pains. He carried them that we might be set free, that we need not bear them.

God made Him to be our sin-bearer and our sickness-bearer. Him who knew no sin was made sin and Him who knew no sickness was made sickness.

In the ministry of Christ, the Father-God revealed that it was His will to heal man physically. Now in Redemption He breaks the power of disease and sickness upon Christ.

Satan, who had the authority in the realm of Spiritual Death, has been brought to nought (Hebrews 2:14).

In that victory, disease and sickness, the works of Satan, were brought to nought also. By His bruising, we are healed from the law of disease.

Healing Today

Christ's ministry upon earth was twofold, constantly affecting the spirits and bodies of men. His death was twofold, bearing our sins and diseases. He is the same today and the twofold ministry of blessing for spirit and body has continued from His earthly ministry to the present time.

He bore man's Spiritual Death that he might have Life, and in His Word He made provision for man's salvation. He bore man's diseases and in His Word He made provision for his healing.

In Mark, the sixteenth chapter, He gave to His disciples the Great Commission. He is going to depart to be with the Father to take up His work at His right hand. His disciples are going to take His place. His representatives are to continue His ministry, do what He would do if He were here.

So in their commission to a world for whom He died He reveals that the twofold ministry will continue.

First, the commission is to meet the spiritual need of man. Mark 16:16, "He that believeth and is baptized, shall be saved." Every child of God applies this portion of the commission to himself, teaching that faith in Christ is essential to salvation and that unbelief excludes one from it. Then comes the second part of the commission, Mark 16:17, "And these signs shall accompany them that believe." The Greek word for "believe" is the same as "believeth" in verse 16, except for the fact that one is singular and the other is plural. What right has anyone had to separate these words of Christ which immediately follow His first part of the commission?

Where in His Word has He ever implied that the first words had reference to all men, and that the last had reference to only the Christians of the Apostolic Age? Both promises hang by the single stem "believing." The act of believing brings one into the family of God. The rich cluster of miraculous promises following, belong to them that believe, or the "believing ones," a literal translation.

Man has held fast to the first promise, because he knew how to use it, and he has flung back the other because he did not know how to use it.

He bore man's diseases that man might not bear them, and the provision for man's healing is in this: "In My Name . . . they shall lay hands on the sick and they shall recover."

The ministry of the disciples under the guidance of the Holy Spirit had the same twofold blessing as had Christ's ministry. A complete Redemption was preached by them, the New Birth for the spirit and healing for the body. The two streams of blessing which began from the personal ministry of Christ, a stream of regeneration and healing have continued from then, through the Apostolic Age, and to the present, wherever Christians have dared to act upon His Word.

Our right to healing given to us in His Redemption has been invested in the authority of His Name. Today He is watching over this Word to confirm it, as He confirmed it in the days of the Apostles (Mark 16:20).

QUESTIONS

1. Name the three present-day attitudes toward healing.
2. Explain why the first attitude is false.
3. If the third attitude is correct, show why the second is false.
4. Explain clearly the origin of disease.
5. How does the life and ministry of Christ reveal the Father's attitude toward disease?
6. Give and explain several incidents in the ministry of Christ which reveal that sickness came from the reign of Spiritual Death.
7. Why must a complete Redemption from Satan include healing?

8. Why do we have a legal right to healing?
9. What provision has Christ made for the continuation of His ministry of healing?

Lesson 27
THE LORDSHIP OF CHRIST

ONE OF THE MOST VITAL TRUTHS in this Revelation to man is the fact that Jesus Christ is Lord of all. Today in this universe He holds the position of Lord. His ministry as Lord is so important that we did not study it in Lesson 25, in which we took up the present ministry of Christ. To know that Jesus is Lord is essential to a victorious Christian life; therefore, we are devoting two complete lessons to its study.

Over seven hundred times in the New Testament, the title, "Lord," is given to Christ.

He has regained the Lordship over creation which Adam forfeited. He is Lord over sin, disease and death and the forces of nature.

He holds the highest position in the universe.

The greatest and most blessed truth of all, however, is that He becomes the personal Lord of man. In previous lessons we have seen man's right to righteousness, eternal life, etc. In this lesson we shall see that every man has a legal right to the benefits of the Lordship of Christ.

We shall study this subject in four divisions. The first division is Satan, the lord; the second is Christ, the Conqueror; the third is Christ made Lord; and the fourth is Christ, man's personal Lord.

In the above outline we have in brief the story of Redemption.

Satan's Lordship

The Word reveals to us, and the facts of life bear witness to it, that Satan is the lord of natural man.

Christ showed that He recognized it, when He called him the prince of this world.

John 14:30, "For the prince of this world cometh: and he hath nothing in me."

In the Revelation which Paul received, Satan is called the god of this world.

II Corinthians 4:4, "The god of this world hath blinded the minds of the unbelieving, that the light of the gospel of the glory of Christ, who is the image of God, should not dawn upon them."

Satan and his cohorts are called the spiritual rulers of this world.

Ephesians 6:12, "For our wrestling is not against flesh and blood, but against the world-rulers of this darkness, against the spiritual hosts of wickedness in the heavenly places."

The natural man is walking according to their rule.

Ephesians 2:2, "Wherein ye once walked according to the course of this world, according to the prince of the powers of the air, of the spirit that now worketh in the sons of disobedience."

However, at the first, Satan did not hold this authority over the human race or creation. Man was the original lord. God gave to him the dominion over the works of creation, making him His under-ruler.

Genesis 1:26-31, "Let us make man in our image, after our likeness: and let them have dominion over the fish of the sea, and over the birds of the heavens, and over the cattle, and over all the earth, and over every creeping thing that creepeth upon the earth."

Man, even yet in his lowered and subjected state, bears within his being traces of his original position as God's under-ruler. In his discoveries in the realm of science, his classifications of knowledge, and his understanding and utilization of the forces of nature, he has shown the capability of his mind in fellowshipping the mind of the Creator.

He who once ruled creation still shows ability as God's under-ruler by multiplying and improving the products of animal and vegetable life.

He has made the waters swarm; he has turned deserts into gardens. His being has thrilled with the harmonies of sound, form, and color of all creation, and he has reproduced them in oratorio, in sculptured marble, on canvas, and in landscape gardening. He was nature's sceptered king; it was for him that the earth was created . . . a home.

One single eternal human being means more to the heart of God than all the universe.

Yet this one obeyed the voice of Satan, committed high treason, and became his subject. Satan desired to rule this world. He desired the position man held. He gained it by becoming man's ruler. He became man's ruler by imparting his nature to man and becoming to man what God should have been, his father (Genesis 2:15-17; 3:1-24).

Through the entrance of spiritual death, which we have studied in the past, and through its reign over humanity, Satan has ruled as lord.

Study again carefully: Romans 5:12, 14, 15, and 17, with Hebrews 2:14 . . . "the authority of death."

What a floodtide of human suffering and misery has the reign of Satan brought to the human heart.

Man was given dominion over the works of God's hands. He turned that vast dominion into the hands of Satan. He went from Lordship to slavery. Even the animal and vegetable kingdoms have groaned under the lordship of Satan (Romans 8:20-24).

But God did not leave man in his hopeless condition to suffer eternally under the reign of Satan. In the very presence of Adam's crime of high treason, He gave the promise of One who would legally break the lordship of Satan over the human race.

Genesis 3:15-18. (We have studied before the full meaning of this prophecy.)

Christ, the Conqueror

God could not annul what Adam had done, and man must wait until the deliverer had come.

Christ has broken the Lordship of Satan over the human race. He has brought to nought absolutely the one who has for ages held the authority in the realm of death (Hebrews 2:14).

Here there are things which we want to note. Christ did not bring Satan to nought for Himself. Satan was never lord over Christ. The Son of God who had lived in eternity on an equality with the Father was not touched by Adam's crime of high treason, which made Satan the lord of the human race (Philippians 2:2-8).

Even when He became a man, Christ was free from Satan's dominion, for He was not born of natural generation. He was God, Incarnate, and by reason of His Deity, He remained greater than Satan and his world-rulers.

Christ said, "The prince of this world comes and has nothing (or no part) in me," in John 14:30.

The Incarnation of Christ gave Him no relationship to Satan. His humanity did not subject Him to the god of this world. He had the same kind of humanity that Adam had before his crime of high treason.

Therefore, in the life of Christ upon the earth, we have a sample life of a man free from the lordship of Satan. Satan obeyed Him, disease and sickness were His servants, and every force of nature obeyed His command.

Therefore, we can see that Christ did not conquer Satan for Himself. He conquered him for man. Although Christ was free from Satan's dominion and man wasn't, Christ could break the power of disease over a man's life and cast out demons, but humanity remained within the authority of Satan. They needed freeing from his lordship. They needed deliverance from his nature out of which came selfishness, jealousy, the reign of sin, disease, and rebellion toward God.

The lordship of Satan over humanity, over the individual, must be broken by a man; therefore, on the cross Christ identified Himself with spiritual death, the nature of Satan, and as one in union with us, He conquered Satan on behalf of the human race.

II Corinthians 5:21, "Him who knew no sin he made to be sin on our behalf; that we might become the righteousness of God in him."

We do not know the exact nature of that combat; we only know that when Christ arose from the dead, as a man, on our behalf, He flung off from Himself the conquered principalities and powers.

Colossians 2:15, "Having despoiled the principalities and powers, he made a show of them openly, triumphing over them in it."

We do not know the exact nature of Adam's treason whereby Satan became his lord and lord of the human race; but we know that when Adam faced God in the Garden, his nature had been changed, and that in his life a new master was reigning, Satan.

220

Although we do not know exactly how, we know that one man crowned Satan as lord of the human race.

Luke 4:6-12, "For it hath been delivered unto me; and to whomsoever I will I give it."

Even so, we do not know exactly how, but we know that one man, Jesus Christ, through His death and resurrection dethroned this man-crowned lord, Satan.

And when Christ entered the Holy of Holies with His own blood, God recognized that complete Redemption from Satan's authority and dominion had been wrought for the human race.

Hebrews 9:12, "But through His own blood entered in once for all into the holy place, having obtained eternal redemption for us."

The first man was cast forth from the presence of God, because Satan had become his Master, and the human race was identified in that rejection (Genesis 3:22-24).

Then the time came when a man who had once been made sin and forsaken of God entered the Holy of Holies and was joyfully accepted, because the reign of Satan over man had come to nought.

Hebrews 10:10, "By which will we have been sanctified through the offering of the body of Christ once for all."

Man had been sanctified by the offering of Christ. To sanctify means "to set apart, to separate." Man had not only been freed from Satan's dominion, but he had also been as separated from Satan's authority as Christ was before He became sin.

There had been made a remission of sins that were the result of spiritual death.

Hebrews 10:18, "Now where remission of these is there is no more offering for sin."

And man had been declared perfect before God.

Hebrews 10:14, "For by one offering He hath perfected forever them that are sanctified."

When Christ was accepted and seated in the very Holy of Holies at the right hand of God, the entire human race was also (Ephesians 2:5-6).

Christ is the conqueror, because He has broken Satan's lordship over man.

Hebrews 2:14, "Since then the children are sharers in flesh and blood, He also Himself in like manner partook of the same that through death He might bring to nought him that had the authority of death, that is the devil."

Christ, Crowned Lord

Because of this victory as a man over Satan, God has crowned Jesus as Lord. When Christ arose from the dead, He arose above every rule, and authority, and power, and dominion (Ephesians 1:12-22).

These "rules," "authorities," and "dominions" were Satan's.

Now, not for Himself, because Christ was always greater, but for man, Christ was raised.

His victory was man's complete freedom from Satan's rule, authority, power and dominion over his life.

The dominion, which man had once had, was not given back directly to him lest he forfeit it again.

Therefore, the lost lordship was given to Christ, who holds it for man. God made Christ "Lord."

"Let all the House of Israel therefore know assuredly that God hath made both Lord and Christ this Jesus whom ye crucified" (Acts 2:36).

The Angel said, "Come, see the place where the Lord lay" (Matthew 28:6).

Christ, the son of man, had risen from the dead and broken the lordship of Satan.

"And what the exceeding greatness of his power to usward who believe according to that working of the strength of his might which he wrought in Christ when He raised Him from the dead and made Him to sit at His right hand in the Heavenly places far above all rule, and authority and dominion and every name that is named not only in this world but also in that which is to come."

God crowns Him as Lord when He gives to Him a name that is above every name, and invests within it the authority of His conquest.

Philippians 2:9, "Wherefore also God highly exalted Him and gave unto Him the name that is above every name, that at the name of Jesus every knee should bow of things in heaven and things on earth and things under the earth and that every tongue should confess that Christ is Lord to the glory of God the Father."

All that He is as Lord is for us, for the authority of His lordship has been invested in His Name, and that Name is ours, as we have seen in a previous lesson. He has been made Lord for us.

Ephesians 1:22-23,"And He put all things in subjection under His feet and gave Him to be head over all things to the church, which is His body, the fullness of Him that filleth all in all."

In our next lesson we shall study, "Christ, our Personal Lord."

We shall see what His Lordship means to us, personally.

QUESTIONS

1. Give three scriptures which show that Satan is the lord of natural man.
2. How did Satan acquire his authority over man?
3. In what way does man still show traces of his original position as God's under-ruler?
4. Show clearly why Christ did not have to conquer Satan for Himself.
5. What scripture shows that Satan never had any dominion over Christ?
6. Explain Hebrews 2:14.
7. What does Colossians 2:15 reveal?
8. What significance is there in the fact that God accepted the blood of Christ when He entered the Holy of Holies?
9. Explain Philippians 2:9-11.
10. Did you study carefully each scripture in the lesson?

Notes

Lesson 28
THE LORDSHIP OF CHRIST
(Continued)

WE ARE CONTINUING our study on the Lordship of Christ. In our last lesson we studied the fact that God had made Jesus "Lord." Acts 2:36, "Let all the house of Israel therefore know assuredly that God hath made both Lord and Christ this Jesus whom ye crucified."

He had died as the Lamb of God. He had been crucified in weakness. II Corinthians 13:4, "For He was crucified through weakness, yet He liveth through the power of God." Yet, when He arose, He arose as Lord.

In His death He was as a lamb that is led to the slaughter. By oppression and judgment He was taken away. Yet, He arose from the dead as a mighty victor. He had defeated Satan who had held the Lordship over man; He had conquered Satan before his own cohorts, his own servants, in the dark region of the damned; and there He had stood, in that dread place, the absolute victor and Master. He stands before the three worlds today: heaven, earth and hell, as the undisputed victor over man's ancient destroyer (Hebrews 2:14).

Is it any wonder that, fresh from such victories, He said to the disciples, "All authority has been given unto me in Heaven and in earth" (Matthew 28:18).

No! He arose as Lord, and today there is no authority in heaven, earth or hell that does not obey the authority of His Name (Philippians 2:9-10).

The Need of His Lordship

Man's personal need of the Lordship of Christ is today practically a lost truth. As a rule, the unsaved man is taught only his need of forgiveness of sins. In reality, the unsaved man needs a new Lord, a new Master.

The natural man lives in bondage to sin and rebellion toward God, because Satan is lord of his life.

Adam's crime was selling out to the lordship of Satan. Satan is lord in the realm of spiritual death. Hebrews 2:14, "Him that had the authority of death, that is the devil."

The human race was identified with Adam in his crime of high treason (Romans 5:12) and as a result of that identification, the human race came under the personal lordship of Satan over their lives.

Man lives in the realm of spiritual death because Satan is the lord of his life. Every spiritual, mental, physical, and material want of man centers in the lordship of Satan over his life.

All human suffering is the result of Satan's lordship over humanity. Human suffering may be caused by the cruelty and selfishness of others, by our own sins, by sickness, by circumstances, yet it may all be traced to the reign of Satan.

Therefore, man's difficulty centers in the need of a new Lord. Satan is a hard taskmaster. He is the one who destroys both soul and body in Hell (Matthew 10:28). Man needs a Love-Lord, a Love-Master.

The purpose of the previous lesson was to show that on legal ground the Son of God has dethroned Satan from his position as lord over man and god of this world. . . . Hebrews 2:14, 15, "That through death He might bring to nought him that had the authority of death, that is the devil; and might deliver all them who through fear of death were all their lifetime subject to bondage."

Another rendering from the Greek is that He "paralyzed him who held the dominion of death." The scripture is clear on the fact that this cruel lord of man was brought to nought. Every unsaved man and woman living in the bondage of spiritual death has a legal right to the Love-Lordship of Christ over his life.

The Lordship of Christ means a New Nature, a New Family, a New Father. Christ died and rose again that He might meet the need of man for a new Lord. Romans 14:9, "For to this end Christ died and lived again that He might be Lord of both the dead and the living."

What a message of joy, what glad tidings we have to bring to an unsaved world, the message of this new Lord for man.

Romans 10:12, "For the same Lord is rich unto all that call upon him." Every need of man may be met according to His riches in glory in Christ Jesus. As the scripture continues (verse 13): "Whosoever shall call upon the name of the Lord shall be saved." By a man's calling unto this new Lord, the power and authority of Satan, the old lord, will be broken over his life. But (verse 14), "How then shall they call on Him in whom they have not believed? And how shall they believe in Him of whom they have not heard? And how shall they hear without a preacher?" Let us be faithful in making known the Lordship of Christ.

Confessing His Lordship, the Way unto Salvation

Because man's need can only be met by the Lordship of Christ over his life, the confessing of that Lordship is the way unto salvation.

Redemption is all of grace. It is God's work, not man's. Ephesians 2:8-9, "For by grace have ye been saved through faith; and that not of yourselves, it is the gift of God. Not of works, that no man should glory."

Man's part is to confess the Lordship of Christ. This is the highest order of repentance. Repentance is not weeping or crying over sins committed in the past. A man may be sorry for the way in which he has lived; although the reign of sin is the result of Satan's lordship over his life.

Repentance is deeper than that. Repentance is to turn from Satan's rule, from following him, to the Lordship of Christ. Repentance is a public confession of the Lordship of Christ. It is confessing in the presence of men and demons that you are following a new Lord and taking Him into your life.

The moment that a man will invite Jesus in as Lord the authority of Satan over his life comes to nought, and he is delivered from bondage to him. To the man who knows his place in Christ, Satan is as nought, as though he did not exist (Hebrews 2:14).

When a man confesses the Lordship of Christ, he is delivered from the authority of Satan into the authority of Christ. Colossians 1:13, "Who delivered us out of the authority of darkness and translated us into the kingdom of the son of His love."

The following takes place in the life of a man when he confesses the Lordship of Christ. He is translated from the authority of darkness into the kingdom of our Lord Jesus Christ.

That means that spiritual death is eradicated from his spirit. Satan's bondage comes to an end. He receives the nature of God when he receives Christ (John 1:12). He becomes a son of God. A love-ruler is his now. He is in God's family and the kingdom of Christ.

Now we can see why confessing the Lordship of Christ is the way unto salvation. Thousands would have been saved years of suffering had they only known this. Confessing the Lordship of Christ is very simple. A man simply confesses, "I will take Jesus Christ as my Lord. I invite Him now into my life."

He gives this to us in Romans 10:9-10, "Because if thou shalt confess with thy mouth Jesus as Lord, and shalt believe in thy heart that God raised Him from the dead, thou shalt be saved, for with the heart man believeth unto righteousness, and with the mouth confession is made unto salvation."

"With the mouth confession is made unto salvation." God watches over His Word to perform it. When a man acts upon it by confessing the Lordship of Christ, God imparts to that one His own Life and Nature. His confession of the Lordship of Christ is the way to the New Birth, the way unto Salvation.

The Benefits of the Lordship of Christ

Just as every spiritual want of man centered in the lordship of Satan over his life, every spiritual blessing centers in the personal Lordship of Christ over a man's life.

Ephesians 1:3, "Blessed be the God and Father of our Lord Jesus Christ who has blessed us with every spiritual blessing in the Heavenly places in Christ."

The man who has taken Jesus as Lord is blessed with every spiritual blessing.

The real man is the spirit. Every impoverished condition of humanity was the result of spiritual death in man's spirit. Being blessed with every spiritual blessing means union with Deity, being brought back into the realm of Deity, the realm of Omnipotence. This results in every need of man being met, whether it be a mental, physical, or material need.

The Lordship of Christ over a man's life means that sin and disease are no longer issues. To the man who knows what the Lordship of Christ means, sin and disease are no longer problems at all.

The Lordship of Christ means freedom from the reign of sin. This Revelation which we have from God gives to us a very clear understanding of the sin problem, its origin, its reign over man, and its destruction.

The Word teaches us that sin entered the world through one man (Romans 5:12). The seventh chapter of Romans gives to us the hopeless cry of a spiritually-dead man for freedom from the bondage of sin. It is the experience of Paul before he was Born Again. His mind had been awakened by the law, but sin which dwelt in him made it utterly impossible for him to keep it (Romans 7:7-24).

Paul's testimony is that he was carnal, sold under sin, or a slave to sin (Romans 7:14).

Then a man appeared for the purpose of putting sin away. I John 3:5 (Weymouth), "And you know that He appeared in order to take away sins, and in Him there is no sin."

He, Himself, was without sin. He knew no sin (II Corinthians 5:21). He had never known its pangs, its reign. He had never known Paul's experience. But this one, Jesus Christ, became sin (II Corinthians 5:21), ". . . God made to become sin on our behalf."

Then He died to sin. Romans 6:10 (Weymouth), "Death no longer has any power over Him. For by the death which He died He became once for all dead in relation to sin." He put sin away. Hebrews 9:26, "Else must He often have suffered since the foundation of the world; but now once at the end of the ages hath He been manifested to put sin away by the sacrifice of Himself."

He put it away as though it had never been, and today in Him there is no sin (I John 3:5).

The Scripture continues in the sixth verse, "Whosoever abideth in Him sinneth not."

The Lordship of Christ means utter oneness with Him. It means a union so close that the oneness of the vine and the branch are used by the Holy Spirit to illustrate it.

To Christ, sin has no power. He is our Lord. It has no more power over us than over Him. To recognize fully the Lordship of Christ is to recognize that sin has no power over you.

A temptation to sin is a bluff of the adversary. Treat it as such. In His earthly ministry, Christ was not concerned with sin or its power over His life. He said, "The Prince of this world cometh and hath no part in me."

I John 3:8 (Weymouth), "The Son of God appeared for the purpose of undoing the works of the devil."

Christ has undone the works of Satan in the human heart. This means that sin has absolutely lost its power over the New Creation, for sin has its origination in Satan.

I John 3:8, "He that doeth sin is of the devil; for the devil sinneth from the beginning. To this end was the Son of God manifested that He might destroy the works of the devil."

If sin has its origination in Satan, and if Satan has been brought to nought, we can readily understand the fact that the works of Satan have been undone and have no power over the New Creation.

The following question may arise: What is sin to the New Creation?

Sin is anything that keeps us from walking in fellowship with the Father and the Master.

I John 1:5-10 reveals to us tnat that which hinders our walking in the light is sin. Walking in the light means "walking in the light of His Word."

Psalm 119:105, "Thy Word is a lamp unto my feet, and a light unto my path." The Word, our Light, reveals to us our place in Christ, our privileges and responsibilities. It reveals our place of victory in Christ.

Walking in the light of His Word is walking in our privileges and responsibilities. Sin, therefore, is anything that would keep us from taking our place. Sin is anything that causes the New Creation to walk in failure and weakness in the presence of the fact that Christ has been made our strength. Unbelief which keeps us from rest and quietness in Him is sin, for "Whatsoever is not of faith is sin" (Romans 14:23).

We have seen that sin, in whatever form it may appear, has no power over the New Creation. The Body of Christ must understand this, taking deliverance from the wiles of the adversary.

II Thessalonians 3:16, "Now the Lord of peace himself give you peace at all times in all ways." Christ is the only one who can give you peace.

QUESTIONS

1. Give a description of Satan's lordship over natural man.
2. What kind of a new lordship did man need?
3. Show why every man has a legal right to the Lordship of Christ.
4. Explain why confessing the Lordship of Christ is the way unto Salvation.
5. What personal experience does Paul give to us in the seventh chapter of Romans?
6. Explain clearly why sin is no longer an issue to the New Creation.
7. Show why disease has no power over the New Creation.
8. Why does the Lordship of Christ mean freedom from want?
9. Explain II Thessalonians 3:16.
10. Did you look up and study carefully every scripture reference in this lesson?

Notes

Lesson 29

THE LAW OF THE NEW CREATION

OUR LAST TWO LESSONS have been on the Lordship of Christ, who is the Head of the New Creation.

Colossians 1:18, "And He is the head of the body, the church; who is the beginning, the firstborn from the dead; that in all things He might have the preeminence."

We have seen that the Lordship of Christ, our head, over sin, disease, Satan and circumstances, means that we are as free from them as He is.

The Lordship of Christ means that sin and disease are no longer problems, no longer issues to the New Creation. There need be no more struggles with sin, no more battles with the Adversary, just an acting upon the Word of God.

As we study the history of the church, we find how little the great spiritual leaders have understood Redemption. For a period of one thousand years during the Dark Ages, the revelation of a Redemption in Christ independent of works was lost to the church. That dark period has had its influence upon the period from the Reformation to the present, so that it has been difficult for the church to see a complete Redemption.

By reading any book on the experience of famous Christians in the past, we can see how the sin and weakness problem was majored in their lives, and how little they understood Redemption.

The message of this Revelation of Redemption is that God is clearly showing us that the sin problem is settled. The book of Hebrews is His commentary upon this fact. He shows us that once and for all Christ put sin away and that there need be no more offering for sin. He is satisfied with His work in Christ.

Read and study carefully the following scriptures: Hebrews 9:12, 26; 10:10, 14, 18.

The church has struggled with the sin problem in the face of the fact that God declares in His Word that He has settled it and that there need be no more offering for sin, no more dealing with it.

God shows us that the New Creation is freed from even the consciousness of sin. Notice Hebrews 10:1-3, "For the law having a shadow of the good things to come, not the very image of the things, can never with the same sacrifices which they offer continually, make perfect them that draw nigh. Else would they not have ceased to be offered? Because the worshippers having been cleansed would have no more consciousness of sins."

Note that the Word declares that the sacrifices under the Old Covenant did not perfect the offerers.

He tells us that if they had, the worshippers would have been freed from the consciousness of sin.

Therefore, God was not satisfied (read the fifth and fourteenth verses of the same chapter) and sent His Son that He might do what the law and its sacrifices could not do, namely perfect those who offered them. He declares in the fourteenth verse, "For by one offering he hath perfected forever them that are sanctified." He has perfected the New Creation by a complete eternal Redemption.

Hebrews 9:12, "But through his own blood entered once for all into the holy place having obtained eternal redemption for us."

He has freed the New Creation from even the consciousness of sin.

Satan has made the church sin-conscious when it should have been love-conscious.

With its mind upon the sin problem, the church has missed the real issue. With a mind ruled by a sin-consciousness, the church has failed to have the mind of Christ.

The Love Issue

There is only one issue to the New Creation, and that is "Walking in Love." There is only one law that governs the New Creation, and that is the law of Love. There is one commandment given, the commandment of Love. John 13:34-35, "A new commandment I give unto you that ye love one another, even as I have loved you, that ye also love one another. By this shall all men know that ye are my disciples, if ye have love one for another."

The one problem that the New Creation confronts is given to us in Philippians 2:5-6, "Have this mind in you which was also in Christ Jesus, who, existing in the form of God, counted not the being on an equality with God a thing to be grasped, but emptied Himself, taking the form of a servant, being made in the likeness of man, and being found in fashion as a man, He humbled Himself and became obedient even unto death, yea, the death of the Cross."

He makes known to us here that He expects the New Creation to be of the same mind that Christ has. This reveals a complete Redemption. The Omnipotent God of the universe is saying, "I have so completely redeemed you from sin, weakness, disease, circumstances, and all the workings of the Adversary, that I expect you to be of the same mind as my Son. As a man thinketh in his heart, so is he."

He is saying, "I want you to think as My Son thinks. I want you to be like Him; to live as He would live if He were in your place, to act as He would act, to be what He would be." "Have this mind in you that was in Christ Jesus." This is the issue that the New Creation faces. The mind of Christ was the love attitude. We know what love is through the Revelation of His life.

I John 3:16, "Hereby we know love, because He laid down His life for us, and we ought to lay down our lives for the Brethren."

He existed in the form of God. All that God was, He was. He was the very image of His substance. Hebrews 1:3. He thought as God thought. He lived as God lived. He loved as God loved. He existed in the form of God.

He was so utterly one with God that He said to Philip, "He that hath seen me hath seen the Father" (John 14:9).

He is really saying, "Philip, during the three years that you have been with me you have seen the Father, the very substance of His nature. In my actions you have seen the Father's actions; in my words you have heard the Father's words; in me you have seen the Father, for we are one."

He existed in the form of God. All the word "God" means, He was. He lived on an absolute equality with Him. Our minds cannot grasp the meaning of the word "God," for our minds are the work of His mind and His hands;

but "the heavens declare the glory of God; and the firmament showeth His handiwork."

We study the Universe around us, conscious of the fact that it is His handiwork. The greatness of the Universe is beyond our comprehension. We cannot fathom the distance of stars that are quintillions of miles away. We know that the Creator of this handiwork is greater. We know that in the domain of the invisible atom there is manifested the same intelligent order that rules the Universe of stars. We know that the Creator is as intelligent as the intelligent order of Creation.

The Universe contains personal beings who think, feel, love, suffer, choose and determine. We know that the Creator of personal beings must be as personal.

The word "God" means that to us. All that it means, He is. He is a God of love, and love compelled Him to do the following: He emptied Himself of his glory. He took the form of a servant, He who was equal to God. He was found in the fashion and likeness of man. He exchanged the form of God for the form of a man.

He, the Creator, took the form of His own handiwork; He, the Creator, emptied and limited Himself to the extent that He lived and walked on His own Creation. He through whom this vast, limitless, measureless Universe had been created, took up His abode upon this small planet, our earth.

Then, He humbled Himself, becoming obedient unto death, yea, the death of the Cross. Then, He, who was as holy as God was, as untouched by sin as He, became sin.

II Corinthians 5:21. This Divine suffering caused by Christ's becoming sin is unique. It has no analogy. We cannot measure it by anything with which we are acquainted. The sin of Adam, the sin-nature that passed upon all men, all its horribleness, penetrates the heart of God, Himself.

Christ's Belief in Love

We ask why He did this, why this tremendous sacrifice by One so great. The answer is, the Son of God believed in love. God is love. Herein is His Love manifested.

Romans 5:6-8, "For while we were yet weak, in due season Christ died for the ungodly. For scarcely for a righteous man will one die; for peradventure for the good man some one would even dare to die. But God commendeth His own love toward us in that, while we were yet sinners, Christ died for us."

Romans 15:3, "For Christ also pleased not Himself, but, as it is written, the reproaches of them that reproached thee fell upon me."

The reproaches of man who had reproached God fell upon Him. The sins of man, who had sinned against God, fell upon Him. The judgment of man fell upon Him. The diseases, the weaknesses of man fell upon Him.

Herein is His love manifested. The son of God faced the problem of sin, its entrance into the world through Adam's crime of high treason, and its reign over the human race.

He knew that by the sacrifice of Himself that He could put it away. He knew He could suffer in man's stead. He knew that He could bring Satan to nought on behalf of man. He believed in love, and He obeyed the dictates of love. He knew love's reward. He knew the joy set before Him when love had triumphed. He knew the harvest that love would reap. He knew that love would conquer.

The Problem of the New Creation

Now, the problem, the issue, that the New Creation faces is the problem that Christ faced.

The man who has become a New Creation in Christ faces the need of spiritually-dead man. It is not given to him to die for them as did Christ, but his place is as essential as was Christ's. Unto the New Creation is given the message of Redemption to be given to humanity.

Study carefully II Corinthians 5:18-19, "But all things are of God, who reconciled us to himself through Christ, and gave unto us the ministry of reconciliation; to wit, that God was in Christ reconciling the world unto Himself, not reckoning unto them their trespasses, and having committed unto us the word of reconciliation, we are ambassadors therefore on behalf of Christ."

Christ's work was to provide the reconciliation between God and man. Colossians 1:20, "And through Him

237

to reconcile all things unto Himself, having made peace through the blood of His cross; through Him, I say, whether things upon the earth, or things in the Heavens."

Also verse 22, "Yet now hath He reconciled in the body of His flesh through death to present you holy and without blemish and unreprovable before Him."

Ephesians 2:11-22 also shows His reconciliation between God and man. God was in Christ reconciling the world to Himself; but He has committed unto us, the New Man in Christ, the message of Reconciliation."

Christ believed in Love and did His part. Seemingly Redemption has failed. How few have been reached with the message of reconciliation. Yet God has not failed; Christ has not failed. It is the Body of Christ that has failed to give the message of Redemption to humanity. If the Body of Christ had been of the same mind as Christ, the world's history would have been different.

Paul saw the real issue which the New Creation faces. He gives it to us in II Corinthians 5:13-14, "For whether we are beside ourselves it is unto God: whether we are of sober mind it is unto you. For the love of Christ constraineth us for we thus judge, that one died for all: therefore all died."

Paul believed in love to the extent that he was believed to be beside himself. Paul's answer was, "The love of Christ has taken hold of my heart. I realize that Christ's death was every man's death." The same love that caused Christ to die for man had constrained Paul's heart and was causing him to live for them.

The attitude of love is this, "I love them as though I had died for them."

Love will make us ambassadors that are as anxious to win men as though we had died to provide the reconciliation. Paul had caught the vision of love. The great Roman Empire was evangelized largely through his efforts. Paul believed in love, so into the pagan world he went as Christ's ambassador, fully conscious that his message would be an offense to the Jew, foolishness to the Greek, and a jest to the Romans.

Yet he knew that only the message of Reconciliation in Christ would meet man's need.

Love's testimony is the following: "I will most gladly spend and be spent for your souls" (II Corinthians 12:15).

God is saying, "I want you to love as my Son loved. You can, for we are one. My nature is yours; My love is yours." He is asking us to yield to the Lordship of His Love within us. Romans 5:5, "Because the love of God hath been shed abroad in our hearts through the Holy Spirit which was given unto us."

Ephesians 3:16-19 is ours, "That He would grant you according to the riches of His glory that ye may be strengthened with power through His spirit in the inward man: that Christ may dwell in your hearts through faith; to the end that ye, being rooted and grounded in love, may be strong to apprehend with all the saints what is the breadth and length and height and depth, and to know the love of Christ which passeth knowledge, and that ye may be filled unto all the fullness of God."

He fills us with His fullness that we might love as He loves. The attitude of love is given in Romans 15:1-3, "Now we that are strong ought to bear the infirmities of the weak, and not to please ourselves. Let each one please his neighbor for that which is good, unto edifying. For Christ also pleased not himself; but, as it is written, 'The reproaches of them that reproached thee fell upon me.'"

Love bears the weaknesses of the weak as though it were its own infirmity. Christ did not please Himself but took over the sins, disease, and judgment of others. Love doesn't criticize or condemn, but love will cause the New Creation in Christ to pray for the one ruled by sin as though he had been made sin for that one. Love will cause us to pray for the sick as though we were the ones who had borne their diseases and carried their pains. To love is to have the mind of Christ. The New Man in Christ, taking Christ's place, has a debt of love to pay to humanity. Romans 13:8, "Owe no man anything, save to love one another." This is the issue the New Creation faces, the debt of love we owe to humanity.

QUESTIONS

1. Why has the church failed to see a complete Redemption?

2. Give and explain several scriptures which show that God considers the sin problem settled.

3. Why has the church missed the real issue that the New Creation faces?

4. Give an explanation of Philippians 2:5-6.

5. What is the work committed to the Body of Christ?

6. What is the meaning of Paul's confession in II Corinthians 5:14?

7. What is love's attitude toward the lost, the sick?

8. How has God made it possible for us to love as Christ loved?

9. Give an explanation of Romans 13:8.

Lesson 30
THE LOVE LAW

IN OUR LAST LESSON we saw that the major issue which the New Creation faces was the Love issue. We shall now see why this is so.

God is Love. I John 4:8. The New Birth which makes a man a New Creation, is the reception of the nature of God. It is the receiving of this love nature. Therefore, the Holy Spirit gives us the following:

I John 4:7-9, "Beloved, let us love one another for Love is of God, and everyone that Loveth is Begotten of God and knoweth God. He that loveth not knoweth not God for God is Love."

The test of the New Birth is the Love Test.

I John 3:14, "We know that we have passed out of Death into Life because we love the brethren. He that loveth not abideth in Death."

These are searching statements of truth. He tells us that if a man loves he has been begotten of God and knows Him, and that if a man does not love, regardless of his religious profession, he is abiding in spiritual death, alienated from God.

If it were not for the understanding of the Greek word for love used here, these passages would be hard to understand; for we are familiar with a certain love that belongs to the man who has never been Born Again.

The word for love used here is "Agape." It seems that Jesus coined this word when He expressed the new law that was to govern the New Creation in the following words: "A New Commandment I give unto you, that ye love one another even as I have loved you, that ye also love one another. By this shall all men know that ye are my disciples if ye have love one for another."

He wanted to express something and there was no Greek word in current use available. He had brought to the world a new thing; something that had been lost to the world since the fall.

It was the Love of God that had been displaced by selfishness in the heart of man. There had been a verb used, but no noun, "Agape."

Man was to receive a new Nature which brought him into a new family and gave to him a new Father. They were to be a new people, a New Creation, and there must be a language to fit this new Kingdom and Family.

They were to be translated out of the kingdom of darkness into the kingdom of the Son of His Love, and in this new realm they must have a language befitting. They must have laws befitting, and so He says, "A new commandment I give unto you. . . . By this shall all men know that ye are my disciples if ye have 'Agape' one for another."

A new love would make known to the world that they had become children of a God of Love.

The disciples did not understand the meaning of this new word until Pentecost.

We catch a glimpse of it in Romans 5:5, "The Love of God is shed abroad in our hearts by the Holy Spirit."

What is this that is shed abroad? It is the Love of God. It is the manifestation of the nature of God within us.

Vegetable life in the peach tree manifests itself first in the leaf, then the blossom, then in the luscious ripened fruit.

The nature of God, Eternal Life, will manifest itself likewise in the Nature, Conduct, and Speech of the child of God.

When one is Born from Above, the Father's nature comes into his spirit. That nature is bound to manifest itself in Love. It is Divine Love which is radically different from our old human love, although it operates through the same faculties.

When the church was born on Pentecost, the phenomena of the Jews deliberately giving their property away and performing other acts as strange, were the first manifestations of this new kind of Love that had come to the earth.

Acts 4:32-35, "And the multitude of them that believed were of one heart and soul: and not one of them said that aught of the things which he possessed was his own; but they had all things common. And with great power gave the apostles their witness of the resurrection of the Lord Jesus: and great grace was upon them all, For neither was among them any that lacked: for as many as were

242

possessors of lands or houses sold them, laid them at the apostles' feet: and distribution was made unto each, according as anyone had need."

This was "Agape" manifesting itself in the lives of the New Creation.

The power of Pentecost was "Love."

We shall now contrast this love that springs from the nature of God, with the love of natural man.

"Agape" and "Phileo"

The common Greek word used in Jesus' day was "Phileo," which means "human love," as the love of a mother for her child, the love of a husband for his wife.

This was the highest type of love that man had ever known. There was no other word for a higher type of love than "Phileo." This common human love of ours is the most blessed asset of the human, and yet the most dangerous. This "Phileo" love is the goddess of the divorce court; it is the High Priestess of human suffering, the parent of most of our tears, sorrows, and heart agonies.

It turns to jealousy and murder at the slightest pretext. It is purely selfishness; it feeds only upon self-gratification.

Jesus brings a new kind of love, a love that seeketh not its own. This kind of love is the real religion of the heart nature of God.

Human love is the interpretation of the human; this new kind of love is the interpretation of God.

The old love springs from the natural heart; the new Love springs from the recreated heart. One is the manifestation of God in the New Man; the other, of natural man. Self is the center around which "Phileo" moves; "Agape" has a new center. This center is God at work through the lives of His children.

There can be no "Agape" manifestation today except through those who have become partakers of the Divine Nature. There is no such thing as a synthetic "Agape." It is the one thing which cannot be duplicated. It is the badge of Christianity. It is God's manifestation in the flesh. It is the heart of God throbbing through the human.

"Agape" is not only the law of the family of God, but it is also the life and joy of the Family.

It makes Christianity more beautiful than all the so-called religions of the earth. It makes the life of the saints the sweetest life and most fragrant of all the human race.

Its prayer under persecution is, "Father, forgive them, for they know not what they do."

It breathes the fragrance of forgiveness. It is bravery, clothed in humility. It is strength, clothed in gentleness. It makes the strong bear the burdens of the weak, the rich pay the bills of the poor; the cultured becomes the companion of the ignorant.

It is Christ manifest among men.

"Agape" Analyzed

It would be hard to define "Agape."

The Holy Spirit, through the Apostle Paul, has shown to us, however, its composition.

The thirteenth chapter of I Corinthians is heavenly. It is untouched by the human mind. It is God's own description of His Life at work through man.

Verse 1, "If I speak with the tongues of men and of angels, but have not 'Agape,' I am become as sounding brass or a clanging cymbal."

The linguistic gift is one of the most highly prized. If I understand all the languages of the earth, and if I am able to decipher the hieroglyphics on monuments reared by the forgotten nations, if I am able to understand the language of the angelic hosts, but have not "Agape," I am become as sounding brass or a clanging cymbal.

This strips Christianity of its verbal garment and leaves it standing naked. This gives the reason for the empty churches, the failure of the Sunday Schools to hold its army of young people, the failure of Christianity in business and social life.

Men have become mere sounding brass and clanging cymbals. This tells why the modern religious periodical goes begging for subscribers. . . . Sounding brass, clanging cymbals, empty words—words, words, words, ever words—only words, empty words.

Verse 2, "And if I have the gift of prophecy, and know all mysteries and knowledge, and if I have all faith so as to remove mountains but have not 'Agape,' I am nothing."

Here is another universal desire of man; the gift of prophecy, the ability to foretell the future events, to know the solution of the world's great problems: the division of the nations, the outcome of the strife between capital and labor, and the solution of the social problem.

If one had the ability to foretell the future, no building ever created would hold the people that would throng to hear him speak. No author has ever been paid per word the immense sum that this writer could demand and receive.

"He may possess this wonderful gift, yet if he does not possess 'Agape,'" God says, and His words drip with tenderness and tears, "he is nothing."

"And if one knows all mysteries and has all knowledge. . . ."

Now He is touching the heart of us all. How we have craved knowledge; how we have yearned to roll the curtain and look behind the scenes, and there read the revelation of the mysteries of nature that surround us.

How we have struggled for this mountain-moving faith, and yet one blow shatters our day-dreams, and cuts the tap root of our ambition.

What a blessing, it seems, that we could become to humanity with an understanding of all knowledge and of all mysteries, and a faith which would remove mountains.

Yet, God says that we would be nothing.

"And if I bestow all my goods to feed the poor, and give my body to be burned. . . ."

That means, if one were able to feed the poor of this generation, to rear libraries and hospitals in every city and town, and if one wears himself out in philanthropic endeavor, and yet does not have "Agape," it profits him nothing.

He has wasted his life. It is poured out like water on a sand pile.

What is this thing without which human endeavor, human learning, human achievements, are failures?

Oh, it is the new Love, the revelation of the heart of God that Jesus brought to the earth.

It is a revelation, but it is more; it is the Life of God outpoured in our heart, manifesting itself through our words and conduct. It is the pulsating of the very heart of God, manifesting itself in an atmosphere that comes from our spirit, blessing and comforting a needy world.

It is God's answer to the broken-hearted human being.

Paul tells us that " 'Agape' suffereth long and is kind."

"Phileo" may suffer, but it grows bitter under the burden.

" 'Agape' envieth not."

"Phileo" has always manifested itself in envy and jealousy.

" 'Agape' vaunteth not itself, is not puffed up."

"Phileo" has forever vaunted itself. Self is the center around which it moves. If you take selfishness from "Phileo," it would crumble and fall to the ground, for that is its strength.

" 'Agape' does not behave itself unseemly."

"Phileo" airs its grievances in the divorce court; it grows wildly jealous and often strikes down in cold blood the object of its affection.

" 'Agape' seeketh not its own."

The struggle of "Phileo" from its birth to its death is to get and hold its own. It becomes unhappy, miserly. It becomes dishonest and treacherous. Its motto is, "All things are fair in love and war." It believes in "doing the other fellow before he does you." It is a cruel despot, but it is the best this old human race had from the fall until Jesus came.

" 'Agape' taketh not account of evil."

"Phileo" is always discussing and feasting upon scandal.

" 'Agape' rejoiceth not in unrighteousness, but rejoiceth in the truth."

"Phileo" cannot understand this. It turns to hatred and revenge at the slightest provocation, and it always rejoices in the fall of its enemy. It cannot rejoice with the truth if the truth does not gratify itself.

" 'Agape' is not provoked."

"Phileo" is sensitive and difficult to handle. It is easily provoked, and tells us that it is very sensitive and must not be neglected. Sensitiveness is, and always has been, of the devil.

" 'Agape' beareth all things, believeth all things, hopeth all things, endureth all things."

"Agape" never goes bankrupt. "Phileo" squanders its fortune in youth in riotous living, and before it comes to manhood strength, it is in danger of being dashed upon the rocks of failure.

What is "Agape"?

John tells us that God is "Agape."

In other words, this new Love that Jesus brought to the world is the nature of the great Creator God which He intended should be the nature of man, and rule the animal kingdom.

But, with the fall, spiritual death took its place, and out of this awful nature of the Devil springs hatred, revenge, and unbelief. A spirit of restlessness grips all nature.

Man and beast today are dominated by this foreign, unnatural power, and yet the heart of the human and the heart of the animal are sobbing for "Agape," when the strong will no longer feed upon the weaker, when the poor will no longer be exploited by the rich, and God shall rule over all.

"Agape" is the new Law of the family of God, the New Creations.

QUESTIONS

1. Why is the test of the New Birth the love-test?
2. Give a definition of "Phileo," of "Agape."
3. When did the disciples first know the meaning of "Agape"?
4. Write an exposition of the thirteenth chapter of First Corinthians.

Notes

Lesson 31
THE HOLY SPIRIT

IN THE OLD COVENANT, God had manifested Himself to Israel as one God. This was a startling revelation to man at a time when he was surrounded by a sea of polytheism.

Then, after many centuries, when God came to earth in the person of His Son, He was presented as Three in One.

As we study the life of Christ, we are conscious of the Three who are One.

At the beginning of His public life, at His Baptism, the voice of the Father spoke out of the Heavens, "This is my beloved Son," and the Spirit descended visibly upon Him in the form of a dove (Matt. 3:16-17). Here a three-fold revelation of God is given to man on the level of his physical senses.

In Christ's teaching, preaching, and private conversation, He constantly spoke of His Father and Himself as two distinct persons, and yet declared equally.

John 10:30, "I and my Father are One." Again He said, "He who has seen me hath seen the Father."

The Trinity Revealed

In His teachings, a Third is brought in as being God also. In His last and longest recorded talk with His disciples in the upper room, the evening before His crucifixion, Christ said, "The Holy Spirit, whom the Father will send in my name, He shall teach you all things and bring to your remembrance all that I said unto you" (John 14:26).

A major part of Christ's last talk with the disciples dealt with the Holy Spirit who was to come to take His place. This message is recorded in the fourteenth and sixteenth chapters of the Gospel of John.

Everything in the description in the Bible of the Three called Father, Son, and Holy Spirit, presents definitely and absolutely no more and no less than Three Persons in the Godhead.

It is what Wood terms in the "Secret of the Universe," an absolute Threeness and an absolute Oneness.

In an absolute Threeness, each one is distinct from the other two; no one of the three could possibly be either of the other two; and no two of the three can exist without the third.

God is manifest as an absolute Threeness; yet, He is also an absolute Oneness. The Three are absolutely One. Each One is represented as God. That does not mean that each one is a part of God, but each one is God. Each one is the Whole of God. Personality is not divisible. God cannot be divided.

God is Three in One. Each One of the Three is God, and each One is the Whole of God.

The Three are represented as Father, Son, and Holy Spirit; Three modes of Beings which God is. It is not primarily three ways in which God acts, but Three modes of Being.

The Word makes clear to us that the Father is first; the Son is second; and the Holy Spirit is third. It does not mean that One is first in Deity, for all are God. It does not mean that One is Greater, for all are Infinite. It does not mean that One is first in time, for all are eternal. It can only mean that the Father is first, the Son is second, and the Spirit is third in logical order.

The Scripture represents the Father as the Source. The eternal Son is begotten of the Father, and the eternal Spirit proceeds from the Father through the Son.

John 14:26, "The Comforter, even the Holy Spirit whom the Father will send you in My Name."

God works through the Son. In Him and through Him He creates.

Colossians 1:16, "For in Him were all things created, in the Heavens and upon the earth, things visible, and things invisible, whether thrones or dominions, or principalities or powers: all things have been created through Him and unto Him."

Christ Works Now Among Men Through the Spirit

The Spirit, like the Father, is unseen. His chief work is to reveal the Son, and in the Son He reveals the Father. Therefore, His ministry, although unseen, is to reveal the fullness of the Godhead to man and through man.

We are living in what is termed the dispensation of the Holy Spirit. It is the Holy Spirit who has made the

Father and the Son so real to us.

Therefore, a knowledge of the Holy Spirit is essential to us. We want to know His Nature, His ministry in us and through us.

Need of a Definite Study of the Holy Spirit

There is today a real need for the definite study of the person and ministry of the Holy Spirit. A small portion of attention has been given to the present day work of the Holy Spirit in comparison to that which has been given to the earthly life of Christ.

A. J. Gordon, in his book entitled, "The Ministry of the Holy Spirit," asks, "Why not employ the same method in writing about the Third person of the Trinity as is employed in considering the Second person."

In his book he follows that method and we wish to use this method here in our study of the Holy Spirit.

Many stories of the life of Christ have been written, beginning with His Incarnation and ending with His Ascension from Mount Olivet.

The Savior lived before His Incarnation and has continued His ministry since the time of His Ascension to the Father; yet it gives to us a definiteness of impression to distinguish His visible life from His invisible.

So also, as we study the Person and ministry of the Holy Spirit, we find it advantageous to separate His special present-day ministry on this earth from His ministry before and after.

That ministry began on the Day of Pentecost and shall continue until the Second Coming of Christ.

When Christ came to the earth as a man, He had a ministry to fulfill, and when He had accomplished it He returned unto the Father. His ministry had a time limit. So also, in His appointed time, the Holy Spirit came into the world, having a certain definite mission to fulfill.

This ministry is being carried on now in us and through us, and shall continue until completed, when He in His appointed time shall ascend into Heaven.

Reality of the Holy Spirit's Ministry

The Advent of the Holy Spirit into the world, and His appointed ministry here is just as real and definite as was the Incarnation and earthly ministry of Christ.

It has been vague and mysterious to us because there has not been a revelation of the Holy Spirit to the physical senses of man as there was of Christ.

Christ's ministry necessitated His becoming man in order to legally take man's place. Therefore, He was revealed to the physical senses of man.

John said, "That which we have heard, that which we have seen with our eyes, that which we beheld and our hands handled concerning the Word of Life" (I John 1:1-2).

Christ as a man could be seen and touched by man; therefore, His ministry has been more real to us than the ministry and Person of the Holy Spirit, who cannot be contacted through the physical senses. We may form a mental picture of Christ, while we cannot of the Holy Spirit.

The purpose of the Holy Spirit's ministry upon the earth is not the same as that of Christ's earthly ministry.

Christ came to pay, as man's substitute, the penalty of Adam's high treason. That demanded that He identify Himself with man.

Therefore, He has been revealed to us as a man, in a body like ours. Christ's earthly ministry was local. He could be in only one place on earth at one time.

Now He has His position as Mediator between God and man.

The Holy Spirit could not come in a human body as Christ came. His ministry could not be fulfilled in that manner. His ministry could not be localized. He came to impart the nature of God to the spirit of man.

He came not in a human body, but to indwell the bodies of those who had become New Creations in Christ.

Yet His coming was as positive, as definite as the coming of Christ in the Incarnation.

He, the Third Person of the Godhead, is actually here upon earth, working in and through the Body of Christ.

The Coming of the Holy Spirit Foretold by the Master

Christ's coming to earth was foretold by prophets and angels.

Christ, Himself, foretold the advent of the Holy Spirit into the world in His last discourses to His disciples. He foretold the coming of the One who was co-equal with Himself, who should take His place.

Read John 14:16-20; 15:26-27; 16:1-16; and Acts 1:4-5.

Do not only read, but also carefully study and meditate upon these scriptures.

The Holy Spirit did not come on this Divine Mission until the Day of Pentecost. He had been the Divine agent in Creation.

In the creation of the physical world, He had imparted life, form, and power of development to dead and formless matter.

Genesis 1:2, "And the earth was waste and void; and darkness was upon the face of the deep; and the Spirit of God moved upon the face of the waters."

He had illumined and inspired the prophets of the Old Covenant.

I Peter 1:10-12, "Concerning which salvation the prophets sought and searched diligently, who prophesied of the grace that should come unto you, searching what manner of time the Spirit of God which was in them did point unto when it testified beforehand the sufferings of Christ and the glory which should follow. To whom it was revealed that not unto themselves but unto you did they minister these things which now have been announced unto you through them that preached the Gospel by the Holy Spirit sent forth from heaven; which things angels desire to look into."

II Peter 1:21, "For no prophecy ever came by will of man, but men spake from God, being moved by the Holy Spirit."

He had descended upon Christ in the form of a dove at His baptism (Mark 1:10) and anointed Him for His earthly ministry.

Luke 4:1, "And Jesus, full of the Holy Spirit, returned from Jordan and was led by the Spirit into the wilderness"; and Luke 4:14, "And Jesus returned in the power of the Spirit into Galilee."

Why the Holy Spirit Had Not Been Given

Now the Holy Spirit had not yet been given. He had not yet come in His real ministry upon earth. Notice carefully John 7:39, "But this spake He of the Spirit which they that believed on Him were to receive, for . . . the Spirit was not yet given, because Jesus was not yet glorified."

Then we note that the Holy Spirit was not yet given because Jesus had not been glorified.

The Holy Spirit could not come until Christ had been glorified. Christ had to die for man's offenses, rise when man had been declared righteous (Romans 4:25), and enter into the Holy of Holies with His own blood, obtaining eternal redemption for man (Hebrews 9:12).

Christ came that man might have Life (John 10:10).

The object of His death and resurrection was to free man from Satan's dominion (Hebrews 2:14) and make it possible for him to receive the life of God (John 1:12).

The Holy Spirit came to impart the nature of God to the spirit of man in the New Birth (John 3:3-8) and then to fill this New Creature (II Corinthians 5:17) with the fullness of God (Ephesians 3:19).

Man could not receive the nature of God until the Father had accepted the blood of Christ. When Christ entered the Holy of Holies, He sat down at the right hand of God (Hebrews 10:12; 9:11-12).

He had put sin away (Hebrews 9:26). The acceptance of the blood of Christ by the Father signified that man's redemption from Satan's authority was complete. Man now had a legal right to receive the nature of God. The blood of Christ became the seal of man's redemption.

Christ became the Mediator between God and man (I Timothy 2:5). Man, a child of Satan, now had a right to approach God through his mediator and receive the life of God.

And now the Holy Spirit could be given. Jesus had been glorified; man's redemption was complete.

No man was Born Again before the Day of Pentecost. The disciples had not become sons of God. They had been called "friends" by Christ (John 15:15).

They were under the Old Covenant. They did not understand the death or resurrection of Christ. They were expecting Him to set up an earthly kingdom even after His Resurrection (Acts 1:6).

The Holy Spirit was not given until Pentecost to reveal these truths and impart God's Nature to man.

The Scripture that shows clearly that they had not been Born Again is Acts 11:17. The Greek reads, "When we first believed."

It is their own testimony to the fact that they had never believed upon Christ, as one believes in order to be Born Again, until the Day of Pentecost.

QUESTIONS

1. In what incident in the New Testament is the Trinity revealed to the physical senses of man?
2. Explain what is meant by the terms: "Absolute Oneness" and "Absolute Threeness."
3. Compare the earthly ministry of Christ with that of the Holy Spirit in regard to time limit.
4. Why has the earthly ministry of the Holy Spirit been more vague and mysterious to us than the earthly ministry of Christ?
5. Why was it that the Holy Spirit could not come in human body as Christ did?
6. In what Scriptures do we have the advent of the Holy Spirit foretold?
7. What was the work of the Holy Spirit before His advent on the Day of Pentecost?
8. Why was it that the Holy Spirit could not come until Christ had been glorified?
9. Why was it that the disciples could not be Born Again before the Day of Pentecost?

Notes

Lesson 32
THE HOLY SPIRIT (Continued)
What Is the Baptism of the Holy Spirit?

THE CHURCH, as a whole, has not understood clearly that the Disciples were not Born Again until the Day of Pentecost. This has led to erroneous teaching concerning the Baptism of the Holy Spirit.

Let us now study carefully all that the Scripture teaches about being baptized with the Holy Spirit.

It is first mentioned by John.

He said, "I indeed baptize you with water unto repentance: but he that cometh after me is mightier than I, whose shoes I am not worthy to bear: he shall baptize you with the Holy Spirit and with fire" (Matthew 3:11).

This statement made by John is also recorded in Mark 1:8 and Luke 3:16.

After His Resurrection Christ refers to this promise made by John, "Commanding them not to depart from Jerusalem but to wait for the promise from the Father, which saith he, ye have heard of me. For John truly baptized with water; but ye shall be baptized with the Holy Spirit not many days hence" (Acts 1:5).

Then the term "baptize" is also used in Acts 11:16 by Peter when he is speaking of the fact that the Holy Spirit came upon the Gentiles in exactly the same manner as He did upon the Jews on the Day of Pentecost.

The word "baptize" is an untranslated Greek word meaning to "immerse." John had merely immersed them in water, but there was to come an immersion in the Holy Spirit.

Then Paul speaks of the baptism with the Holy Spirit in I Corinthians 12:13, "For by one spirit are we all baptized into one body."

Galatians 3:27, "For as many of you as have been baptized into Christ have put on Christ."

These are the only places in the Scriptures where the term "to baptize" or "to be baptized" with the Holy Spirit is used.

Let us now examine them carefully in order to learn the Scriptural meaning of the term.

257

John said, "He shall baptize you with the Holy Spirit."

Christ came to bring the nature of God to man. John 10:10. John 1:12, "But as many as received Him to them gave He the right to become the sons of God, even to them that believe on His Name, which were born, not of blood, nor of the will of the flesh, nor of the will of man, but of God."

Is this New Birth the thing to which John is referring?

Now, let us carefully examine this Scripture to see.

John is comparing his ministry with that of Christ. The baptism that he, himself, brings is physical. It is external. It does not touch the spirit, the real man. It is just a type of the work that Jesus is to do within the spirit of man.

Of what is baptism in water a type?

What spiritual significance is given to it in the Scripture?

It is a type of the New Birth. This fact is revealed to us in Romans 6:1-4. Paul is using their baptism in water to illustrate what took place in their lives by the New Birth.

Romans 6:3, "Or are ye ignorant that all we who were baptized into Christ Jesus were baptized into His death that like as Christ was raised from the dead through the glory of the Father so we also might walk in newness of life."

Being buried with Christ in water is typical of our burial with Christ in His death whereby the old man was crucified and put off.

Being raised out of the water is typical of our resurrection with Christ out of Spiritual Death into Eternal Life, that we might walk in newness of Life.

This is what takes place in the New Birth. Spiritual Death is eradicated from the Spirit, and Eternal Life, the nature of God, is imparted to man, and then he walks in the newness of that life.

After we have been Born Again we are baptized in water as a witness of what has taken place in the spirit.

So John is saying, "My baptism is external, physical; it is just a type of what He shall do in the spirit of man. I baptize the physical body with water, but He shall immerse the spirit with the Holy Spirit, and out of that

258

immersion shall come the New Birth, and man shall begin a new life."

It was for this New Birth that Christ was to bring to spiritually-dead man that the Disciples were told to tarry in Jerusalem (Acts 1:5).

We remember from our last lesson that the Holy Spirit could not be given, could not come to make man a child of God, until Christ had been glorified.

Let us now examine the Scripture in I Corinthians 12:13 to see whether or not it also refers to the New Birth.

"For by one spirit are we all baptized into one body."

When does a man become a member of the Body of Christ? When he is Born Again.

Again, we see that the term "baptism" refers to the New Birth. The Baptism into the Body of Christ is the birth into the Body of Christ.

Galatians 3:27, "For as many of you as have been baptized into Christ have put on Christ."

This refers to the New Birth. "For if any man have not the spirit of Christ, he is none of His" (Romans 8:9).

The Baptism with the Holy Spirit has been taught as a second experience because, as before mentioned, the church as a whole has not realized that no man could be born out of death into Life until Christ was.

Man had to be legally redeemed from Satan's authority before God could impart His Life to him.

Christ was the firstborn from the dead (Colossians 1:18). He was the firstborn of many brethren (Romans 8:29).

Therefore they looked upon the baptism that was to occur as the second experience, while in reality it was the first.

Let us now see what actually took place on the Day of Pentecost.

What Took Place upon the Day of Pentecost?

The Disciples were gathered in the upper room . . . Acts 2:1-2, "And when the Day of Pentecost was fully come they were all with one accord in one place. And suddenly there came a sound from heaven as of a rushing, mighty wind, and it filled all the house where they were sitting."

The Holy Spirit entered the world for His special ministry. It was as definite a coming as was the birth of Christ as a babe in Bethlehem.

He filled the room where they were sitting. What happened?

The room was filled with the Holy Spirit, and they were immersed, or baptized, with the Holy Spirit.

The Baptism in the Holy Spirit is reversed from baptism in water in a certain sense.

In water baptism there is a plunging down into the water.

In the Spirit baptism there is a "coming down upon" of the Holy Spirit.

The result is the same, however—immersion.

There are several phrases used in reference to Pentecost: "coming upon," "pour out," "fallen upon," "fell upon," "poured forth," "fell on them," "came upon."

The result was immersion in the Holy Spirit, out of which came the New Birth.

The Body of Christ was born on that memorable day.

As the manger had been the cradle of the Son of God, so also the upper room became the cradle of the mystical Body of Christ.

One hundred and twenty became New Creations in Christ on that day.

Then they were filled with the Holy Spirit. This is the second experience: to be filled with the Holy Spirit, to be indwelt by Him.

There is a vast difference between being baptized, immersed, in the Holy Spirit, and being filled with the Holy Spirit.

We may illustrate it by the following: if a tank were filled with water, and a man immersed in the water, he would be in the water, but the water wouldn't be in him.

After those in the upper room had been born out of death into Eternal Life by the Spirit, they were filled with Him.

Acts 2:4, "And they were all filled with the Holy Spirit and began to speak with other tongues as the Spirit gave them utterance."

They could not be filled with Him until they had been born again.

Christ said that the world (or spiritually-dead man) could not receive Him. John 14:17, "Even the Spirit of Truth: whom the world cannot receive."

He can only make His home in the bodies of those who have been Born Again.

Our conclusion is this: The term "baptism in the Holy Spirit" literally and scripturally refers to the New Birth, and the second experience is to receive, or to be filled with the Holy Spirit so that our bodies can be indwelt by Him, and become His Temple.

I Corinthians 3:16, "Know ye not that ye are a temple of God, and that the Spirit of God dwelleth in you?"

It is clear that the early church did not use the term "baptism" in referring to the second experience, or filling of the Spirit.

For, after the Day of Pentecost, the term is used only once. It is evident from Peter's words that they had not used the term as it is being used now by many groups. For, when relating what happened when the Gentiles first received the Gospel, he tells that the same thing that took place when they first believed upon Christ occurred then, and he remembered or recalled the words of John, that Christ should baptize with the Holy Spirit.

Just as the Holy Spirit came upon the Jews, making them New Creations in Christ and filling them with Himself, He came also upon the Gentiles when they first received Christ.

We note here that the Gentiles did not have to tarry as the Jews had had to before the Day of Pentecost; for the Holy Spirit had come, and He "fell upon them" as Peter was speaking to them.

How Does One Receive the Holy Spirit?

The Scriptures clearly teach that the receiving of the Holy Spirit occurs separately and after the New Birth.

Peter said, "Repent ye and be baptized everyone of you in the Name of Jesus unto the remission of sins, and ye shall receive the gift of the Holy Spirit" (Acts 2:38).

261

The remission of sins signifies the New Birth, and then comes the receiving of the Gift of the Holy Spirit.

Christ said, "If ye then being evil, know how to give good gifts unto your children, how much more shall the Heavenly Father give the Holy Spirit to them that ask Him." The Heavenly Father gives the Holy Spirit to His children who ask for Him.

After the city of Samaria had received Christ through the preaching of Philip, John and Peter came down and laid hands upon them that they might receive the Holy Spirit (Acts 8:14-16).

The Holy Spirit is received by Faith.

Galatians 3:2, "This only would I learn from you, received ye the Holy Spirit by the works of the law or by the hearing of faith?"

Also Galatians 3:14, "That upon the Gentiles might come the blessing of Abraham in Christ Jesus; that we might receive the promise of the Holy Spirit through faith."

What is the evidence of the Holy Spirit's coming in?

The evidence is the Word of God alone. Many teach that the evidence is the speaking in tongues, yet this teaching is not supported by the Word of God.

The book of Acts is not a doctrinal, but a historical book. It relates that upon several occasions, during a period of thirty-five years, certain ones spoke in tongues when they were filled with the Holy Spirit.

Acts 2:4, the Day of Pentecost.

Acts 19:6, when the Gentiles received Christ at Ephesus.

Nowhere is it taught that we should look upon tongues as the evidence of the fact that the Holy Spirit has filled us.

The speaking in tongues is mentioned in several other places in the Scripture.

Paul speaks of it in I Corinthians 14 when writing to the church at Corinth to reprove them for their abuse of tongues.

I Corinthians 12:30 shows clearly that all do not speak in tongues; and I Corinthians 14:22 shows that tongues is not a sign for the believer but for the unbeliever.

Not only does the Scripture fail to teach that tongues is the evidence of the indwelling of the Holy Spirit, but to make tongues the evidence of the Holy Spirit's indwelling would be contrary to the law of God's dealing with the New Creation.

The speaking in tongues is a physical manifestation. It is an evidence to the senses of man. God has nowhere put a premium upon sense evidence or ever permitted us to trust it. He is a Faith God. The law of His dealings with man and with the New Creation is the Faith law.

We are Born Again through faith (Ephesians 2:8).

We live by faith (Romans 1:17).

Everything we receive in prayer we receive by faith.

God has not changed the law of His dealing with us in the incoming of the Spirit, for He tells us in Galatians 3:2 that we receive the Spirit by faith also. What is faith, but acting upon the Word without the evidence of the physical senses? A man is Born Again when he says, "I have Eternal Life because the Word declares it."

A man is healed when he says, "I am healed because the Word declares that 'by His stripes ye are healed.' "

In the case of a financial need, we receive the answer when we say, "The need is met because the Word declares that 'My God shall supply every need of yours according to His riches in glory in Jesus Christ.' "

So we also receive the Holy Spirit when we say, "I have the Holy Spirit because I have asked the Father for Him, and He has promised to give the Holy Spirit to them that ask Him."

QUESTIONS

1. In what Scriptures do we find the Baptism of the Holy Spirit mentioned?
2. What does the word "baptize" mean in the Greek?
3. Show why baptism in water is a type of the New Birth.
4. What did John mean when he said that Christ would baptize man in the Holy Spirit?
5. Explain I Corinthians 12:13.
6. What happened to those in the upper room when it was filled with the Holy Spirit?

7. What Scriptures show that the receiving of the Holy Spirit is separate from and follows the New Birth?
8. How does one receive the Holy Spirit?
9. Show why God has not put physical evidence upon the receiving of the Holy Spirit.
10. Have you received the Holy Spirit?

Lesson 33
THE HOLY SPIRIT (Continued)

IN OUR LAST TWO LESSONS on the Holy Spirit we have seen that the Holy Spirit, the Third Person of the Godhead, entered this world on the Day of Pentecost to fulfill a definite, appointed mission.

He is in the world today in as much reality as was Christ during His earthly ministry, although He cannot be contacted by the physical senses of men.

We have seen why it was that He could not come before the Day of Pentecost and what took place in the Upper Room upon that day.

In our concluding lesson upon this study of the Holy Spirit we shall study further His ministry today.

Ministry of the Holy Spirit to the World

Christ taught His disciples that another Comforter would come to take His place. If the Holy Spirit takes the place of Christ, we know that He is doing what Christ would do were He here.

If Christ were here in a human body as He was before His Ascension, His ministry would be to reveal to man what He had wrought for him by His death and Resurrection.

His aim would be to show every man that He had become sin on his behalf that he might become righteous, and to make every man see the tragedy in rejecting that substitutionary sacrifice.

So the Holy Spirit today is making real to human hearts the work of the Son of God. The Spirit's teachings and communications are not His own; they are Christ's (John 16:13-14).

Christ gave to us the threefold method of the Holy Spirit in making His work real to the world in John 16:7-11.

It was expedient for Christ to go to the Father and the Holy Spirit to take His place, for Christ's ministry to man through a human body would have been localized.

The Holy Spirit, however, can reach the world.

It is necessary that we understand how the Holy Spirit deals with an unsaved man so that we can let Him work freely through us.

As we study His method of presenting the work of Christ to them, we shall see how wrong has been most of our evangelistic preaching.

John 16:8-11. Note: The Holy Spirit convicts the world of judgment because the prince of this world has been judged. What has the judgment of Satan to do with man? Everything, because man has become his child, and Satan's eternal home has become man's eternal home.

After the Holy Spirit shows a man that he is a child of Satan, not only now but for eternity, He convicts him of righteousness, because Christ has gone to the Father.

He shows man that he has a Mediator before God, One who, with His own blood, after providing an eternal Redemption for man, entered Heaven on his behalf.

He shows man that he may become the righteousness of God, and that he possesses the legal right to become God's child.

Then, He convicts man of the sin of rejecting Christ, the only way of Redemption from Satan's authority—the sin of choosing to remain a child of Satan after he has learned that he may become a child of God.

How out of harmony with the Holy Spirit's method has been our preaching. We have not shown man that he was a child of Satan, nor have we shown to him his legal rights to righteousness and the nature of God.

We have preached him under condemnation because of the sins he had committed. God does not condemn a man because of what he does, but because of what he is, and convicts him of only one sin, the sin of rejecting Christ, the choosing to remain a child of Satan.

The Holy Spirit works through the Word. . . . It is His Sword (Ephesians 6:17).

It is through the Word, God's Revelation to man, that the Holy Spirit shows an unsaved man his need of Christ. We are the instruments that the Holy Spirit uses, for we have had committed unto us the Word of reconciliation (II Corinthians 5:18-19).

If we do not know how to rightly divide the Word, and intelligently present it to an unsaved man, we cripple the ministry of the Holy Spirit.

266

After the Holy Spirit has convicted one of his need of Christ, if that one believes upon Christ, the Holy Spirit imparts to that one the nature of God (John 1:12).

Christ said, "I am come that they may have life, and have it abundantly."

Christ came to make it possible for man to actually receive the nature of God, Eternal Life (I John 5:11-13).

The man who receives Christ receives this nature of God and actually becomes His child. The blessed, faithful Holy Spirit is the Mediator through whom this life is transmitted.

Christ said, "Except one be born of water and of the Spirit, he cannot enter the Kingdom of God. That which is born of flesh is flesh, and that which is born of spirit is spirit. Marvel not that I said unto you ye must be born from above. The wind bloweth where it will and thou hearest the sound thereof, but knowest not whence it cometh, and whither it goeth, so is everyone that is born of the *spirit*."

The New Birth is a hidden action, yet the greatest of all miracles.

The Holy Spirit overshadows the one who believes on Christ and imparts to that one the life of God, and he becomes a New Creation in Christ (II Corinthians 5:17).

John 1:13, "Who were born not of blood, nor of the will of the flesh, but of God."

We see that it is the Holy Spirit who convicts natural man of his need of Christ and then imparts the nature of God to his spirit when he accepts Christ.

Then the Holy Spirit, if intelligently invited, indwells the one whom He has made a New Creation in Christ. The body of the child of God becomes His temple.

During this period of the Holy Spirit's residence upon the earth, His home and place of abode is the body of Christ.

Just as Christ's physical body was the temple of God while He was here upon earth, His body, the Church, is the temple of the Holy Spirit during His ministry here.

Let us note the comparison. A literal translation of John 1:14 is, "The Word was made flesh and 'tabernacled' among us."

"Tabernacled" is the word used in the Scripture for the place where God dwells among men. God's dwelling place is a temple.

Then, when God was tabernacled in Christ, Christ's body became His temple. Christ, when speaking to the Jews, called His body a Temple. He said that if they would destroy His body, this Temple of God, that He would raise it up again.

When God was tabernacled among men, the Shekinah glory rested above the Mercy Seat.

So also when God was tabernacled among men in Christ, they beheld His glory, "the glory as of the only begotten of the Father, full of Grace and Truth."

When God was Tabernacled among us in Christ it was God's coming into union with perfect and sinless humanity; for Christ had not partaken of spiritual death, or come under its influence.

So also now when the Holy Spirit becomes Tabernacled in the Body of Christ, it is God's coming into union with the New Creations who have been delivered completely from Spiritual Death and Satan's authority.

The new man is created in "Righteousness and Holiness of Truth," ready to become the Temple of God.

Ephesians 2:21-22, "In whom each several building fitly framed together groweth into a Holy Temple in the Lord; in whom ye are builded together for a habitation of God in the Spirit."

I Corinthians 6:19, "Or know ye not that your body is a Temple of the Holy Spirit which is in you, which ye have from God, and ye are not your own."

As with Christ the Head, God has become incarnated in the Church.

Because of the Indwelling of God in Christ, He could say, "He who hath seen me hath seen the Father."

For the first time, God was actually revealed to man. No man had beheld God at any time, but in Christ He was made known to man.

When Christ left the world to take His place at the Father's right hand where He would have no more personal contact with man, He sent the Holy Spirit to become incarnated in His mystical body, the Church, that the revelation of God to man might continue.

It is the desire of the Father that the body of Christ through the Holy Spirit be filled with the fullness of God.

Ephesians 3:19, "That ye may be filled unto all the fullness of God."

Ephesians 5:18. In fact we are commanded to be filled with the Holy Spirit that He might be revealed to the world.

Christ has no contact with the world today except through His Body. He cannot work independently of it.

If our lives are not filled with the Holy Spirit so that He can work freely through us, we tie the hands of Deity.

This is the dispensation of the Holy Spirit. It is through Him that the Father and Son are working, and He works in and through the body of Christ. There cannot be a true manifestation of Christ to the world if His body is not indwelt with the Holy Spirit.

In connection with this thought there is a serious lesson found for us in I John 4:12, "No man hath beheld God at any time; if we love one another, God abideth in us and His love is perfected in us."

If God abides in us through the Holy Spirit, His love is perfected in us.

The word "perfect" means "complete." The thought is that if God dwells in us, that His love can be completed through our lives.

The implication is that His life cannot be made complete except as it finds expression through us. There is something lacking in it except as it works through our lives.

This is true. God's grace has abounded toward man in Christ. John 1:16, "For of His fullness have we all received, and grace upon grace."

Grace is love at work. God's love has wrought a complete Redemption for man. By His grace, Christ has tasted death for every man. He has borne the diseases and pains of all humanity.

Yet, the word of reconciliation which will bring to man the Redemption which is in Christ can only be given through the Body of Christ. God has reconciled all humanity

269

to Himself through Christ and has given the message of reconciliation to the Body of Christ (II Corinthians 5:18-21).

If the Body of Christ is not, under the direction of and through the Holy Spirit, taking its place in the world, God's love cannot be expressed.

No man hath beheld God at any time, but if He can indwell the Body of Christ as He did Christ, His love can find expression and reach humanity.

His message to us is, "I will dwell in them and walk in them" (II Corinthians 6:16). If we let Him, then the world can behold His glory today and behold the works of His love as they did when God "tabernacled" among men in Christ.

The Holy Spirit, the Revealer of Christ

When the Holy Spirit began His ministry on the day of Pentecost, He began it under a new name. Christ had called Him the "Paraclete." It is a Greek word derived from the verb meaning "to call to one's aid."

The sorrow that had come to their hearts through the death of Christ had been turned into joy at His Resurrection.

However, there was to come a longer separation, His going to take His place at the Father's right hand.

The Third Person of the Trinity is the One called to their aid. He came to fill the vacant place of their Master.

What great expectations must have arisen in their hearts. They had been thrilled by the coming of the Son of God to earth; now another, on the same plane as the Lord, Himself, is to come to abide with them forever.

John 14:16, "And I will pray the Father, and He shall give you another Comforter, that He may be with you forever."

Christ is to come to them in the Holy Spirit.

John 14:18, "I will not leave you orphans: I come unto you."

The Paraclete is to take the things that are Christ's and reveal them to man. John 16:13-14, "Howbeit when He, the Spirit of Truth, is come, He shall guide you into all the truth: for He shall not speak from Himself. He shall glorify me: for He shall take of mine and declare it unto you."

We note here that the Holy Spirit does not reveal the earthly Christ to man. . . . It is the glorified Christ at the Father's right hand whom the Holy Spirit reveals.

He reveals the Christ who has conquered death, grave, and Hell, and been given a name above every other name.

He has revealed to us all of Christ's ministry that could not be disclosed to the senses of man. He is the One who gave to Paul the tremendous revelation of the substitutionary sacrifices of Christ, His conquering of Satan in Hell, His entrance into the Holy of Holies with His own blood, having obtained Eternal Redemption for man, and His present ministry at the Father's right hand.

He has revealed to us the riches of His Grace (Ephesians 1:7), and the riches of His Glory (Ephesians 3:16).

There are many scriptures that reveal to us different phases of the Holy Spirit's ministry.

As we observe the ministry of Christ, who is our example, we find that His ministry was wrought in the Holy Spirit. Read Matthew 12:28, Hebrews 9:14, Acts 1:2, Isaiah 11:2.

We find that the early church went forth also in the power of the Holy Spirit.

Read Acts 4:8, 31; 6:5; 13:2, 4, 9, 52; 15:8, 28; and 16:6, 7.

QUESTIONS

1. What is the ministry of the Holy Spirit toward the world?
2. What is His threefold method of presenting Christ's work to an unsaved man?
3. What person of the Trinity is the Active Agent in the New Birth?
4. What are the instruments of the Holy Spirit?
5. What, today, is the habitation of the Spirit?
6. Why is it essential for every child of God to be filled with the Holy Spirit?
7. Explain I John 4:12.
8. Why did Christ call the Holy Spirit the "Paraclete"?
9. What of Christ's ministry has the Spirit revealed to man?

10. Give scriptures to show that Christ's ministry was in the power of the Spirit.

Lesson 34

THE SECOND COMING OF CHRIST

OUR LAST TWO LESSONS have been upon the Ministry of the Holy Spirit. We have seen that He came at an appointed time to fulfill a definite mission, and that when He has accomplished His ministry upon earth He will return unto the Father as did Christ.

II Thessalonians 2:7 reveals that there is a time appointed for His being taken away from this world.

"For the mystery of lawlessness doth already work; only there is one that restraineth now, until he be taken out of the way." This One who is restraining the work of Satan is the Holy Spirit, but there is a time when He shall be taken away.

There are a few facts which we want to note about His return or Ascension to the Father.

In our study of His ministry during this dispensation, we have seen that when the Holy Spirit entered the world, He became incarnated in the mystical body of Christ, His church.

Since that time the Body of Christ has been His habitation. Ephesians 2:22, "In whom ye also are builded together for a habitation of God in the Spirit."

We want to note the following fact: now, when the Holy Spirit leaves the world He will not disembody Himself, but He will leave in the Body of Christ.

This will constitute the Rapture. The church will be taken up in the Spirit to be united in glory with Christ, the Head of the Church, Himself the Saviour of the Body.

The Holy Spirit has been forming the Body of Christ and He will present it to Him "a glorious church, not having spot or wrinkle" (Ephesians 5:7).

Writing upon this subject, A. J. Gordon has said the following: "The translation of the church is to be effected by the Holy Spirit who dwells in her.

" 'But if the Spirit of Him that raised up Jesus from the dead dwell in you, He that raised up Christ from the dead shall also quicken your mortal bodies by His Spirit that dwelleth in you.'

"It is not by acting upon the Body of Christ from without, but by energizing it from within, that the Holy Spirit will effect its glorification.

"In a word, the comforter, who on the Day of Pentecost came down to form a body out of flesh, will at the Rapture return to Heaven in that Body."

The Certainty of Christ's Return

This will take place at the return of our Lord. We want to study the Scriptures upon His return before we close this course.

In prophecy, in parable, and in teaching, Christ revealed that He is coming again. Over three hundred verses in the New Testament deal with this tremendous fact.

God's prophecies never fail in their fulfillment. Every prophecy of Christ's first coming was definitely fulfilled. So will every promise of His Second Coming be fulfilled.

We see Isaiah's prophecy come to pass (Isaiah 7:14), when a virgin conceived and bore a Son whose name was Immanuel.

Christ was born in Bethlehem in fulfillment of Micah 5:2. The "whole world" had to be "enrolled," however, to bring it about.

Twenty prophecies of the 22nd Psalm were fulfilled when Christ died upon the Cross.

Isaiah 53 was fulfilled as He was made sin in our behalf.

The Holy Spirit revealed to the prophets of old these events hundreds of years before Christ came.

I Peter 1:10-11, "Concerning which salvation the prophets sought and searched diligently who prophesied of the grace that should come unto you, searching what time or manner of time the Spirit of Christ which was in them did point unto when it testified beforehand the sufferings of Christ and the glories that should follow."

As we see the exact fulfillment of all the prophecies of Christ's first coming, what an incentive it gives to our searching the Scriptures to learn of His coming again.

As we study the prophecies that foretell the second coming of our Lord, we see that there are two phases of that coming.

(1) The Rapture, in which the Church is caught up to meet Him in the air, and

(2) The Revelation of His coming to earth with His Church in a display of His Power and Glory, when "every eye shall see Him." At this time He shall set up His kingdom on earth for a thousand years.

What Will Take Place in the Rapture?

The Holy Spirit, through the Apostle Paul, gives us a startling picture of what will take place when Christ returns. His coming will affect every member of the Body of Christ, whether they are with the Lord or alive, awaiting His return.

I Thessalonians 4:15-17, "For this we say unto you by the Word of the Lord that we that are alive and that are left unto the Coming of the Lord, shall in no wise precede them that are fallen asleep. For the Lord shall descend from heaven with a shout and with the voice of the archangel and with the trump of God: and the dead in Christ shall rise first; then we that are alive that are left shall be caught up in the clouds to meet the Lord in the air, and so shall we ever be with the Lord."

Our Lord, who has ascended into Heaven and taken His place on our behalf as Mediator, Intercessor, Advocate, and Lord, "will descend from Heaven with a shout."

Every living believer will hear that shout; the unbelievers have no part in this; and the shout will be a signal for the resurrection of the bodies of those who have died in Christ.

The bodies of those who are with Christ shall rise first. They, with all living believers, shall be caught up (the Greek reads, "in clouds") to meet the Lord in the air.

We want to note here that it is the Resurrection of the bodies of those in Christ who have died that will take place at the Rapture. It is not that the spirit will be raised.

The spirits of the departed saints are already with Christ in heaven.

The spirit of the believer in Christ Jesus can never die, and therefore can never need a resurrection. The dead in Christ are not in the grave, but alive with Christ.

I Thessalonians 4:14 shows that those who have died in Christ shall come with Him at the rapture to receive their glorified, immortal bodies.

The term "clouds" does not necessarily mean the clouds of the air. It probably means that clouds of believers shall arise from every nation to meet the Lord in the air. We find the term "clouds of witnesses" mentioned in Heb. 12:1.

Let us notice the Greek meaning of the word "caught up." We are told that "it indicates a mighty, decisive act of God which none can resist and which none will desire to resist. It means a 'taking by force.' "

The word is used in Matthew 11:12, when Christ says that men of violence take the kingdom of Heaven by force, and in Acts 23:10, when the soldiers were commanded to take Paul by force.

What a joyful compulsion that will be! "Caught up to meet our blessed Lord and Saviour, whom not having yet seen, we love."

A change shall take place within our bodies.

Paul says that "flesh and blood cannot inherit the kingdom of God . . . but we shall be changed in a moment, in the twinkling of an eye, at the last trump" (I Corinthians 15:50-51).

Philippians 3:20-21, "For our citizenship is in heaven; whence also we wait for a Saviour, the Lord Jesus Christ: who shall fashion anew the body of our humiliation. . . ." We shall actually receive a glorified, immortal body like our Lord.

The Holy Spirit, through John, tells us that "we know that when He shall be manifested we shall be like Him." We have been translated from Satan's authority into Christ's.

We have already been conformed in spirit to the image of Christ (Romans 8:29). We are waiting now for the Redemption of our bodies, the receiving of a glorified body like unto our Lord's.

Paul mentions this hope in Titus 2:13, "Looking for the blessed hope and the appearing of the glory of our great God and Saviour, Jesus Christ."

Christ speaks of His coming in Luke 17:30-35.

"In the day that the Son of Man shall be revealed . . . in that night there shall be two men in one bed, the one shall be taken, and the other left. There shall be two women grinding together; the one shall be taken, and the other left."

Also Matthew 24:40, "There shall be two men in the field; one is taken, and one is left." Here is revealed an eternal separation of the Body of Christ and the world.

The Marriage Supper of the Lamb

The meeting of Christ with His Body will be a time of great rejoicing. The members of the Body of Christ shall be welcomed by Him. Rewards will be given. The rewards may consist of various appointments of office for the millennium period. We do not know definitely.

II Corinthians 5:10, "For we must all be made manifest before the judgment seat of Christ; that each one may receive the things done in the body, according to what he hath done whether it be good or bad."

Romans 14:10, "But thou, why dost thou judge thy brother? or thou again, why dost thou set at nought thy brother? for we shall stand before the judgment seat of Christ."

This meeting is called the marriage supper of the Lamb.

Revelation 19:7-8, "Let us rejoice and be exceeding glad, and let us give the glory unto him; for the marriage of the Lamb is come, and His wife hath made herself ready. And it was given unto her that she should array herself in fine linen, bright and pure: for the fine linen is the righteous acts of the saints."

Revelation 19:9, "And He saith unto me Write, Blessed are they that are bidden to the marriage supper of the Lamb!"

It will last during a period of several years. The spiritually-dead people shall continue living upon the earth. In the meantime, the tribulation prophesied by our Lord shall take place upon the earth.

The Coming of the Antichrist

It will be led by Satan who has been cast down to earth. The following Scriptures refer to this great tribulation: Isaiah 26:16-21; 27:1.

We note the silence of the epistles upon this subject. It is not mentioned in any of them, because it will not affect the Body of Christ.

From our Lord's words in Matthew 24:21-30, it seems clear that the greatest tribulation the world has ever known will take place, and especially fall upon the Jews just before His coming in glory at His Revelation.

During this time the Antichrist shall appear.

The word "Antichrist" is used only by John. Other Scriptures refer definitely to him, however.

Paul refers to him as the "lawless one," "the man of sin," and "the son of perdition" (II Thessalonians 2).

Daniel refers to him as a king that shall magnify himself above every god.

Daniel 11:36, "And the king shall do according to his will; and he shall exalt himself and magnify himself above every god, and shall speak marvelous things against the God of gods; and he shall prosper till the indignation be accomplished; for that which is determined shall be done."

It seems that the Antichrist shall be some sort of a Christ.

The prefix "anti" means either "against" or "instead of." Both conceptions may be contained in one word.

Westcott says that it means far more than the adversary of Christ; it means one who, under the same character, opposes Christ.

During the tribulation, not one single believer will be left upon the earth. Every person will be a child of Satan. The world will be his. Then Satan will come in personal form. The Antichrist will be an incarnation of Satan and imitate Christ in many ways.

We must remember that the desire which caused the downfall of Satan and changed his nature, was the desire to be like the Most High.

Isaiah 14:13-14, "And thou saidst in thy heart, I will ascend into heaven. I will exalt my throne above the stars of God: and I will sit upon the mount of congregation, in the uttermost parts of the north: I will ascend above the heights of the clouds; I will make myself like the Most High."

He promised Adam and Eve that they should be as God (Genesis 3:5). He desires to take God's place in the life of man.

He even tried to secure the worship of Christ. So in this period of unrestraint, he will sit in the temple, setting himself as God.

It seems that the Jews will make a pact with the Anti-Christ for one week (it may refer to a period of seven years), who will permit the sacrifice and the oblation.

Daniel 9:27, "And he shall make a firm covenant with many for one week: and in the midst of the week, he shall cause the sacrifice and the oblation to cease, and upon the wing of abominations shall come one that maketh desolate; and even unto the full end, and that determined, shall wrath be poured out upon the desolate."

However, he breaks this covenant in the middle of the week and demands that he, himself, shall be worshipped.

Then will come the time of Jacob's trouble. All those who then refuse to worship the beast will be killed. No one will be able to buy or sell without the mark of the beast upon his hand or forehead.

The most stupendous triumph of Satan shall come when he shall appear as Antichrist and exalt himself above every other god, compelling men to worship him.

However, his triumph shall be short-lived; and he shall be conquered by Christ. Scriptures which tell of the Anti-Christ are the following: Revelation 13; Daniel 7:8-20, 21-25; 8:23, 24; 11:36-37.

We shall continue this study in the next lesson.

QUESTIONS

1. What Scripture shows that there is a time appointed for the Holy Spirit's leaving the world?
2. Why is it that the Body of Christ will leave when the Holy Spirit leaves?
3. Discuss the certainty of our Lord's return.
4. What are the two phases of the second coming of Christ?
5. What will happen to the living believers when Christ comes?

6. What will happen to those who have fallen asleep in Christ?
7. What will take place at the meeting of Christ and His bride in the air?
8. What will cause the tribulation upon the earth?
9. Why are the epistles silent about the Tribulation?
10. What is the ambition of Satan in assuming human form in the person of the Anti-Christ?

Lesson 35

THE SECOND COMING OF CHRIST (Continued)

SINCE OUR STUDY of the coming of the Incarnate One and the Redemption wrought in Him and the making of a New Covenant in His blood, we have not dealt with God's Old Covenant people, the Jews.

However, as we approach in our study the tribulation period, the Jew is again brought into the picture. The Tribulation is the time of Jacob's trouble, the greatest tribulation that has ever been faced by the Jew. Before we take up the study of the part that the Jews play in the Tribulation, it would be well to briefly survey the history of the Jew—the fulfillment of God's prophecy about him.

As we studied the Covenant that God made with Abraham and his descendants we saw that the Covenant people were to be a witness for Him upon the earth. Although in broken fellowship in his covenant relationship with God, the Jew is still a witness. His history is a fulfillment of God's prophecy concerning him.

God's Prophecy Concerning the Jew

Let us examine certain prophecies that have already been fulfilled before we deal with prophecies whose fulfillment is still future.

God prophesied through Moses that they should be scattered throughout the world and that wherever they went in their scattering that they should be persecuted.

Leviticus 26:33, "You will I scatter among the nations, and I will draw out the sword after you." This prophecy has been fulfilled, for no nation has ever been scattered so widely and extensively over the earth as the Jew.

History reveals that wherever they have gone that they have met with exile, captivity, confiscation of property, torture and massacre.

The above prophecy alone does not seem impossible of fulfillment—that the Jew should be scattered and per-secuted — but in the light of it there are several other prophecies concerning them which would surely seem void of all possible fulfillment.

The natural outcome of the scattering and persecution of the Jew would be his being absorbed by other nations so that he would lose his identity.

However, Numbers 23:9 has been fulfilled: "It is a people that dwell alone, and shall not be reckoned among the nations." Wherever the Jew has gone he has been recognized except in a very few exceptional cases.

God also declared that although the Jew will be widely scattered and persecuted, he should never become extinct and that He, Himself, would avenge the nations that persecuted him.

Jeremiah 30:16, "All they that devour thee shall be devoured—and they that spoil thee shall be a spoil."

The great empires of Babylon, Greece, and Rome, which persecuted the Jews, have passed away. Yet wherever Jews are found, they are prospering and holding leading positions in every sphere of life.

One writer said, "The Jews, braving all kinds of torments, the pangs of death, and the still more terrible pangs of life, have withstood the most awful persecutions. Yet mighty nations whose power has embraced the whole inhabited world have vanished; whilst the little handful of scattered, subjugated and hunted folk still flourishes after the organized and worldwide persecutions of eighteen centuries preserving their laws and customs given them in the infancy of the world, and preserving their unique nationality among the changes of the centuries."

Present-Day Fulfillment of Prophecy

Prophecy now being fulfilled is the one saying that the Jew will go back to his own land.

"And as the Lord liveth I will bring them back again to their land that I gave to their fathers."

"I will plant them upon their land, and they shall no more be plucked up out of their land which I have given them" (Amos 9:15).

Since the close of World War I the Jews have been going back to Palestine in large numbers.

Eleven days after the deliverance of the Holy Land from the Turks, the war suddenly ended. This deliverance of

Palestine from the Turks made it possible for the Jews to return.

Future Prophecy Concerning the Jew

Prophecy also declares that the Temple will be rebuilt after the return of the Jews to Palestine.

"After these things I will return, and I will build again the tabernacle of David . . . and I will set it up; that the residue of men may seek after the Lord and all the Gentiles upon whom my name is called" (Acts 15:16-17).

In our last lesson we studied the rise of the Anti-Christ during this period. (The Rapture will already have taken place.)

Then will come the time of Jacob's trouble. The nations of the world, although glad to be rid of the Christians, will become bitter toward the Jews because of their prosperity. The nations of the world, with their armies gathered together, will come arrayed against Jerusalem.

They will capture the city, and at the time when everything seems to be absolutely hopeless for the Jews, Christ will return. This will be what is termed as the Battle of Armageddon.

We want to note that as Christ with His Saints comes to deliver the Jews that a bloody combat will not take place between Christ and the nations. The Saints will not take part in the battle.

II Thessalonians 2:8 tells us that the Lord Jesus will slay the "lawless one," the "son of perdition" with the breath of His mouth. The implication is that Christ will slay with his mouth His enemies before He reaches the earth.

After Jerusalem has been taken by its enemies, the very presence of Christ will defeat them. Then, when the victory is gained, His feet shall stand upon the Mount of Olives.

Zechariah 14:2-4 tells us of Christ's return at the time the nations are at war with Jerusalem.

"I will gather all nations against Jerusalem to battle; and the city shall be taken and the houses rifled . . . and half the city shall go forth into captivity, and the residue of the people shall not be cut off from the city. Then shall the Lord go forth and fight against those nations . . . and

His feet shall stand in that day upon the Mount of Olives."

The Revelation of Christ

This Revelation of Jesus Christ is the second phase of the second coming of Christ. The marriage supper of the Lamb will have taken place and the Church will return with Him.

This is the time that every eye shall see Him and the time that the Jews will recognize Him as their Messiah and mourn for their rejection of Him.

Then shall be fulfilled Zechariah 12:10, "And I will pour upon the house of David and upon the inhabitants of Jerusalem the spirit of grace . . . and they shall look unto me whom they have pierced; and they shall mourn for Him, as one mourneth for his only son, and shall be in bitterness for Him, as one that is in bitterness for his firstborn."

Isaiah 25:9 will be fulfilled, "And it shall be said in that day, So this is our God; we have waited for Him; we will be glad and rejoice in this salvation."

The Jews will mourn over their rejection of Christ, but not for long. Their deliverance from their earthly enemies and their spiritual darkness will bring great joy to their hearts. God has foretold in many scriptures of the joy of His people.

Isaiah 60:1, "Arise, shine; for thy light is come, and the glory of Jehovah is risen upon thee."

Isaiah 60:20, "Jehovah will be thy everlasting light, and the days of thy mourning shall be ended."

Isaiah 60:21, "Thy people also shall be all righteous, they shall inherit the land forever, the branch of my planting, the work of my hands, that I may be glorified."

Then Christ will establish His earthly kingdom.

The Millennium

To His Old Covenant people God gave a twofold prophecy concerning His Son. One was the prophecy of His first coming, as the Lamb of God to bear sin away. The other was His coming as King, to set up an earthly kingdom.

The Jew seemed to overlook what God said about the first coming and saw only His kingly appearing and reign.

This is why they did not recognize or accept Christ as the Son of God. The first coming has been fulfilled.

Therefore, we, with the Jews, are looking for His glorified appearing.

The Bible speaks time and time again of the period when Christ shall reign for a thousand years upon the earth. There will be a temporary cessation of the reign of Satan.

In our last lesson we saw that the taking away of the Holy Spirit from the earth was naturally to be followed by a great tribulation, for Satan would be an unrestrained god of this world.

On the other hand, the end of Satan's reign caused by his being bound and shut away for a thousand years from all access to the earth will be followed by a glorious era of peace.

Satan is the author of sin, disease, suffering and misery and when he is banished from the earth, these will leave, too.

There are many scriptures which describe the millennial period. We shall give a few of them:

There will be no more war (Micah 4:2-4), "They shall beat their swords into ploughshares and their spears into pruning hooks; nation shall not lift up sword against nation; neither shall they learn war any more."

Isaiah 33:24, "The inhabitants shall not say, I am sick; the people that dwell therein shall be forgiven their iniquities."

Isaiah 35:5-10, "Then the eyes of the blind shall be opened, and the ears of the deaf shall be unstopped. Then shall the lame man leap as an hart, and the tongue of the dumb sing: for in the wilderness shall waters break out, and streams in the desert. And the parched ground shall become a pool, and the thirsty land springs of water: in the habitation of dragons where each lay, shall be grass with reeds and rushes, and an highway shall be there, and a way . . . and it shall be for those: the wayfaring men, though fools, shall not err therein. . . ."

"And the ransomed of the Lord shall return and come to Zion with songs and everlasting joy upon their heads: they shall obtain joy and gladness, and sorrow and sighing shall flee away."

Habakkuk 2:14, "For the earth shall be filled with the glory of the Lord as the waters cover the sea."

Isaiah 65:19, "And I will rejoice in Jerusalem and joy in my people: and the voice of weeping shall be no more heard in her, nor the voice of crying."

During the millennium, the Jews as a nation will be following Christ and will become the missionaries of the world. The Jews will become a great blessing to the world. "If their fall is the riches of the world and their loss the riches of the gentiles, how much more their fullness?"

The center of the world's worship will be Jerusalem; and Isaiah 2:3 will be fulfilled, "And many people shall go and say, come ye and let us go to the mountain of the Lord, to the house of the God of Jacob; and he will teach us his ways and we will walk in his paths: for out of Zion shall go forth the law, and the Word of the Lord from Jerusalem." All men will be able to witness and to realize what the Lordship of Christ will mean to humanity.

However, this reign of peace shall end when Satan is loosed from his prison. He shall gather for war all those whose hearts have not really been in harmony with Christ's reign, although they have been under His subjection.

Revelation 20:7, 8, "And when the thousand years are finished, Satan shall be loosed out of his prison, and shall come forth to deceive the nations which are in the four corners of the earth, Gog and Magog, to gather them together to the war; the number of which is as the sands of the sea."

Again Jerusalem will be attacked, but God will intervene with fire sent down from heaven, and Satan will be cast into the lake of fire, nevermore to have access to the earth, or the new heaven and new earth. A record of what will take place is given to us in Revelation 29:9-10.

"And they went up over the breadth of the earth, and compassed the camp of the saints about and the beloved city: and fire came down out of heaven and devoured them. And the devil that deceived them was cast into the lake of fire and brimstone, where also are the beast and the false prophet; and they shall be tormented day and night forever and forever."

Then eternity will arrive. There will be the second resurrection, the resurrection of the unbelieving dead, and the Great White Throne Judgment.

Revelation 20:11-15, "And I saw a great white throne and him that sat upon it, from whose face the earth and the heaven fled away; and there was found no place for them. And I saw the dead, the great and the small, standing before the throne; and the books were opened; and another book was opened, which is the Book of Life: and the dead were judged out of the things which were written in the books according to their works. And the sea gave up the dead that were in it; and death and Hades gave up the dead that were in them; and they were judged every man according to their works. And death and Hades were cast into the lake of fire."

"This is the second death, even the Lake of Fire. And if any was not found written in the Book of Life he was cast into the Lake of Fire."

The New Heaven and the New Earth

When this has taken place, then will come forth the New Heaven and the New Earth, and the first heaven and the first earth shall pass away and the sea shall be no more.

Revelation 21:1, "And I saw a new heaven and a new earth for the first heaven and the first earth are passed away; and the sea is no more." Read Revelation 21:1-8.

The church will then completely enter into its vast inheritance. Paul tells us in Ephesians that in the days to come the great Father-God is going to give us the wealth and riches that He has stored up in His great love during the Eternity of the past for us.

Oh, the glorious truth of the wealth, the riches, the joy that belongs to God's family.

Through the ages of the ages we are going to know one another, talk with one another, enjoy heavenly bliss eternally.

Blessed be the hope of the New Heaven and the New Earth.

QUESTIONS

1. How is it that the Jew, today, is still a witness?
2. Give three prophetic scriptures concerning the Jew that have been fulfilled.
3. What prophecy concerning the Jew is now being fulfilled?
4. What will take place at the revelation of Christ?
5. Give four scriptures that refer to the Jew receiving Christ.
6. Why will there be no sin, nor suffering, during the millennium?
7. Who shall be in the army that Satan shall gather upon his release?
8. How will God save Jerusalem?
9. What will take place at the second resurrection?
10. Tell what you can of the New Heaven and the New Earth.

Lesson 36

"TWO KINDS OF KNOWLEDGE"

WE ARE NOW COMING to the conclusion of our course. It has been a study of Redemption in Christ. Our study of the Old Testament was in the light of God's preparation for that Redemption. Our study of the New Testament has been a study of the consummation of that Redemption in the New Creation in Christ.

Our hearts have been thrilled as we have studied the privileges of the New Creation and the authority invested in the Name of Jesus that is legally ours.

Now, as we finish this course, we face the problem of putting into action in our daily living that which we have learned. Knowledge that is not usable is of no value to us.

Can we act upon the knowledge of Redemption and the New Creation that we have learned in this course as we act upon our knowledge of the world around us? The authenticity of this Redemption is dependent upon the authenticity of the Word.

Why is it that the Bible is not given its place in the world as a Revelation from God to man? Why is it that the scholastic world does not consider it authentic?

It is because there are two kinds, two distinct classes of knowledge: The knowledge of natural man and the knowledge coming from Revelation.

The Knowledge of Natural Man

Let us examine the knowledge the world has, the knowledge of natural man, and as we examine this knowledge we will ask ourselves three questions: What is its source? What are its limitations? To what extent is it sufficient as an answer to life's problems?

The Source of Man's Knowledge

The first question concerns the source of man's knowledge. The source of man's knowledge is man's physical body and the material universe around him. All that man knows about Reality, the great accumulation of knowledge that fills our libraries, our textbooks, has grown out of man's contacts with the physical world. These contacts are based upon man's sense perceptions.

We shall explain this further. Every contact that man has with the world comes to him through his five senses. The five senses belong to the central nervous system and are the following: the sense of sight, the sense of hearing, the sense of touch, the sense of taste and the sense of smell. Man knows nothing about Reality except that which he has gained through these senses. You could picture for yourself how much a man would be able to know if he could not see, hear, touch, taste or smell.

I have here a definition taken from a book dealing with physiology that bears witness to this fact:

"But no broadly philosophic view of the human organism can fail to assign the central nervous system the place which is that of the Holy of Holies. Without it we should be senseless, sightless, soundless, motionless masses of multiplying protoplasm. Everything else about the body is vegetative, which means like a plant. A plant can neither move, nor feel. Its life processes are carried on in response to the most primitive chemical and physical changes in its immediate environment. The central nervous system gives us every contact which we ever possessed with the rest of the world."

We can see from this that man can know nothing at all about the world, the sky, the grass, the sea and other human beings except through his five senses.

Let us take Miss Keller, for example. She possessed only three senses: The sense of touch, the sense of taste, and the sense of smell. Her sense of touch was so developed that through it, under the direction of those who possesed the five senses, she gained a wide knowledge of the world and life.

However, if it were possible for a person to be born who possessed none of the senses, he would never be able to be taught a thing. He could learn absolutely nothing of the outward world. In this we can see how dependent the mind is upon the material of sensation brought to it through the five senses.

To aid his senses in their search for Reality, man has developed the microscope, the spectroscope and the telescope; yet these instruments have only aided his senses in their contact with the physical world. Through them he has been able to study the universe and forms of life that are invisible to his sense of sight. Through the microscope and the ultramicroscope he has been able to study the most minute forms of life. He has been able to come to a knowledge of bacteria, and a knowledge of realms, that otherwise he would never have been able to contact.

With the aid of the telescope, he has been able to come to a knowledge of the heavenly universe. With his naked eye man can only see from two to four thousand stars. With the aid of the telescope, he can see hundreds of thousands of stars, and with the photographic plate, millions. By using the spectroscope, he has been able to know and study the composition of the stars.

There are many physical forces that we cannot perceive with our senses, but man has developed instruments that are sensitive to these forces and are able to record them.

We could mention other inventions that have aided man in his acquisition of the knowledge of the universe in which he lives. He has made great progress. He has become familiar with the laws and processes of the forces of nature. He has made them obey his command and utilized them, and out of the great accumulation of knowledge gained through his physical senses, out of years of research and study he has built the great civilization that we have today.

Yet we repeat that the source of this knowledge is based upon man's sense perception of the physical universe; and these senses belong to the physical body. They are only able to contact matter, and man's every contact has only been with a material realm.

The Limitations of Man's Knowledge

Our second question is: "What are the limitations of the knowledge of natural man?" The preceding makes them evident.

We can illustrate the limitations of our senses in giving to us a true picture of Reality by the following: a blind man who had never possessed the sense of sight, and who had never come into contact with men who did possess it would think that through his four senses he had a true picture of the world around him. He would never be able to know what color was or light was because he had no sense that could perceive it or admit an understanding of that quality to his mind.

A man who had never possessed the sense of hearing and never contacted men who did would think that he knew the universe as it was through his four senses. He would never imagine that the universe was filled with music.

So it may be that man with his five senses does not possess a true picture of Reality of the universe around him. We do know that man's five senses limit him only to the knowledge of matter. Every invention that he produces to aid his senses in receiving a true picture of the universe is a physical one and only aids in this knowledge of the physical.

Reason for Atheism and Materialism

It is because of this fact that materialism and atheism have developed. Man has said that there is nothing in the universe but matter and its properties. He has said that man does not survive the existence of his body because there is no spiritual quality in man to exist after the body has disintegrated. We can see that such an attitude upon the part of man toward life is a natural attitude, for with his five senses to which he is absolutely limited, he can contact nothing but a physical world.

It would be just as logical for a blind man to refuse to believe that color existed as for man with his five senses to say that the spiritual does not exist.

A fish might just as well say that there is nothing outside of water, as for a man to say, "In this universe there exists nothing but matter."

Two of our questions are answered. The source of man's knowledge is the central nervous system of his physical body, and its limitations are the physical universe and matter alone.

Rational Thinking and Sense Perception

We do not want to give a wrong impression when speaking of the source of man's knowledge. Thinking does not arise out of sense perception. Man has capacities for thinking, reasoning, reflecting and memorizing that are not based upon sense perception; yet man's mental powers and reasoning faculties have only the material of sensation from which to draw their conclusions.

Animals have sense perception, yet they do not have rational thinking. Rational thinking does not arise in sense perception; yet our statement is true: man knows nothing except as it comes to his mind through one of his five senses. Now we come to our third question: To what extent will the knowledge that man has gained through the medium of his five senses satisfy his hunger for Reality? To what extent is this knowledge sufficient in answering the most vital problem that man faces?

As Voltaire has said: Man has been able to measure the distance of the stars, and yet himself he has not come to know. The problems that concern a man the most have been left unanswered. He has not been able to find the reason for his own existence, and until man knows the reason for his own existence he cannot know the purpose or meaning of life.

Man's Hunger for God

As man studies creation through his five senses, he sees marks of design and intelligence that compel him to believe in an intelligent Creator, and yet he cannot find Him. This search for God has been the greatest problem of his life. Langdon Davies writes that the greatest hunger and the greatest thirst of man is a hunger for God. He believes that the motive that has been behind all scientific research has been man's hunger for God. He has explored Creation; he has desired to acquire a technical knowledge of nature in an effort to find the Creator.

Cotton has written a book entitled, "Has Science Discovered God?" This book is a symposium of modern scientific opinion which points to the fact that scientists today are becoming God-conscious. He said that the search for science has been a search for Reality, and that it was really a search for God.

The first tendency of science was to give a mechanical explanation for the universe, to rule God out; but as it has developed and come to a knowledge of the wonders of Creation, it realized that the great mechanical design of the universe must have a designer. The author felt that in time,

293

perhaps, science would discover God; but science can never discover God, for God is a spirit and He can never be found or discovered by the sense of sight, or hearing, or touch, regardless of the aid of the telescope and the microscope or spectroscope.

Mr. Cotton said that the greatest benefits that science could ever confer upon the human race would be the finding of God and a discovering of the fact that man survived death.

However, science will never be able to do this. Man will never be able to locate with his physical instruments the spirit in man, or contact it after it has left the physical body. So we see that although science has given to us our civilization, a vast knowledge of the heavenly universe, a knowledge of the earth and a knowledge of our own physical bodies and the care they should have, it must always leave untouched the two most vital problems that the human being faced. So much for the knowledge of natural man.

The furthest point to which science can bring us is the acknowledgement of an intelligent Creator, and with that there arises the problem of knowing Him. Is it reasonable that a God should create a man whose primeval and greatest hunger was to know Him and then leave that man to grope in the darkness of his physical body, unable to ever find Him?

In our first few lessons of this course we saw the reason for man's present alienation from God, man's treason. Man, with his physical body and five senses, can never contact God. and God did not intend that man should know Him in this manner. The real man is the spirit, created in the image of God with the capacity to know Him and to fellowship Him.

Man, as he came forth from the hand of God in creation, knew Him. Christ revealed to us that they that worship God, worship Him in spirit. Man's physical body was given to him only as a home for the spirit in this physical universe. It fit him for his life upon the earth and through it he contacted the physical world and the physical world alone. It was through his spirit that he was to know and to fellowship God.

The senses of sight, hearing, touch, taste, or smell were to make known to man the physical world which was his home. They were not given to him for the purpose of revealing God to him.

When man died spiritually as a result of his treason he became alienated from God and absolutely estranged from the ability to know Him. Since then, man, spiritually dead, left with only the senses of the physical body, has learned the wonders of the universe to which that body can belong, but never the Creator.

We can see by this that if man is ever to know God, a new knowledge must be given to him, a knowledge that cannot come through sense perception, a knowledge that man cannot gain by his study of the world.

The Creator has understood man's need and has given to him a revelation of Himself. He has brought that Revelation down to the level of man's senses that spiritually dead man might contact this revelation and through it come to a knowledge of his Creator—the Bible.

QUESTIONS

1. Why must we learn to act upon what we have learned?
2. What is the source of natural man's knowledge?
3. Why is it that all the inventions that man produces cannot lift him above a material realm?
4. Discuss the limitations of man's sense knowledge.
5. Why have materialism and atheism developed?
6. Why is sense knowledge not sufficient as an answer to life's problems?
7. What is man's greatest hunger?
8. Why is it that science will never be able to discover God?
9. What condition of natural man keeps him from knowing God?
10. What is the only way in which his need can be met?

Notes

Lesson 37
"MAN'S NEED OF A REVELATION"

IN OUR LAST LESSON we studied the knowledge that man has gained through his physical senses. We saw its limitations and the need of a Revelation from God.

So we have in reality two classes of knowledge: the knowledge of natural man and the knowledge that has come from God. We can see now why this Revelation is not recognized by the scholastic world. It is not given its place among the textbooks that fill our colleges, because it does not belong to the realm of knowledge that man has gained through his physical contacts with matter.

Even in our contacts with one another, limited to sense knowledge, we cannot know the thoughts of a man's spirit. However, he, through the medium of words, can make them known to us (I Corinthians 2:10-13).

In a like manner, limited to sense knowledge, we cannot know God, who is a spirit; but He has given to us in human words a knowledge of Himself. The Spirit has combined spiritual truths with spiritual words.

Authenticity of the Revelation

However, the problem that was set forth at the beginning has not been answered yet. It was this: Can we act upon the Bible, which tells us of so complete a Redemption in Christ, as we act upon our knowledge of the world around us? Can we act upon this Revelation as we act upon sense knowledge?

Many say this: "You cannot prove that the Bible is a Revelation from God. You ask me to act upon it, to assume first of all that it is true; but I do not believe anything that I cannot prove."

It is not a very thorough science that will not believe anything which it cannot prove. We have no knowledge in any sphere or realm that is not based upon assumptions.

The very same doubt and criticism that is applied to this revelation may be applied to the knowledge of natural man. We could not prove that our knowledge is accurate. At the very basis of our knowledge of the outward world is the assumption that our senses and memory do not deceive us.

Although we could never prove that our senses are telling the truth, we do not for a moment question the fact.

As Mr. R. A. Armstrong has said, "There are precisely analogous reasons for doubting whether there is any external world at all, whether there are any tables or chairs, any great cities and green fields, any wide waters and mighty mountains, any stars or moon or sun, to those for doubting that there is any God. In both cases the doubt is simply a doubt whether our own natural faculties are instruments that tell us the truth; whether our own apparent experiences may be trusted as real and actual."

Although we could never prove that our senses do give to us a true picture of reality and that all our experiences with the outward world are anything more than just action-reaction in our central nervous system, we believe in the external world, because **to do so works.**

As Mr. R. A. Armstrong again says, "These beliefs (referring to our belief in an external world, the veracity of memory, etc.) are justified in that they work, they never **land us in** confusion, they never break down; as the daily haps of life turn up, a myriad an hour, in infinite diversity, these beliefs fit into them all without a jar or a contradiction; while if for a moment we attempt to depart from them, we fall into utter confusion. This is the highest evidence we can have."

We can apply this same test to this revelation that we have from God. Does it work? Can we act upon its veracity as we act upon our knowledge of the outward world? Does the Word never break down? Do we never land in confusion when we take what He says to be true?

In all the experiences of life can we act upon what God says that He has wrought for us in Christ?

If, when we act upon what God has said, we find that Omnipotence comes upon the scene to make His Word good, then we are justified in assuming that it is a revelation from God.

This Revelation declares that which would be utterly impossible if it were not a revelation from God. It would be absurd to even consider its authenticity. It declares that if a man will believe with his heart that God raised Christ from the dead, and confess with his mouth that he will take Him as Lord, that he shall be saved, become a New Creation (Romans 10:9-10).

We have seen thousands whose lives have been changed instantaneously as they acted upon this Word. The power of sin has been broken over their lives; they have been freed from habits that have kept them in bondage years and years. Old desires have passed away, and things they have loved they now hate, and the things they have hated they now love.

The Word declares that in the Name of Jesus we shall lay hands on the sick and that they shall recover. When Jesus said this, He put His reputation at stake, for if His Name should fail to possess authority, His Deity would be repudiated.

We have seen this Scripture fulfilled in thousands of lives also. The power of incurable diseases has been broken by a simple prayer in the authority of Jesus' Name. Daily, weekly, those miracles are being performed.

This last week we have received testimonies of cancers being healed within a period of a few days.

The only explanation is that this Bible is God's Revelation to man.

The Faith Walk

The fact that there are two kinds of knowledge is one of the basic truths underlying the faith walk.

Many times the faith walk has seemed difficult. We have wondered why God has put faith as the requirement for all that we receive. It has many times seemed unnatural. It has made blessings unattainable. It seems to put them just beyond our reach.

When we understand clearly the fact that there are two kinds of knowledge, and learn to distinguish between the two, the faith walk becomes the natural walk for us.

This can be explained by our referring to the eighth chapter of Romans. The first eight verses of this chapter are hard to understand except in this light. We have here the contrasting of two walks—the walk by the flesh (senses) and the walk in the spirit.

The ninth verse reveals to us that the term "flesh" is applied to the man who has not been Born Again; for he writes. "But, ye are not in the flesh (physical), but in the spirit, if so be that the Spirit of God dwelleth in you. For if any man hath not the Spirit of Christ, He is none of His."

For a long time I could not understand the Spirit's using the term "flesh," but now in the light of the two kinds of knowledge I can understand it. The man who has not been Born Again lives purely in the realm of the physical senses.

We took this up more fully in the last lesson. We saw that every contact that man has with the world is through the central nervous system. Man lives in the physical: by sense evidence, he cultivates the arts that please the senses. Because man lives in a physical realm, civilization will not raise him above that level. Every rise in civilization has been accompanied by a decline in morals. This, however, is not the natural or normal realm for man.

We remember that man was created in God's image, a spirit being. He was created to walk with God, who is a Spirit. Man belongs to God's realm, the realm of Omnipotence. It is the faith realm. It is the realm of the One "Who calleth the things that are not as though they were." In that realm, words hold a strange power, for they are filled with Omnipotence.

When man died spiritually, he became alienated from God. He ceased to live in the spirit. He became estranged from God's ability.

He then began to walk in the flesh, the realm of the physical. We have reference to this walk in the eighth chapter of Romans. He had fallen from the realm of Omnipotence to the realm of human ability. Words lost their power. He was dependent upon his own ability which was really the ability of his physical body, dependent upon its strength in his struggle for existence and his combat with the forces of nature. . . . All that he should know about the world in which he lives, was dependent upon his five senses.

We can see by this that the walking in the flesh or senses, expresses the walk of spiritually dead man.

But we who have been Born Again have come back into our rightful realm, the normal realm. By being made alive spiritually through the impartation of God's life to our spirit, we can walk again in His realm. It is the realm of the spirit—the realm of Omnipotence; for man's spirit is one with Him—and the realm of faith, where words filled with Omnipotence call the things that are not as though they were and they become.

These are the two walks that we have contrasted in the eighth chapter of Romans. Let us notice the comparison:

Romans 8:5-7, "The mind of the flesh is enmity against God." It is the mind that lives alone by the evidence of the five senses, excluding God, excluding the spiritual and the faith life.

Its end is death (verse 6) for it belongs to a death-doomed body and cannot reveal God to man, that he might receive His life.

The mind of the spirit is the mind of the one who has received God's life and come back into the normal realm for man.

The mind of the spirit is the mind that lives by the Word rather than the evidence of the physical senses.

The Life of the New Man

We do not mean to discredit the knowledge that we have through our five senses. It is only that we have come into contact with God, and we can no longer be dependent upon human ability; for we have now dwelling within our bodies the ability of God.

We belong to a New Creation and are freed from the laws of sin, weakness, want and disease that belong to the Old.

God has wrought man's Redemption in Christ that frees him from the dominion of Satan.

That we might know the things that He has freely given to us, He has given us this revelation. I Corinthians 2:12-13, "But we received, not the spirit of the world, but the spirit which is of God; that we might know the things that are freely given to us of God. Which things

301

also we speak, not in words which men's wisdom teacheth, but which the Spirit teacheth, combining spiritual things with spiritual words."

The man who has been Born Again lives by this Word. Christ said, "Man shall not live by bread alone, but by every word that proceedeth out of the mouth of God."

By the term "bread," Christ has reference to the physical. The new man is not limited to sense evidence or the realm of weakness and defeat.

He lives in oneness with God and by the authority of what God has revealed him to be in the Word.

This constitutes the faith life. Faith is fearlessly acting upon what God has said.

Luke 1:37, "For no word from God shall be void of power." Every word that has been spoken from God is a part of Himself. It is filled with His Omnipotence. The word "power" means "ability." No word is void of ability to bring Life, healing, blessing for every need.

Isaiah 55:11, "So shall my word be that goeth forth out of my mouth; it shall not return unto me void, but it shall prosper in the thing whereto I sent it."

No word that goes forth from Him shall fail to accomplish that for which He sent it forth. It will not return to Him void. No man will be able to bring His Word to Him, saying, "It failed. I could not act upon it."

The Renewed Mind

After a man has been Born Again, his first need is the renewing of his mind. It is the renewing of his mind that enables him to walk no longer conformed to the old life.

Romans 12:2, "And be not fashioned according to this world, but be ye transformed by the renewing of your mind, that ye may prove what is that good and acceptable and perfect will of God."

The renewing of the mind is necessary to the walk in the New Creation.

Ephesians 4:23-24, "And that ye be renewed in the spirit of your mind and put on the new man that after God hath been created in righteousness and holiness of truth."

Before a man can live in the fullness of his privileges, his mind must be renewed.

The renewed mind is the mind that has learned to live by God's Word.

The mind of the old creation lives by sense evidence; the mind of the new, by the Word.

Let me illustrate it. A Christian who is walking in fellowship has a financial need that he must meet. He does not have the money. He can see no means through which it can come to him. If he were not a child of God he would have no hope. He would be dependent upon his own ability.

But the Word declares, "My God shall supply every need of yours." The integrity of God is behind that Word.

Even though Heaven and earth should pass away, that word cannot fail. If this Christian's mind has been renewed, he will have as much joy in what the Word says as he would in the actual possession of the money, for he would know that God will make it good. God's Word means as much to him as sense evidence.

In the case of sickness, a child of God is overcome by disease; but the Word declares that by His stripes we are healed. That scripture should bring as much joy to him as the actual symptoms of healing, for God's ability is behind it to make it good.

In conclusion, the renewed mind is the mind that lives utterly by the Word.

In this course you have learned of what you are in Christ; now live by it and God's ability will be yours.

QUESTIONS

Discuss:

    (a) Man's need of a revelation.
    (b) How God has met that need.
    (c) The need of our living by the Word.